India

Brief History of a Civilization

THOMAS R. TRAUTMANN

New York Oxford
OXFORD UNIVERSITY PRESS
2011

Oxford University Press, Inc., publishes works that further Oxford University's objective of excellence in research, scholarship, and education.

Oxford New York
Auckland Cape Town Dar es Salaam Hong Kong Karachi
Kuala Lumpur Madrid Melbourne Mexico City Nairobi
New Delhi Shanghai Taipei Toronto

With offices in
Argentina Austria Brazil Chile Czech Republic France Greece
Guatemala Hungary Italy Japan Poland Portugal Singapore
South Korea Switzerland Thailand Turkey Ukraine Vietnam

Published by Oxford University Press, Inc.
198 Madison Avenue, New York, New York 10016
http://www.oup.com

Library of Congress Cataloging-in-Publication Data
Trautmann, Thomas R.
India : brief history of a civilization / by Thomas R. Trautmann ;
drawings by James A. Cogswell, Jr. ; maps by Elisabeth Paymal.
p. cm.
Includes bibliographical references and index.
ISBN 978-0-19-973632-4 (alk. paper)
1. India—Civilization. 2. India—History. I. Title.
DS423.T735 2010
954—dc22 2010024466

Printing number: 9 8 7 6 5 4 3 2 1

Printed in the United States of America
on acid-free paper

CONTENTS

ILLUSTRATIONS

Figures

Maps

Drawings by James A. Cogswell, Jr.
Maps by Elisabeth Paymal

ABOUT THE BOOK

I wrote this book for my students in a large introductory Indian Civilization course at the University of Michigan.

There are many introductory works on Indian history, books that I like, by authors whose scholarship I respect. I have prescribed several of them to my Indian Civilization students over the years, but students regularly complained they were too long, too detailed, and had too many names and terms to master for students new to the subject. They convinced me that my colleagues and I, believing that the key to historical explanation is in the details, have been overwhelming our students by giving them more detail than they can digest at the beginning. They convinced me that what is needed is a first book, one that is short enough to read in a few sittings but is comprehensive in coverage—five thousand years of India in brief. They convinced me that I needed to learn the art of how to make a better introductory book by subtraction, and to rein in my historian's tendency in the opposite direction. What was needed, they taught me, was a book that will give newcomers a quick overview of a very long period, so that in a short time they will acquire a mental map of the history of Indian Civilization as a whole, a basic stock of names and technical terms and a rough sense of the chronology. It should give readers the means to tackle more advanced works. It should be an hors d'oeuvre, not a full meal. I began writing this book and course-packing it for my students only after I had tried and failed to find the ideal first book. Their feedback on this work has been positive, encouraging me to think that others might find it useful.

The gap I found between detail-loving history professors such as myself and our students' unmet need for an elementary work without too many speed bumps to get over while pursuing an overall sense of Indian Civilization and its history resulted in this book. No doubt it falls between the wishes of both parties and will leave them something to complain about. I have kept the book reasonably short by omitting everything I felt I could; colleagues will think it omits too much, and students, too little. It is meant to be elementary, but I have tried not to sacrifice complexity of interpretation and "dumb down" the ideas. It is short, but not easy.

The book also tries to strike a balance between briefness and being comprehensive in chronology. In carrying out this balancing act I have departed again from existing practice. Most comprehensive histories devote a few chapters to the early period and an increasing number of pages to the more recent period, up to independence. This plan gives an unfortunate impression that the early period is mere background to the present, and that Indian Civilization finds its fulfillment in the nation-state, something I want to avoid. I want to give the early period its due weight and significance, not as a matter of doing justice to the past, but because I believe that the deep past lives on in the present, and is a valuable resource for understanding the present and finding ways to a viable future. Believing this, I have made the chronological profile of the book somewhat the reverse of the usual, devoting more nearly equal attention to the earlier phases of the story. Not exactly equal, however: Eight chapters are devoted to the first four thousand years, four chapters to the last thousand. In purely numerical proportions even that seems to privilege recent history far too much, but some will think that recent history gets too little coverage. I freely concur, and encourage them to supplement the book with companion readings, as I have in my own course.

I wanted the book to be illustrated by pen-and-ink drawings that were appealing as well as informative, and had the unity of style that comes from being made by a single artist. James Cogswell was my choice, and he responded magnificently. Elisabeth Paymal made the maps and was my artistic director for the book. To both I am profoundly grateful for their skill and their enthusiasm for the project. Having been an editor myself I appreciate more than many authors the value of good editing. David Akin brought to the manuscript his superb editing savvy, tightening the text and making it better in many ways. Brian Wheel,

Charles Cavaliere, and Marianne Paul for Oxford, shepherded the project from acceptance to publication, giving invaluable help and direction at every juncture in the process. I know how much I owe these editors, and I thank them warmly. Sudipa Topdar did excellent work for me as research assistant, and the College of Literature, Science, and the Arts of the University of Michigan gave support. Robbins Burling gave comments on the entire text that were most helpful because they were completely frank. Azfar Moin, who had taught the course pack version, gave comments on the whole manuscript, and more especially gave me the benefit of his innovative ideas on Mughal kingship, which are only beginning to appear in print. Carla Sinopoli helped me greatly on the Indus Civilization chapter. I am deeply in their debt. Anita Nahal Arya, Sumit Guha, Arnold Kaminsky, Mithi Mukherjee, Peter Schmitthenner, David Stone, Rachel Sturman, and anonymous reviewers for Oxford gave me suggestions that proved immensely useful, some of them very detailed, all of them thoughtful and constructive, for which the book is much better than it might have been, and for which I thank them. I am grateful to Anjali Pathak, Parna Sengupta, Maitrii Aung-Thwin, Janam Mukherjee, Azfar Moin, Rebecca Grapevine, and Anshuman Pandey, who taught the text as graduate student instructors in History 206, Civilization of India, for giving me their readings of the classroom effectiveness of chapters. Above all I thank my students in the course for their help, sometimes unwitting and certainly involuntary, but always useful, in the making of the book.

CHAPTER 1

Introduction

India, Indians, Indian Civilization
The History of Indian Civilization
The Landscape of Indian Civilization

The civilization of India occupies a long period of about five thousand years, in a large part of the inhabitable earth's surface, and it has had large influences on the world around it. Before getting to the details, we need to begin with some "big-picture" examinations of the time and the place within which our study will unfold, and the terms through which it will proceed.

India, Indians, Indian Civilization

The first thing we need to do is to examine the terms of the investigation, for we cannot take it for granted that we know what we mean—or that we all mean the same thing—when we speak of India, Indians, and civilization. Such words are ambiguous not because the things they refer to are fictions, but because they are complex, and complex objects cannot be easily apprehended or described. Our attempts to understand the simplest aspects of the world involve making generalizations that, by simplifying, both make the world intelligible and falsify it to some extent by editing out some of its complexity. How much more difficult it is, then, to describe something as multifaceted as Indian civilization, involving as it does millions of people living in a large portion of the earth's surface over several thousand years, without severely distorting and misrepresenting it. This problem is general and inescapable, and we must always keep in mind the simplifying nature of all our generalizations—that is to say, of everything we say or write. It is equally important to remember that what we are trying to describe is real, even though we can never capture it fully in words because of its intricacy.

This being so, we start by specifying what we mean when we speak of India, Indians, and civilization. We take them up in the reverse order.

Civilization

We use the word *civilization* to express at least two different meanings. In one sense it denotes a *quality* that is admirable and of which a person or a group can have more or less; in the other it denotes a *way of life* distinctive of a particular complex society, and accordingly it is, as the linguists say, a "count noun," meaning there are a number of different but parallel civilizations, in the plural.

In the nineteenth century, Europeans liked to speak of the *scale of civilization,* a kind of staircase or ladder, and to arrange the societies of the world at different steps, with Europe at the top. We often feel uneasy about using the word civilization in this sense because it so evidently embodies a European sense of superiority over everyone else. All civilizations have this internal sense of the superiority of a familiar way of life. The idea that civilization denotes a quality such as civility, refinement, or politeness, opposed to rudeness and the like, has two advantages that we cannot do without, namely, that it reveals a scale of value from the inside, so to say, and that it helps us identify powerful centers of diffusion for ideas of good behavior and comportment, mostly religious elites and ruling classes. It reminds us that civilization is unevenly distributed within a society.[1]

On the other hand, we also use the word civilization in ways that make it similar to what anthropologists mean when they speak, from the outside, of a *culture* or of cultures. That is, it can denote a patterned way of life distinctive of a certain society, about which, in our analysis, we make no moral judgments as to whether it is better than another. As a nonjudgmental way of speaking this has a strong appeal, but we need also to be aware that it lends itself to a "clash of civilizations" kind of thinking, which takes the civilizations to be sharply bounded, homogeneous within, and mutually incompatible.[2] Each one of these attributes is entirely false; all civilizations have fuzzy boundaries, are unevenly spread and "lumpy," and continually mingle with and draw on other civilizations.

A civilization is usually thought of as having three attributes. In the first place it has a common culture in the anthropologist's sense; that is, a patterned set of beliefs, values, and rules of behavior that are distinctive. In the second place it has a social system that is complex, with a certain degree of social ranking, and privileged and unprivileged classes. In the third place it pertains to a large geographical area. We can think of humanity, at least before Columbus, as containing a finite number of civilizations in this sense. Although this statement relies on the outsider view of civilization, it has a tincture of the first meaning in the attribute of social complexity, so that the insider and outsider views of civilization are connected.

When we take the second, "anthropological" sense of the word and look at it in the light of history, we see that the civilizations are extended in time but there is a point in the past when they did not exist, and after which they came into existence. At some time since the last ice age, and for reasons we only dimly perceive, the human race has developed, for the first time in its long history, certain types of complex, large-scale, culturally patterned social systems that did not previously exist, and that spread and multiplied, these being the ancient civilizations. The story of the civilizations fills several thousand years of history, but of course that constitutes only the very recent history of humanity. The far longer part of human history occurred before the invention of the civilizations, and their invention in turn built on several prior inventions, especially agriculture and animal domestication, also after the last ice age and only a few thousand years before the first civilizations. Taking advantage of this clue we can form a historical sense for the word civilization, by which we will mean a certain kind of society having the attributes we have named that has arisen in the recent history of the human race. Indian Civilization is one of these. Like all the civilizations it had a beginning in time, however difficult in practice it might be to pinpoint the time of that beginning.

Indians

It follows from what has been said that the object of our study is a kind of society (complex, large-scale...), and that Indians are the people making up the society we call Indian Civilization. It is worth saying at the outset that Indians are not a *race,* and that in the physical features considered markers of race Indians are neither internally homogeneous (and in fact they vary enormously among themselves) nor, in respect to outsiders, distinctive. There is a standard but mistaken view about the genesis of Indian Civilization, which can be called "the racial theory of

Indian Civilization." According to this theory, Indian Civilization came into being through a clash, and subsequent mixture, of a light-skinned, civilized race with a dark-skinned, barbarous race. As we shall see in the course of this book, the racial theory was exploded by the discovery of the Indus Civilization, which pushed back the beginnings of civilization to a very distant past. At the same time it is clear that at least three different, previously distinct groups combined to create Indian Civilization, as indicated by the existence in India of three major language families that are not related. They are, in order of size, the Indo-Aryan, the Dravidian, and the Munda language families (Map 1).

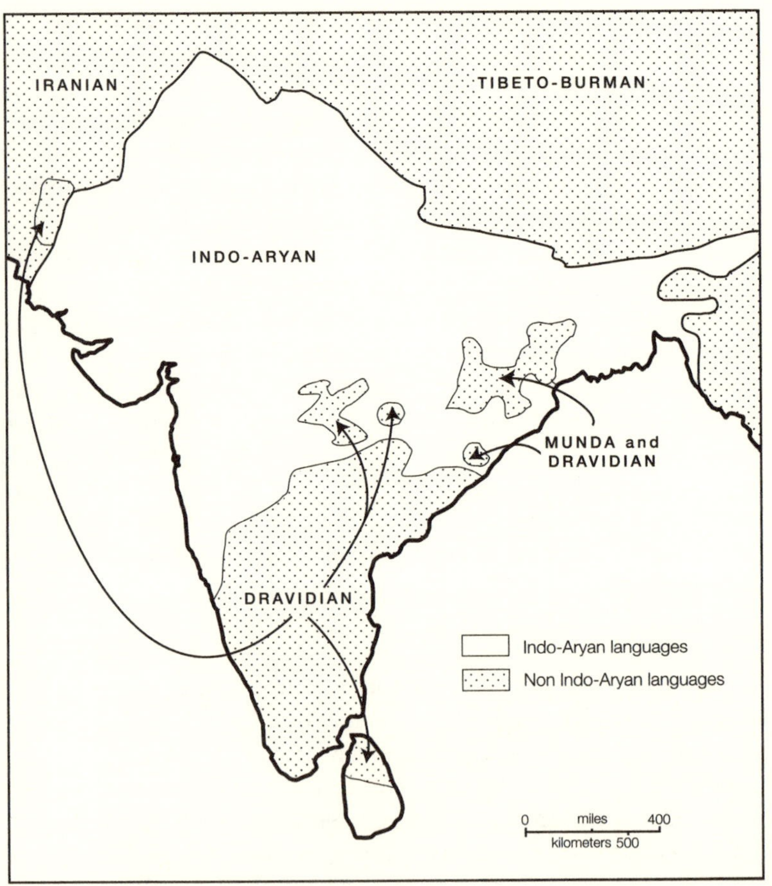

MAP 1 Languages

The *Indo-Aryan* family consists of the following languages: Hindi and Urdu are spoken in the upper Gangetic basin, Hindi being the official language of the Republic of India. They are, in effect, two dialects of a single language, although they differ in script (Hindi is written in a script called Devanagari, descended from the ancient Indian script called Brahmi shown in Figure 11, whereas Urdu is written in a modification of the Arabo-Persian script) and vocabulary (Urdu has a large component of Persian and Arabic loan words), and they tend to be used by Hindus and Muslims, respectively. Other Indo-Aryan languages have names indicating their regional locations: If we read a map of North India in an arc from west to east, we find the Marathi language (of Maharashtra), Gujarati (of Gujarat), Sindhi (of Sindh), Punjabi (of the Punjab), Hindi (in the valley of the Ganga River), Nepali (of Nepal), Bengali (of Bengal and Bangladesh), and Oriya (of Orissa), to name only the more salient ones. The Sinhalese language of Sri Lanka is a far southern outlier of this family.

All of these descend from the Sanskrit language, in which the sacred books of Hinduism are written, brought to India by peoples calling themselves Arya in about 1400 BCE. Sanskrit in turn is part of a larger language family called Indo-European, comprising, approximately, Sanskrit and its descendants in the modern nations of Indian Civilization; Old Persian and its descendants in Iran, Afghanistan, and Pakistan; and the languages of Europe, including English.

The *Dravidian* and *Munda* language families were already established in India before the arrival of Sanskrit speakers. The major Dravidian languages today are those of South India: Tamil (of Tamil Nadu), Telugu (of Andhra Pradesh), Kannada (of Karnataka), and Malayalam (of Kerala). There are altogether some twenty Dravidian languages, some of them spoken by tribal peoples of central India (such as Gondi, with more than five million speakers). There is an island of Dravidian speech in the Ganga Valley (Malto), and another in the Indus Valley (Brahui). Dravidian languages were established all over India before the coming of Sanskrit, but in the North they gradually gave way to Indo-Aryan languages. Because of this there are several features of Indo-Aryan languages, and many loan words, that have been absorbed from Dravidian ones. Scholars do not agree about where Dravidian came from; some think it was related to the Finno-Ugric family (which includes the Finnish language), others to Elamite (an ancient language of southwest Iran). There is general agreement, however, that it arrived in India before Sanskrit, and that it entered India from the west or northwest.

Munda, on the other hand, is a family of languages related to the Austroasiatic languages of Assam and Indo-China (including Mon-Khmer of Cambodia) and it is reasonably certain that it entered India from the east, also before the arrival of Sanskrit, which has early loan words from Munda and Dravidian languages. Munda languages are spoken by tribal peoples of central and east central India.

Over the centuries Indian peoples and their languages have mixed greatly and the amalgam is what we call Indian Civilization. The discernible difference among these three language families remains as a very conservative trace marking the three major components that went into the mix. One other feature tracks the linguistic boundaries, approximately but not exactly: kinship and the rules of marriage. North Indian peoples follow rules of marriage that vary greatly from place to place and caste to caste, but the general drift of them is that one must marry a "stranger" so to say, a nonrelative and someone living in a different village. The Dravidian kinship system has a very different effect. There is a positive preference for marriage between what anthropologists call "cross cousins," the type of which is the son and daughter of a brother–sister pair (that is, the children of opposite-sex siblings). The rule structures the language such that all the people of my own generation are either categorized as my brothers and sisters (and so are unmarriageable to me) or my cross cousins (and so marriageable). Similarly, because one marries one's mother's brother's child or father's sister's child, the words for "uncle" and "aunt" are also words for "father-in-law" and "mother-in-law." This pattern is widely spread in South India and Sri Lanka. It extends into regions of Indo-Aryan language in certain places, notably Sri Lanka and certain castes of the Marathi- and Gujarati-speaking areas, suggesting that the pattern of kinship might be even more resistant to change than language. The Munda pattern of kinship is different from the other two. In most other respects, though—in religious ideas, economies, and political forms—the boundaries of kinship systems and language families are overridden. That these traces remain of the "pre-Indian" situation out of which Indian Civilization emerged shows that language and kinship do not determine the other structures of which that civilization consists.

India

Because Indian Civilization is a particular society or social system, we should understand India not as a physical fact, a landscape, but as a landscape in relation to that society. This landscape has certain very important structuring or constraining effects on Indian Civilization that we must look into. It is important to keep in mind that India is not a permanent place on the map of the world with fixed boundaries, but a place that comes into existence with Indian Civilization, with boundaries that shift and expand with its growth. In particular it has an internal frontier as well as an external one. In very early writings of Indian Civilization we see the recognition of the idea of the barbarian, Sanskrit *mleccha,* and the recognition of an inner, Central India zone of people as yet unassimilated to Indian Civilization.

It is important, too, to remember that when we speak of India we mean Indian Civilization and its landscape, and not the Republic of India, created about sixty years ago with the end of British rule. The political map of today is divided into seven nation-states occupying the territory of India in the civilizational sense:

- The Republic of India
- Pakistan
- Bangladesh
- Sri Lanka (formerly Ceylon)
- Nepal
- Bhutan
- The Maldives

As political entities these nation-states are for the most part quite new: India (the republic) and Pakistan were created by the division of British-ruled India in 1947, Ceylon was given independence from Britain in 1948, the Maldives in 1965, and Bangladesh broke away from Pakistan to become an independent state in 1971. Nepal considered itself the last Hindu kingdom until a revolution established a republic in 2008. Although Nepal retained its sovereignty during British rule of India it was under British influence. Bhutan, a small kingdom of Buddhist majority in the east, had its first nationwide elections to parliament in 2007.

To avoid confusion between Indian Civilization and the Republic of India, some have abandoned using the word "India" and use the phrase "South Asia" to refer to the region occupied by these modern countries. This latter has the advantage of being politically neutral, but the disadvantage that no one uses it except scholars specializing in the study of that region. The advantage of "India" is that it is the name used for thousands of years by the Greeks, the Persians, the Arabs, and the Chinese to denominate

Indian Civilization and its landscape. We use India to mean what other scholars mean by South Asia—the territory and civilization in question—except when we speak of the modern republic bearing that name.

The History of Indian Civilization

India, in the sense of Indian Civilization, had a beginning in time and therefore it has a history. The history we tell of India's Civilization itself has a history, and the main outlines of the story were formed in the last two centuries. The history of Indian Civilization was very largely formed through the work of European scholars of India and the Indian intellectuals who were their teachers in the period of British rule, beginning in the 1760s. This new combination of scholars thrown together by colonial rule brought about a new narrative of India's past that was unlike what had gone before. The new narrative was the effect of two things. First, India's ancient past was brought into relation to the pasts of other ancient societies, such as those of the Egyptians, Chaldeans, Greeks, and Persians. Second, the contents of ancient Sanskrit literature were read in a new way, making a distinction between what was regarded as myth and what was regarded as history.

At the beginning of the British period it was recognized that the Sanskrit language was related to Greek and Latin, and it was believed that the Sanskrit speakers first brought civilization to India, and that, therefore, India's history began at that point. For a while it was thought that all the languages of India were descendants of Sanskrit, but then it was discovered that the languages of the South formed a separate family of Dravidian languages. This led to the previously mentioned racial theory of Indian civilization, which remained the view until about 1924, when remains of an earlier civilization in the Indus Valley, which we call the Indus Civilization, were identified and assigned to an early period contemporary with the Bronze Age civilizations (Sumerian, Akkadian, and Elamite) of Mesopotamia and Iran. Since then our knowledge of the history of India has involved two beginning points and two civilizations, the second built on top of the first, so to say. The experts are still arguing about the relation of the two, as we shall see.

Indian Civilization's long period of development had many inputs from foreign sources through trade, war, and the travels of religious teachers, and in its mature form it had a very large presence in Asia. It is the homeland of two world religions: Buddhism, which spread to East

Asia, Central Asia, and Southeast Asia, and Hinduism, which spread to parts of Southeast Asia. With them went other elements of Indian Civilization, including writing systems, grammar, astronomy and astrology, mathematics, medical practices, codes of law, mythology and story literature, sculpture, and dance.

Indian Civilization lay in the path of two far-reaching imperial expansions that had deep effects on India, that of Islam and the countries formed with its spread, and that of Christian Europe, both through trade and through the conquest states formed by Turks, Mughals, and the British. In the course of the period of British rule, a nationalist movement formed around the new notions of popular sovereignty and the nation-state, leading to the pattern of seven self-governing states that now prevails.

Here is a brief chronology, with approximate dates, to give you a rough picture of the whole:

1. The beginnings of Indian civilization, from c. 2500 BCE
2. The Vedic age, from c. 1400 BCE
3. New religions and empires, from c. 500 BCE
4. The classical age, from 320 CE
5. Turks and Mughals, from c. 1200 CE
6. British rule, from c. 1760 CE
7. The formation of nation-states, from 1947 CE

The Landscape of Indian Civilization

The name "India" comes from the Sanskrit word for river, *sindhu,* which was the name given to the Indus River—that is, it was called The River, perhaps because it was so large. In Old Persian the initial "s" of Sanskrit words is changed to an "h," so that the Persians called the river and the country that it ran through Hindush, and the Greeks, dropping the initial "h" had Indos and the like. A whole set of English words for India, its people, religion, and language derive from the Sanskrit name for the Indus through Persian and Greek:

- Through Greek: India, Indian, Indus River
- Through Persian: Hindu, Hinduism (religion), Hindi (language), Hindustan (India), Hindustani (language)

This doubling of the vocabulary also occurs in Chinese, where we find two names for India, Sin-tu and Yin-tu, the first obviously from Sanskrit, the second from either Persian or Greek. The Arabs, following the Persians, spoke of al-Hind. The Chinese, Persians, Arabs, and Greeks registered the existence of Indian Civilization in the past and gave it the name we derive from them and, ultimately, from the Indus River.

The landscape of Indian Civilization (Map 2) divides into three parts: the Peninsula, called the Deccan, the Himalayan Mountains, and the Indo-Gangetic Plain. The Deccan is a block of granite that is extremely old. The experts on plate tectonics tell us that this block was

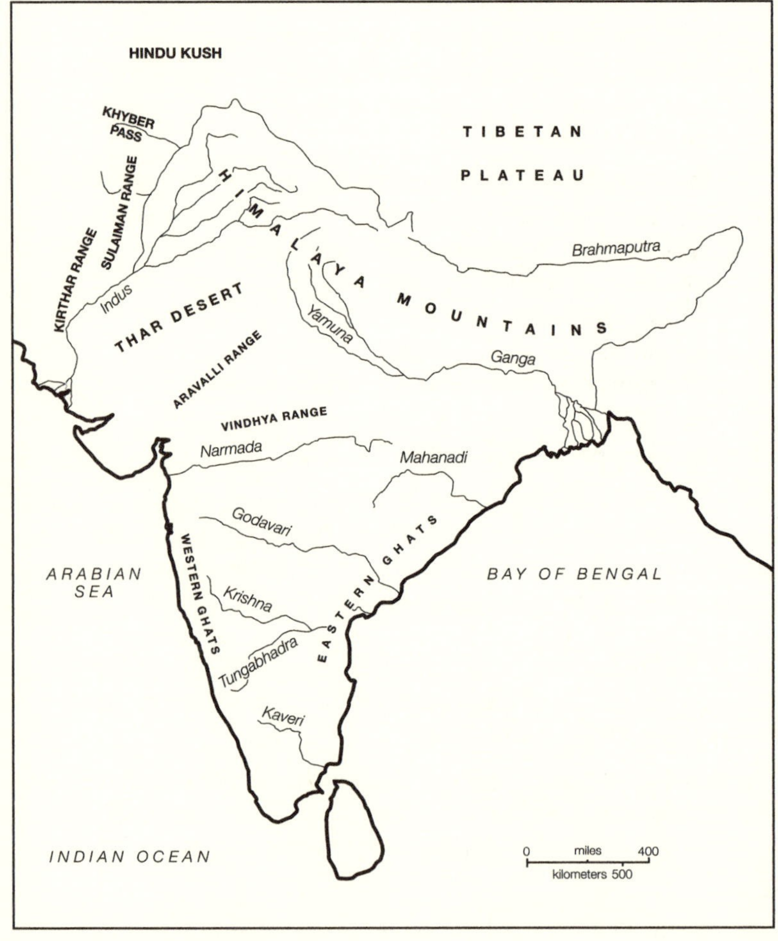

MAP 2 Physical features

once a free-floating large island that, moving northward over a very long period of time, collided with the landmass of Eurasia, creating the Himalaya as it did so, and pushing it ever higher. The Deccan, as one can see from the direction of the rivers, is a plateau tilted toward the southeast, and has hilly ridges parallel to the coasts, called the Eastern and Western Ghats. The coastal districts are well watered by the monsoon rains, but the interior is dry and its rivers tend to reduce to a trickle in summer. For those reasons, agriculture, and hence population, tends to concentrate on the coasts and to be more limited in the interior. Sri Lanka lies off the southern coast, separated from India by little more than 40 kilometers (25 miles) at the narrowest point.

The Himalayas (*Himalaya* is a Sanskrit word meaning "abode of snow") are the tallest mountains in the world, the highest peak, Mount Everest, being over 8 kilometers (5 miles) above sea level. Because the Peninsular block continues to push northward into the Eurasian landmass, raising the mountains faster than erosion lowers them, they add a few millimeters each year. This forbidding and difficult terrain serves to separate India fairly sharply from Tibet, but its passes have been corridors for trade and the transmission of Indian Buddhism to Tibet for a very long time, and languages of the Sino-Tibetan family on the Indian side of the Himalaya, in Nepal, Bhutan, and the western fringes of the Himalaya show that they are by no means impassable. The mountainous boundary of India continues eastward until it nearly joins the north–south-running ridges that make up the Indo-China Peninsula. To the west of the Indus River there are less formidable mountain chains, called Kirthar and Suleiman, giving definition to the northwest side of the Indian diamond. Famous passes through these mountain ranges, especially the Khyber and the Bolan passes, make for communication with Afghanistan and, from there, northward to Central Asia and the Silk Road joining China to Europe, or westward to the Middle East and the Mediterranean Sea.

The Indo-Gangetic Plain, as its name implies, is made of the basins of the two great rivers of the North, the Indus and the Ganga (Ganges), to which we should add the third great river to the east, the Brahmaputra. The Indus and the Brahmaputra start within a few miles of each other on the Tibetan Plateau, one flowing west and the other east, and descend into India on opposite ends of the Himalaya. The Indus Valley makes up the whole of Pakistan and a part of the Republic of India. The upper Indus and its tributaries are called Punjab, "the five (*panch*) rivers (*ab*)," and the region of the lower Indus bears its ancient name, Sindh. The Ganga and its twin, the Yamuna, form between them the rich land called the Doab, the land between "the two (*do*) rivers (*ab*)" that was the agricultural heartland for North Indian empires, so that it is here we find the capitals of ancient and modern India, of which Delhi is the most recent. The mouths of the Ganga and the Brahmaputra make eastern India a very rich agricultural region.

The plain is formed at the juncture of the Deccan block and the Himalaya, and over the ages it has filled with alluvium—eroded rock turned to soil—favorable to agriculture. The alluvium deepens as one goes eastward down the Ganga, until, in West Bengal and Bangladesh, one needs to dig down one hundred meters or so before finding bedrock; consequently there are few stone buildings there, and everything is made of brick, from the fine clay soil. The rivers, besides making and distributing soil, favor agriculture by supplying water for irrigation to supplement the monsoon rains, and because they have their roots in very tall, snowy mountains, they remain much fuller all year than do the rivers of the South, and much more dependable as sources of irrigation.

Climate: The Monsoon

The other great factor for agriculture is rainfall, which in India is seasonal. The southwest monsoon is a moist, rain-bearing wind that blows from the Indian Ocean over the land in summer, from southwest to northeast, dropping its rain as it is heated and rises over the land.

The mechanism of the monsoon has come to be understood only recently. Suppose (to start with a simplified model) the earth was entirely covered with water, and that its axis was not tilted, so that the equator was always closest to the sun. Then the air would be hottest directly over the equator and would rise; to replace the rising hot air, cooler air would flow from the poles toward the equator, be heated, rise, and flow back to the poles till it sank, so that there would be two convection currents of circulating air, one to the north and one to the south. The zone of rising hot air over the equator, where the two systems of convection touch, is called the intertropical discontinuity (ITD)—the discontinuity, that is, between the northern and southern convection currents.

The earth is tilted on its axis, however, and in summer the Northern Hemisphere is closer to the sun, so that the ITD moves northward, over India, drawing Indian Ocean air currents toward it. The eastward rotation of the earth deflects the north-going air currents to eastward, so that the general direction of flow is from southwest to northeast. Moreover, the earth's surface consists of land as well as water, and the land heats up the air above it, much more than the ocean does, in the daytime summer sun. The moist sea breezes are heated more when they blow landward and as they rise they lose their capacity to retain moisture, and it rains.

The monsoon concentrates the rainfall in a rainy season, so that from ancient times the Indian year has been divided into three (or six), rather than four, seasons: the rains, the cold season, and the hot season. The rainy season is the main agricultural season, and the season of warfare was in the cold season, after the harvest. In many places irrigation or the winter rains of the less bountiful retreating monsoon make a second crop possible in a single year. Double-cropping has been going on in India for a very long time, and the Greek geographer Herodotus (fifth century BCE) noted it as something he had not seen elsewhere, and as a sign of India's wealth.

Because the rainfall is concentrated in a rainy season, agriculture is greatly extended if the water can be controlled by works of irrigation that manage the supply of water and deliver it (or drain it away) when needed. These include the riverine irrigation typical of parts of North India, the "tanks" or reservoirs typical of the South where rivers fall very low in summer, and wells, with various devices for raising water by human or animal power, or, in the tube wells of today, by electrical pumps. For this reason the great divide in types of agricultural land is between wet land and dry land; that is, land that is irrigated as opposed to land that is watered by rainfall only. Large portions of India fall within the arid zone, which continues across Eurasia through Afghanistan, Iran, Arabia, and northern Africa, a zone of pastoralism and irrigation agriculture (Map 3).[3] The making of irrigation works greatly increases the productivity and value of agricultural land, by as much as five times over the value of dry land, and wet land therefore supports denser aggregates of people. Consequently the features that make for civilization—complexity of social ranking, cities, states, monumental constructions requiring the marshaling of large numbers of workers and resources—are especially tied to the distribution of wetland in the Indian landscape.

The monsoon falls on the Indian landscape unevenly, and the better watered portions (or places that have riverine irrigation) have the

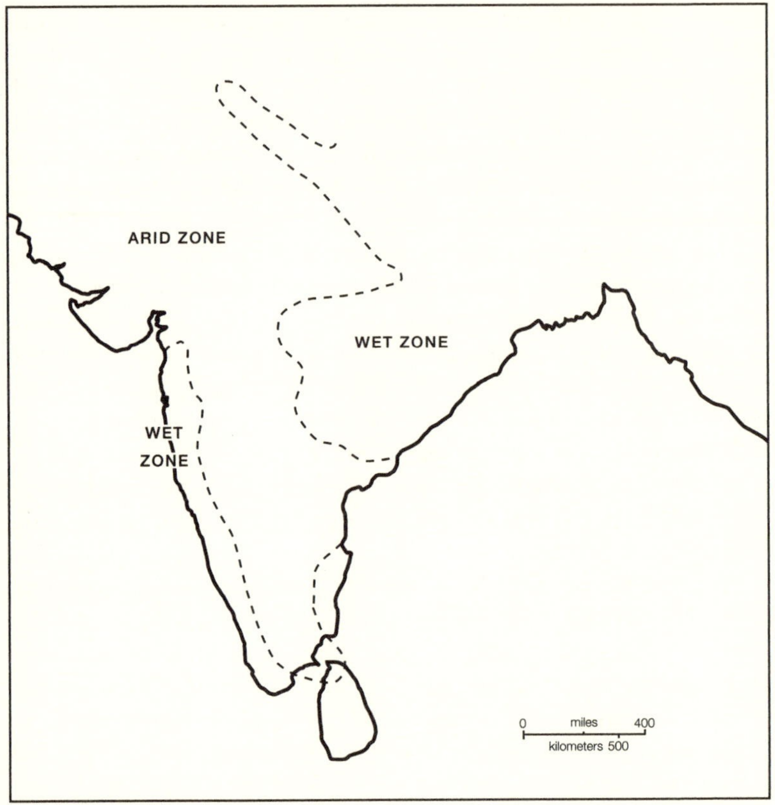

MAP 3 Arid and wet zones

greatest population densities: in the Deccan, along the coasts, and in the North, along the Indo-Gangetic plain. The driest areas are the Rajasthan Desert and the lower Indus (Sindh), and the interior of the Deccan plateau. It is in the areas of denser population that Indian Civilization sprung up in the first place (the Indus Valley and the Indo-Gangetic Plain generally) and took root (the coastal regions and river deltas of the Peninsula). It is here that agriculture yields a surplus large enough to sustain a complex social structure including kings and priests, and to finance the building of palaces, temples, and monasteries. By contrast, the drier areas or areas of rainfall agriculture are typically inhabited by peoples with a tribal organization, far less complex and far more egalitarian, very often practicing a "slash-and-burn" form of agriculture, which sustains far lower densities of population. Societies of this kind exist in many variants in many parts of India, but the great concentration of them is in the central and east-central zone, which, therefore, constitutes a kind of interior frontier for Indian Civilization, a place of exile for princes in disgrace, a wilderness conducive to the meditations of a religious hermit, the home of forest peoples and wild animals, a place of magic and of danger.

CHAPTER 2

The Beginnings of Indian Civilization

The rivers and tributaries of the Indus, flowing in a southwesterly direction, and of the Ganga flowing southeasterly, comprise the two great river basins that form the alluvial plain of Pakistan, North India, and Bangladesh. Of these two great rivers, the greater population densities are today found along the Gangetic basin. It is favored not only by its rivers but also by the monsoon (and cursed periodically by its absence, which spells famine), which reaches the head of the Bay of Bengal in June, drives up the Ganga from its mouth, dropping its rain in decreasing amounts on the plains until, about September, it depletes itself over the upper Indus region. Thus in West Bengal (India) where the Ganga enters the ocean, and in Bangladesh watered by the adjacent delta of the Brahmaputra River, population densities average over 1000 persons per square kilometer; further up the Ganga, in the Indian states of Bihar and Uttar Pradesh, they drop to 900 and 800 persons; in the Punjab (upper Indus basin) they are in the 500 to 400 range; and in Sindh (lower Indus basin), which the monsoon never reaches, they drop to just over 200.

Yet it is in the more arid Indus Valley and not the humid Ganga and Brahmaputra valleys that urban civilization began in South Asia. The Indus Valley divides in two. The upper region, called the Punjab or "Land of Five Rivers," takes its name from the five Indus tributaries (from west to east: Jhelum, Chenab, Ravi, Sutlej, Beas) that fan out across it. Not only do these perennial, snow-fed rivers permit extensive canal irrigation, but the winter monsoon blowing from the Eurasian landmass supplements the modest rainfall deposited during the summer monsoon, making this region highly favorable to agriculture, with two main growing seasons in the year. Today the rivers also power hydroelectric projects. The lower Indus region of Sindh, which bears the ancient name of the great river itself, is ignored by both monsoons. Its annual rainfall at places is below a paltry 13 centimeters (5 inches), so that agriculture is more or less impossible beyond the areas serviced by irrigation canals. Summer temperatures reaching 50°C (120°F) in the shade are normal. At places the salinity of the soil is so great that the landscape is a silvery and infertile waste. Sindh sustains the lowest population densities of a very crowded subcontinent, but appearances are misleading. The Indus meanders lazily toward its mouths above the level of the surrounding plain, contained within embankments of its own alluvium. From time to time it breaks through these natural dikes and spreads rich new soil across the plain until it forms a new channel. Less predictable than the Nile in its flooding, but twice as rich in its burden of soil, the Indus created a habitat for archaic civilization not unlike that of Egypt or Mesopotamia. The arid zone of India, with its reliance on wheat, barley, and millet (as opposed to the wet rice-growing regions to the east, and the coastal regions of the south) is continuous with the arid zone of Western Asia and the Mediterranean, where agriculture and animal domestication began (Map 3).

Mohenjo-daro and Harappa

In this setting lies the ruins of a city of the third and second millennia BCE called Mohenjo-daro; some 550 kilometers to the north lies another, called Harappa, near the Ravi River in the Punjab. The general disposition of these cities is strikingly similar, consisting of three main elements: (1) a lower city, not known to be walled, divided by major avenues into city blocks; (2) a raised mound to the west of the lower city; and (3) a granary complex or warehouse contiguous to the old bed of the river. Excavation of these sites is far from complete, but we can get a composite picture of the cities by taking them together.

The Lower City

The residential area of Mohenjo-daro (very little of Harappa's having been excavated) was divided by major avenues 10 meters wide, running north–south and east–west, creating something like city blocks. These blocks, 350 by 250 meters and oriented north and south, are cut up by narrow, angular lanes on which opened the entrances to the closely packed but comfortably commodious dwellings of the Indus people. On the sides fronting the main street we meet blank brick walls, with little suggestion of windows and doors, but there is evidence that the brickwork was plastered within, and it is likely enough that the brick facades that lined the main arterials were enlivened with plaster, paint, and carved timbers. Masonry screens, and probably screens of perishable materials such as reeds and bamboo, served to admit ventilation while minimizing sunlight, highly desirable in these latitudes. The blank and noncommittal exterior, opening via a small doorway, with adjoining room for a night watchman, to a courtyard leading to small rooms, is a plan typical of the residences still seen in South Asia's old cities. Remains of staircases show that the dwellings had one or more upper stories. Among the inner rooms we find a well room, a bathroom, and a toilet with seat latrine rather than the "squatters" of contemporary South Asia. The Indus cities as a whole show a remarkable grasp of and dedication to the principles of public sanitation in the supply of clean water and removal of wastewater. Courtyards and bathrooms drain by means of earthenware pipe enclosed in brickwork into the covered drains of the streets. Drains enclosed within the brick walls serviced the upper stories. In the streets, brick manhole covers permitted the public drains to be unblocked or periodically cleaned, presumably by municipal workmen. Sewage was drained into soak pits. Rubbish chutes conveyed household refuse into rectangular bins outside, doubtless to be emptied by city garbage crews. Public wells in the streets supplemented those of the larger houses.

In these mundane details of street arrangement, waterworks, and sewage, the Indus people reveal themselves as committed city dwellers. Working evidently from a plan—for a rectilinear pattern of main streets oriented to the cardinal points requires conscious decision and collective cooperation—they built, not overgrown villages, but South Asia's first cities. They were in several respects the most modern cities in the world, and they remained unsurpassed in South Asia long after their demise. These people understood that the health and well-being of large concentrations of people require sanitation works of a type and scale quite different from what suffices for a village or hamlet.

The Granaries

At Harappa, just north of the raised mound (in the city's northwest sector), lie two rows of small, identical two-room dwellings, no doubt laid out by the government. That they were the barracks of slaves or semiservile workmen is shown by the regimentation of their plan and their close proximity to the citadel. To the north of these barracks are circular brick milling platforms and the remains of twelve granaries. One of the platforms yielded remains of wheat and barley in the central hollow, where the grain was probably ground by a wooden pestle. The wooden granaries were built on brick-faced earth podiums with three parallel joists, assuring sufficient ventilation to prevent mildew. Just beyond lies the old bed of the river, suggesting that grain was brought as tax or tribute from the peasant communities of the hinterland by boat, stored in the granaries for the payment in kind of state servants and the provisioning of the city, and ground into meal by the occupants of the workmen's barracks on the milling platforms as needed. The granary complex as a whole calls to mind the palace and temple granaries of Egypt and Mesopotamia, with their staffs of bakers, brewers, and slaves.

At Mohenjo-daro a single granary (or at any rate a warehouse of some sort), greater in area than the twelve Harappan granaries put together, was found within the citadel itself; whether there were others in the lower city remains to be discovered. Twenty-seven rectangular brick platforms, set up in a grid with ventilation channels between, was the substructure on which the wooden granary was erected. A large staircase nearby gave access to the raised mound and its great granary, perhaps from riverside. A group of sixteen workmen's huts, comparable to the barracks at Harappa, is found within the lower city. Although the occupation of the inhabitants of these 6 by 4 meter, two-room dwellings cannot be determined, they are further evidence of a regimented labor force, implying the presence of some kind of government authority.

The Raised Mound

In both cities the most imposing and intriguing complexes are raised mounds on their western perimeters. At Harappa the entire complex rests on a platform of mud and mud brick, rising some 10 meters above ground level. Around this platform was thrown a massive wall of mud brick, more than 10 meters thick at the base, inner and outer planes tapering together; its outer surface is faced with a revetment of burned brick.

Bastions surmounted the wall at various intervals and at the angles. The main entrance lay to the north, with subsidiary gateway and terraces to the west. The area enclosed was in the shape of a parallelogram, approximately 350 by 200 meters, the long axis oriented north and south. At Mohenjo-daro very little of the comparable structure has been excavated, although enough to show that it was of similar type, and the buildings making up the mound there are much more fully known than those of Harappa. Besides the granary of the Mohenjo-daro citadel, there are three structures: the great bath, the "college," and the assembly hall.

The bath, 2.5 meters deep and approximately 12 by 7 meters in plan, is of careful construction, made of bricks set on edge with a layer of bitumen (tar) for waterproofing covered with further layers of brick, a drain in the corner, and brick steps leading into the bath. Surrounding the bath on three sides are small cells, "cloisters" or changing rooms depending on whether one puts a religious or a secular interpretation on the bath's functions. Ritual bathing and the pollution it is supposed to remove are central concepts in domestic Hinduism as we know it.

Northeast of the bath is the "college," a complex of rooms similar to those that surround the bath itself, in this instance bordering a courtyard 10 meters square. The excavator speculates that it housed a college of priests, hence its name. Toward the southern end of the complex stand the remains of a hall, nearly 30 meters square, with four rows of five brick piers, like the later Achemenid audience halls of Iran. The raised mound evidently had several functions, perhaps religious ones associated with purification with water, and perhaps civic ones having to do with collective deliberation. It might also have served as a defensive citadel within which the population could withdraw when the city was attacked; no defensive wall has been found around the lower city.

Other Indus Sites

Fairservis estimated the population of the lower cities of Mohenjo-daro and Harappa at about 41,000 and 23,500, respectively.[4] As such they were the most populous, but by no means the only settlements of the Indus Civilization . More than a thousand Indus Civilization sites have been found. A whole cluster has been found on the dried-up bed of the Saraswati River, and the largest of these, Ganweriwala, is nearly as

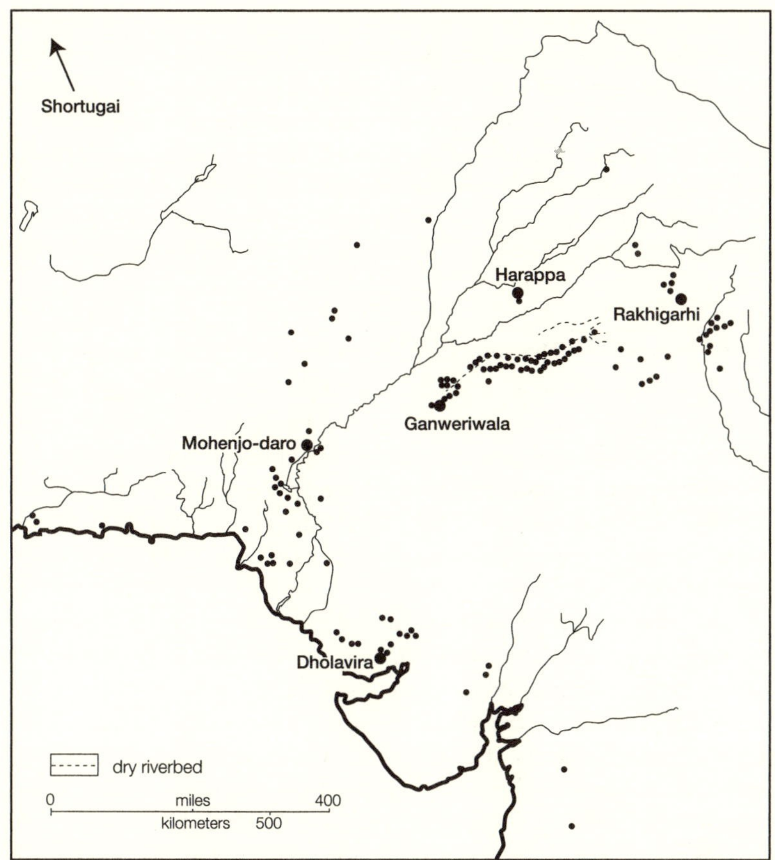

MAP 4 The Indus Civilization

large as Mohenjo-daro and Harappa; so is Rakhigarhi in Hariyana, in the Republic of India, and Dholavira in Gujarat is only slightly smaller. Thus we have identified at least five cities, plus many towns and many, many villages (Map 4).

The area over which these sites are distributed is astonishingly large. Eastward from Harappa in the Punjab we find Indus sites as far as the basin of the Ganga; south of Mohenjo-daro in Sindh they reach the Arabian Sea and spread west and southeast along 1,300 kilometers of Pakistani and Indian seaboard, from Makran to the Kathiawar Peninsula and the Gulf of Cambay. Its most widely separated settlements are more than 1,600 kilometers apart. Shortugai is a remote Harappan site in northern Afghanistan. A substantial similarity of style unifies the material remains from site to site. Mohenjo-daro and Harappa give evidence of a stratified society with a complex division of labor, commanding the agricultural surplus of a large hinterland, perhaps through tax or tribute. It seems reasonable to infer that the Indus cities constituted a state or states, although archaeologists differ on this question.

Economy, Technology, Writing

Of the peasants whose precious agricultural surplus fed the great Indus cities and villages and of their methods of farming we know very little. They must have been numerous; country people outnumber city dwellers by four times in modern India. In Sindh the flooding of the Indus enriched and replenished the topsoil from time to time. In addition, irrigation must have been necessary then as now, but we do not know what form it took.

The principal crops were wheat and barley (perhaps domesticated in place), and also millets (from Africa), but not rice, except perhaps in Gujarat. Bits of cotton cloth have been preserved. Cotton is native to this area, and did not reach the Mediterranean until much later: Herodotus, nearly a thousand years after the Indus Civilization had disappeared, wrote wonderingly of the wool-bearing trees of Sindh. Domesticated animals were above all cattle (humped and unhumped), sheep, and goats, and also probably the camel and the ass but not the horse (no wild species here) or the elephant (which is no longer found in the Indus region). Bullock carts with heavy solid wheels, still to be seen in Sindh, must have been the principal means of rural transport, judging from the terracotta models of them the Indus folk made, perhaps for the amusement of their children (Figure 1).

The tools of the Indus people show that they are still using stone, but are very much a bronze-age society. Stone tools abound, whereas the rarer metal tools are of copper or a bronze containing very little of the tin that toughens the alloy, and their shapes are often copied from stone prototypes. The axe blades, for example, are flat without sockets, so that they had to be lashed to the haft with a thong, just as a stone axe head would. Spearheads were leaf shaped and lacked a thickened midrib, so that they can hardly have withstood the first impact unless

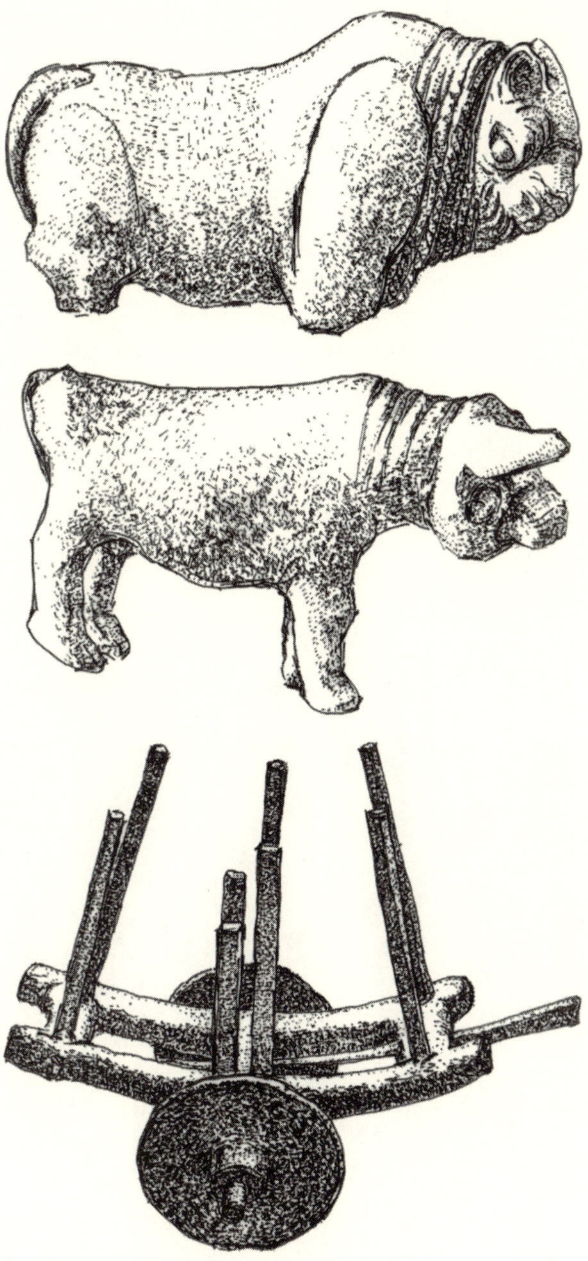

FIGURE 1 Toy ox cart and oxen, Indus Civilization

deeply embedded in the split ends of the shaft. Copper arrowheads with deep barbs but no tang are fairly common. Other metal tools include knife blades, chisels, saws, and fishhooks.

An inventory of Indus crafts reveals a fairly wide range of materials that entered into their manufactures: mirrors and pins (copper), cosmetic boxes (steatite), beads beautifully made of many different substances (gold, silver, copper, faience, steatite, semiprecious stones, shell, pottery), and sculpture (limestone, alabaster, bronze, terracotta). Some of these materials are unavailable locally, and it is clear that Indus cities had trading connections with distant regions including Persia (the Elamites), Afghanistan, and various regions of India to the east of the Indus settlements. Indus seals and other items found their way to Mesopotamia, and the Indus Civilization was known to the Sumerians and Akkadians of Mesopotamia under the name Meluhha, as a source of rare trade goods. Excavations in southeastern Iran suggest that the early Elamite cities there might have traded their products—metal ores, steatite, lapis lazuli,

FIGURE 2 Seals of the Indus Civilization

FIGURE 2 *Continued*

and alabaster—to both Mesopotamia and the Indus, and also have served as an entrepôt for trans-shipment of Indus goods westward.

The most intriguing artifacts of the Indus sites are rectangular steatite seals, because of the writing on them (Figure 2). These seals, little more than 2.5 cm square, generally bear an incised image, beautifully carved, of which the humped bull is a common type; other animals (tiger, elephant), composite mythological beasts, and the rare human form are figured on other seals. They also bear a short inscription across the top, in a script that has defied many attempts to decipher it. This script contains more than four hundred signs, too many to be purely alphabetic or syllabic because no language is known to have more than a hundred phonemes. Although many of the signs are obviously pictographic, other elements act as modifiers, perhaps as word endings, and others are clearly numerals. The seals were meant to be pressed into soft clay as a mark of ownership, in all likelihood. The inscriptions are short, presumably recording little more than the owner's name. The language of the script is unknown; a Dravidian language would be our best guess because of islands of Dravidian language in the Indus and Ganga valleys, but other languages cannot be ruled out. We do not have a bilingual inscription, like the Rosetta Stone by which the Egyptian hieroglyphics were deciphered, or the Greek and Prakrit inscriptions on coins by which the inscriptions of Ashoka were read. However, because the Indus people were involved with seagoing trade with other literate people, especially the Elamites and perhaps the Mesopotamians, there is a chance that a bilingual inscription will be found one day. It is clear that the Indus people were literate, and that their script became extinct in time; attempts to show that it evolved into the Brahmi script of Ashoka have not convinced the community of scholars.

Religion

Our inability to read the Indus inscriptions has hampered the analysis of Indus religion. There is a strong temptation to interpret the material finds of the Indus Civilization by means of the known content of historic Hinduism, on the assumption that some elements of the Indus culture must have continued and shaped that of historic India, but we need to be cautious. Certain Indus objects lend themselves to the idea that the religion of their makers might be ancestral to certain specific features of historic Hinduism. Three groups of such objects are of interest to this hypothesis.

First there are a number of cheaply made terracotta figurines of women heavily ornamented with necklaces, earrings, and fan-shaped headdresses. It is natural to think that these are votive figures, mass produced for popular worship, and that their function is to promote the fertility of crops, livestock, and humans. Mother goddess figurines are commonplace all across Neolithic Western Asia, and even prehistoric Europe. It is reasonable to hypothesize that the Indus figurines depict the local version of this cult, and that this is the prototype of the Great Goddess of Hinduism, the wife of Shiva. On the other hand it is entirely possible that these images are not objects of worship but toys for children.

Second, there are the seals with their theriomorphic, anthropomorphic, and composite images, which might well represent divinities because of their nonnatural form. On one of the seals we find a man with a horned headdress, perhaps three-faced, seated with the soles of his feet touching, hands on knees, surrounded by two gazelles, a buffalo, a rhinoceros, an elephant, and a tiger. John Marshall, who first expounded the theory of Indus survivals in Hinduism, called this figure "Proto-Shiva."[5] The Shiva of later Hinduism is indeed called "Lord of Beasts," which seems appropriate to the figure on the seal, surrounded as he is by various animals. The posture of the figure, which cannot be imitated without considerable practice and much muscular discomfort, suggests the postures of *yoga* and another of Shiva's epithets, "Lord of Yogis."

Finally there is a group of stone artifacts that can be interpreted as conventionalized representations of the phallus and the vulva, perhaps to be associated with the phallic stone or *linga* sacred to Shiva in Hinduism as we know it.

Indus religion appears to have had images of divinities (the existence of temples is not proven), embracing a pantheon partly animal and partly human in form. The case for seeing here an early form of the "Shiva complex"—*yoga,* Shiva Lord of Beasts, his spouse the Great Goddess, and emphasis on the functions and organs of generation and fertility—can be regarded as a reasonable hypothesis to be tested by further research.

Origin and Destiny of the Indus Civilization

The Indus Civilization is an enigma placed between the two question marks of its origin and its destiny. Little as its mute remains tell us of its economy, social organization, and culture, we know even less of how it began and how it ended.

Radio carbon dating had placed the mature phase of the Indus Civilization between 2300 BCE and 1700 BCE. Those dates were subsequently pushed further *back*, to 2500 and 1900, due to a recalibration of radio carbon dates after checking them against the exactly-datable tree rings of the bristlecone pine of the American Southwest. These dates show that the civilization of the Indus is, together with the civilizations of the Tigris-Euphrates and the Nile, one of the three earliest civilizations of the Old World. Civilized life began somewhat earlier in Mesopotamia (3100 BCE), but not by a great deal. The Indus remains, moreover, resemble those of Mesopotamia in a general way, including the use of seals, the central granaries, and the combination of lower city and raised mound. The grid pattern of its main thoroughfares contrasts with the meanderings of Mesopotamian city streets as the streets of New York contrast with those of London. Evidently the Indus cities, so far as we know them, did not simply grow, they were planned, an impression that is strengthened by the fact that many of them were planted on virgin soil and were not growths of ages. Did their planners come from Mesopotamia?

Probably not. Indus techniques might be similar, but their products are quite different in detail and possess a style uniquely their own. It is more likely that the founders of the Indus cities came from among the bronze-age peasant cultures whose remains are to be found in the hills of Baluchistan, west of the lower Indus in Pakistan. These cultures are named from the places at which their pottery types were first found, following archaeological convention: Zhob, Togau, Quetta, Amri-Nal, and Kulli. These pottery types show similarities to those of Iran, whence presumably they derive, and some of these sites are known to predate the Indus Civilization by as much as a thousand years and more. Excavations at Mehrgarh in Pakistan now show that agriculture was practiced in the region three thousand years *before* the building of the Indus cities, so that the indigenous growth of civilization seems more likely than borrowing from Mesopotamia. The picture we get of these communities, reconstructed from surface finds supplemented by a small amount of excavation, is quite uniform in its broad features: small fairly isolated hill villages subsisting on agriculture of barley and wheat and stockraising of humped cattle, sheep, and goats, watering their fields from stone check dams thrown across the gullies to impound the precious rainwater, grinding their cereals with mano and matate. The great variation in detail from culture to culture and site to site, as seen principally in their pottery, contrasts with the generic similarity of the Indus pottery style across its vast area.

Gregory Possehl points out that the invention of agriculture and domestication of animals in Western Asia and the Mediterranean grew out of human interactions with wild varieties of wheat and barley, cattle, sheep, and goats indigenous to the region.[6] He further says that barley, cattle, sheep, and goats are also indigenous to the Indus Valley, and wild wheat might have once existed there, and that there is good archaeological evidence of local domestication of these crops and animals in the Indus settlements prior to the mature phase of the cities (2500–1900 BCE). He suggests that, instead of positing the diffusion of techniques from Western Asia to the Indus, we should think of the Indus as a part of the same arid zone in which domestications first occurred, in various localities, including the Indus itself.

The End and Aftermath of the Indus Civilization

The Indus cities came to an end in about 1900 BCE. Many of the towns and villages of the Indus Civilization settlements carried on as before, some of them until the Iron Age (1000 BCE), but city life was at an end, and had to be reinvented in the second urbanization of the fifth century BCE. The Indus script became extinct, and writing had to be reinvented in the time of Ashoka or possibly somewhat before. The Indus cities, which appeared rather abruptly in about 2500 BCE, had a six-hundred-year span, very long indeed, but not nearly so long as the cities of Egypt and Mesopotamia.

We do not know what brought about the death of the Indus cities, or whether they ended with a bang or a whimper. Bang theories concentrate on evidence for a major disaster, natural (flood) or human (military invasion), whimper theories center on ecological (desiccation) or internal causes (stagnation, loss of morale).

In Sindh where the Indus flows between embankments above the level of the plain, flooding is a boon to agriculture but a constant danger to settlements. Parts of the lower city of Mohenjo-daro were flooded and rebuilt at least three times. R. Raikes, a hydrologist, believes that a catastrophic flood caused the abandonment of Mohenjo-daro and other sites.[7] The fact that Indus sites along the Arabian Sea lie some 40 or 50 kilometers inland suggests that they were originally coastal sites separated from the sea by a major uplifting of the coast at some time in their existence. As this is in the earthquake zone, the uplifting could have been sudden. If it occurred when the Indus cities were inhabited, and if the uplift was sudden enough, as Raikes believes, it would reverse the flow of the lower Indus, flooding the plain and the settlements on its banks without warning. Whole civilizations, however, as opposed to individual cities, do not perish all at once in natural calamities, and the Indus sites in the Punjab could not have been affected, even if Raikes is correct in believing the southern cities of Sindh were.

Late strata of Harappa and other Indus sites have yielded evidence that they were taken over by squatters who built squalid huts from the bricks of the ruins (the Jhukar culture). Here and in general the appearance of copper or bronze shaft-hoe axes coincides ominously with the end of Indus habitation levels. Mohenjo-daro's uppermost stratum showed skeletons of people who had died in the streets and houses, in circumstances strongly suggestive of violence, and left unburied. Sir Mortimer Wheeler pinned the responsibility on the early Aryans, whose sacred collection of hymns, the *Rig Veda,* speaks of the hundred-walled forts of the Dasyus, their enemies, which Indra their warrior-god destroyed.[8] On present evidence, however, the end of the cities must be put at about 1900 BCE, and the Aryan arrival four or more centuries later.

Reid Bryson, a meteorologist, holds in effect that the Indus people wore out their environment, with agriculture on the large scale stripping the soil of its natural cover, creating dust clouds that turned a favorable climate arid and made a desert of Rajasthan to the east of Sindh.[9] Clearly Sindh once supported a more luxuriant fauna than now, including species such as the elephant (if it was not imported) that require shade, water, and abundant green fodder to survive, and also the rhinoceros and tiger.[10] All three are today are found together in the wet, grassy floodplain of the Brahmaputra River in Assam, for example. Like the flood theory, however, this does not by itself account for the disappearance of the upper Indus cities of the Punjab.

Each of these theories implies that the Indus people were unable to respond with countermeasures to an external force so strong that it overwhelmed them, that they had become unable to adapt to new and pressing circumstances and became demoralized before the challenges that confronted them. Although they had rebuilt flooded cities before, rebuilt and improved defensive works against military attack, and spread agriculture across the face of Sindh and the Punjab, they were now dealt such a blow that they lacked sufficient inner resources to rebuild or defend their settlements or relocate them in more favorable places. All the foregoing theories are reducible finally to the question of inner resources, material, and morale.

The cause of the cities' demise, then, is still to be determined. What is more important, however, is the question of what continuities there might have been between the Indus Civilization and later historic India, given the rather sharp discontinuity of city life and writing. In addition to speculations about religious continuities, especially concerning the worship of Shiva, the practice of yoga and the conception of a mother goddess, about which we have already spoken, some scholars think the Indus Civilization was created by the Sanskrit-speaking Aryans of the Veda, whose settlements centered on the Saraswati River, the site of Ganweriwala and many lesser Indus sites.[11] The theory of an Indo-Saraswati Civilization has many difficulties, the most notable of which is the near complete absence in the Indus cities of remains of horses and chariots, abundantly spoken of in the earliest Vedic texts.

There was, then, a period of several centuries before writing and city living were revived again in the Indian subcontinent, some time after the arrival of the Aryans. The Aryan contribution to the formation of classical Indian Civilization is the most readily identifiable component of a culture that synthesized the techniques, practices, and beliefs of many previous cultures, and the cultural survivals of the Indus Civilization are the most open to speculation. On the mundane level, the solid-wheeled ox cart that can still be found in Sindh, long after the rest of South Asia exchanged it for the spoke-wheeled vehicle introduced later from the northwest, is probably such a survival. On a more sublime plane, the Hindu worship of images such as those of the Great Goddess and of Shiva are possible survivals. For the present, however, the history of the Indus civilization is largely a chapter of its own, its connection with the story of Indian Civilization that follows still uncertain. Only further archeological field work can unearth the facts by which our speculations can be tested.

CHAPTER 3

The Vedic Age

The *Rig Veda*
Indo-European, Indo-Iranian, Indo-Aryan
The Later Veda

So long as the Indus script remains undeciphered, the history of the Indus Civilization must be read from its material remains. Just the opposite is the case with the Aryans, with whom the next age of South Asian civilization opens. Although their earliest settlements—probably humble affairs—have left little for archeologists to discover, their religious literature, called the Veda, is a rich source from which to reconstruct their inner life. As a consequence, we are able to know a good deal more about the religion of the Aryans than about their patterns of settlement, economy, or technology. In the Vedas we have the mind, but not the body, so to speak, of the early Aryans of South Asia.

The *Rig Veda*

The oldest work of this literature is the *Rig Veda*, a collection of 1,028 hymns addressed to the gods, arranged in ten sections. Within this collection we can distinguish strata of different ages: The central core consists of those sections that were once the private liturgical collection of old priestly families or clans, later joined to form a single collection; to this were added a section consisting of hymns entirely devoted to the god Soma, and at a still later date the first and last sections in which the most speculative and philosophical of hymns are found.

Reconstructing the society and life of the times of *Rig Veda* is difficult because it is a collection of hymns, not a sociological treatise. We begin with mythology and religion before sketching what may be known of Aryan society, economy, and technology.

The gods of the *Rig Veda*

The hymns of the *Rig Veda* are directed principally to beings called *devas,* the "shining ones," gods associated mostly with the sky, not so much with the soil and the mysteries of fructification. From the same root comes the name of the Sky Father, Dyaus Pitar, whose union with Mother Earth is probably the oldest conception of the world's creation to which the Vedas allude. Already in the *Rig Veda* Dyaus has yielded pride of place to Varuna as sovereign of the universal order. Varuna is one of the few Vedic gods of a pronounced ethical character, whose thousand eyes the wrongdoer cannot hope to evade. Varuna, in turn, is in the latest section being replaced by Prajapati, Lord of Creatures, who, as the Primordial Man, creates by self-sacrifice the phenomenal world from his own dismembered body. Beside these august divinities we find Mitra, friend of the good and guarantor of compacts; Agni (Fire), who eats the sacrificial oblation and conveys the offerings of men to the gods; and Soma, who takes his name from an inebriating drink made of the juice pressed from a hallucinogenic plant (a certain mushroom, according to some scholars; ephedra according to others), and is the object of an important series of sacrifices in later times.[12] Yama, the first man to die, presides over the spirits of the dead gathered in the World of the Fathers.

Many and important as these gods were to the Vedic Aryans, Indra was their hero, the type of the warrior. Wielding the thunderbolt, he kills the demon Vritra, releasing the pent-up waters of life that flow forth lowing like cattle. As king of the devas he leads them in battle against the *asuras* (demons). On behalf of his Aryan followers, Indra destroys the walled fortresses of the enemy. Other passages speak of his drunken carousing when he has overindulged in soma. Ever victorious over the enemy, succumbing only to soma in his heroic drinking bouts, Indra is the Vedic warrior as he would like to be, drawn larger than life.

The Vedic pantheon is strongly associated with the sky, the sun, and the weather. It is preponderantly masculine, although there are several important goddesses, notably Earth; Ushas, the lady of the Dawn; and Vach, or speech. Of the two greatest gods of later Hinduism, Shiva and Vishnu, we find very little. Rudra, the Howler, in whom are later incorporated other ideas in the Hindu conception of Shiva, is a turbulent god more to be propitiated than petitioned, and Vishnu is in Vedic literature a dwarf who with three giant strides wins earth, air, and sky for the gods and consigns the demons to the nether world.

Religion of the *Rig Veda*

Outside the three-tiered universe that Vishnu won for the gods is the realm of order or *rita,* presided over by the sovereign deity Varuna. The concept of rita is rather like the scientific concept of the laws of nature, except that rita has a moral as well as a physical content. Departure from ancient custom amounts to deviation from rita and invites chaos. Order had constantly to be reestablished, as it had first been instituted, through the sacrifice, which reenacted Prajapati's original act of creation.

Unlike the Indus people, the Aryans had no temples or images. Theirs was a religion of sacrifice in which Agni, the sacred fire, was the focal point. This fire was either the sacred fire in the household, or specially kindled fires in the open air, with, at best, a few temporarily constructed huts within the sacred ring that demarcated the sacrificial field from the profane world; there was nothing like the temples of later Hinduism. The gods were invisibly present, seated on strewn grass provided for them, and invisibly partook of the offerings of butter, milk, fruits, cereals, and meat, transmuted into a subtle form the gods can ingest by Agni. The Fathers or ancestors also had to be fed by the living through sacrifice. Already in the times of the *Rig Veda* as many as four priests were required to aid the sacrificer in the more complex rites, and the number of priestly officiants continued to grow as the sacrifice grew more elaborate in succeeding times.

At the simpler level the sacrificer hoped for earthly benefits: long life, the birth of many sons, riches, preeminence among men, and power over enemies. After death he hoped to journey to the World of the Fathers and feast with King Yama. At a more philosophical level, the universal order itself was continually recreated, and chaos averted, through the sacrifice.

Economy, Technology, Society

The people of the *Rig Veda* were stock breeders and farmers. Teams of horses drew the chariot of the Sun daily across the heavens, as they drew the chariots of the Aryans in battle against their enemies. The yoke by which their animals were harnessed to the chariot was better adapted to the massive shoulders of the ox, and had a tendency to choke the slender necks of their horses; but the light spoked wheels of their chariots were a distinct improvement over the heavy solid wheels of the Indus carts (Figure 3)[13]. Horseback riding was known but was practiced only by the lower classes or individuals needing to make a fast getaway. The Vedic

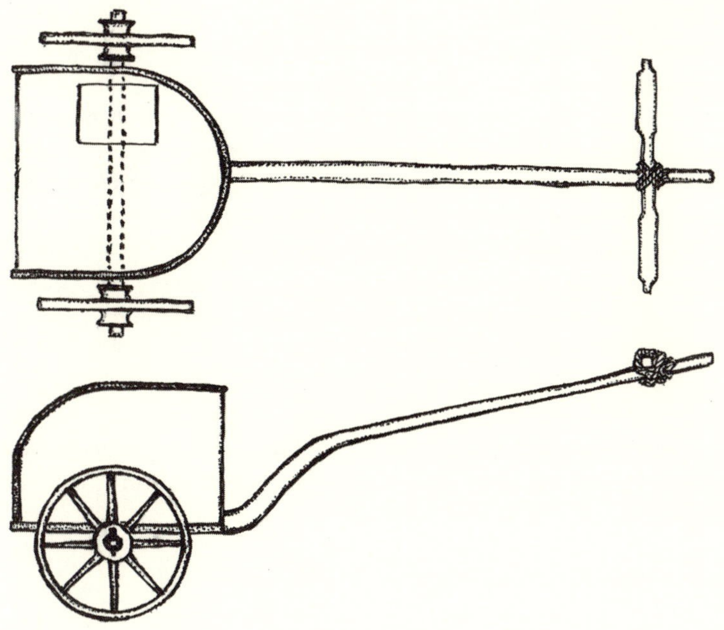

FIGURE 3 Vedic chariot

aristocracy rode chariots, as did their gods; the gods of later Hinduism ride on the backs of animals once the chariot gives way to the mounted cavalry as the elite corps of Indian armies.

The chief form of wealth, however, was cattle, which were highly valued as sources of draft, meat, and milk. A synonym for war was "desire for cattle" (*gavishti*), and cattle rustling must have been a constant source of friction between the tribes of the *Rig Veda.* Cattle are among the offerings of the Vedic sacrifices, and the Vedic tribesman was obliged by custom to show honor to a guest by roasting an ox. Cattle were already animals of considerable sanctity but only later did their flesh become taboo for Hindus. Other domesticated animals included goats, sheep, and dogs.

The *Rig Veda* speaks of carpentry and weaving. Metals were known, copper or bronze certainly, and probably iron at an early date, as well as silver and gold. Dwellings were probably small and of perishable materials.

The *Rig Veda* gives a picture of a people very different from those of the Indus cities and towns: They were militaristic, wandering tribes tending their flocks and herds when their warriors were not stealing those of other tribes or confronting the walled cities of their enemies, apparently the indigenous people they called Dasyu, or Dasa, a word that quickly became a synonym for "slave." Although they seem quite mobile it is a mistake to think of them in the same category as the classic Central Asian nomad. They were not true nomads, for they practiced agriculture as well as animal husbandry, and agriculture is the antithesis of nomadism. Barley and perhaps wheat were cultivated (rice was taken up later), and it is probable that they used a wooden plow, to the tip of which somewhat later they fastened an iron point. The T-shaped, pointed plow of North India has scarcely changed in thousands of years, but in Vedic times it represented a decisive advance over the stone hoes and garden agriculture of prehistoric India, though we do not know what implements the Indus folk used.

Indo-European, Indo-Iranian, Indo-Aryan

Who were the Aryans of the *Rig Veda,* and where had they come from? To answer these questions we must first understand the position of their language, Sanskrit, among the other languages to which it is related. Sanskrit and its descendants, the modern languages of North India (Hindi, Bengali, Punjabi, and so forth) are collectively called Indo-Aryan. The Indo-Aryan group is most closely related in structure to the languages of Iran, with which it forms the larger language group labeled Indo-Iranian, and this group in turn is one of the nine branches of the large family of historically related languages called Indo-European, six of them found in Europe (Celtic, Germanic, Italic, Albanian, Greek, and Balto-Slavonic), two in Central Asia (Armenian and an extinct branch family called Tocharian), and one in Iran and South Asia (Indo-Iranian, with its two subbranches, Iranian and Indo-Aryan). To this list we must also add Hittite, an extinct language of Western Asia spoken in the second millennium BCE, which is a member of the Indo-European family or closely related to it.

The modern languages of this large family are very different from branch to branch, yet comparison shows such systematic equivalences of sound systems, vocabulary, and grammatical structure that we must presume they are all descended from an extinct parent language that we call Proto-Indo-European. From this parent language the daughter languages differentiated themselves and spread to different regions. In the course of these movements, Indo-Iranian further separated into two: one branch establishing itself in Iran, the other migrating to North India. The *Rig Veda* was composed in the upper Indus region shortly after Indo-Aryan-speaking peoples entered the Indian subcontinent.

Languages do not speak themselves; they are spoken by people who are organized into societies and possess certain common symbols and values—religion, mythology, laws—that constitute a distinctive culture. If we must infer the existence of a Proto-Indo-European language, we must also infer the existence of a Proto-Indo-European society and culture, in which this language was spoken (although nothing permits us to speak of a homogeneous Indo-European or Aryan "race"). The separation of the tribes speaking Proto-Indo-European, and their migrations to different regions, isolation from one another and intercourse with peoples of differing non-Indo-European languages, societies, and cultures brought about the evolution of distinct daughter languages, societies, and cultures, of which the Indo-Aryan is one.

Proto-Indo-European society and culture can to some extent be reconstructed through a comparison of the vocabulary, religion, myth, and law of its descendants. The Proto-Indo-European speakers were above all herders of cattle and horses. They had carts of some sort, and probably had a hand in the improvement of the solid-wheeled, ass-drawn chariot of the ancient Near East, through the introduction of the lighter spoked wheel and the horse. Although this gave them considerable mobility, they were not true nomads, a style of life that was developed later in Central Asia (and in which Iranian-speakers such as Scythians participated). The Proto-Indo-European speakers practiced some form of agriculture and lived in semipermanent dwellings of wood and thatch, rather than tents, all of which indicates a somewhat sedentary existence rather than a life of continuous, seasonal movement. They drank mead (fermented honey); used implements of stone, copper, and bronze; and knew the arts of pottery, weaving, and carpentry.

The Proto-Indo-European tribe was divided into patrilineal extended families in which the sons, grandsons, unmarried daughters, wives, and perhaps servants were considered legal minors under the authority of the household head. A large part of their religious life consisted of offerings of food to the sacred fire of the household for the benefit of the deceased patrilineal ancestors of the family. Similar offerings were made to the gods (Latin *deus,* Greek *theos,* Sanskrit *deva*), who for the most part were associated with the sky, the sun, and the weather. The Sky Father (Latin Jupiter, Greek Zeus Pater, Sanskrit Dyaus Pitar) was one such, whose sexual union with the Earth Mother brought about the creation of the world. The goddess Dawn is one of the few other Proto-Indo-European divinities that can be reconstructed with confidence.

According to Georges Dumézil, the Proto-Indo-Europeans conceptualized their gods and their society in terms of three functions, organically related and ordered in a hierarchy: magic and juridical administration, military force, and fertility. Relics of this ideology are found, he believed, in the Roman triad of Jupiter, Mars, and Quirinus, for example, or the Indian series Mitra-Varuna, Indra, and the Nasatyas, who represent these respective functions.[14] It is certain that the Indo-Aryans brought their conceptual division of society into the priest, the warrior, and the herdsman-agriculturalist with them into India, for they share it with their Iranian cousins; and if Dumézil was correct in attributing this ideology to the Proto-Indo-Europeans themselves, it implies that a certain degree of functional differentiation and stratification had already entered the internal organization of their tribes.

This culture developed in the third millennium BCE to the north of the primary centers of civilization in Western Asia. We now have good archaeological evidence to locate the Indo-European homeland in the steppes of southern Russia. There, burial mounds containing human skeletons have been found, together with the remains of domesticated sheep, cattle, and horses; chariots; clay models of wagons; and implements of flint, bone, and copper. Remains of this kind can reasonably be identified with Proto-Indo-European society as reconstructed through language.[15]

The earliest documents showing the existence of Indo-European speech come from Western Asia in the second millennium BCE. At the beginning of this period we first hear of the Hittites, who formed an important empire in Asia Minor and whose language was Indo-European or closely related to it. As the second millennium progressed, the dynasty of Hammurabi succumbed to invaders from the mountains to the north, probably including speakers of Indo-European languages, for from the early sixteenth century BCE we find the Kassites, some of whose kings bore Indo-European names, in control of Babylon. The small Mitanni kingdom of upper Mesopotamia in the fifteenth and fourteenth centuries left documents that show that although the language of its people was non-Indo-European, there was an Indo-European-speaking element in its ruling elite, as shown by the names of its gods, its kings, and a few technical terms in a curious treatise on chariot racing.

From this meager evidence it is clear that the Indo-European speakers among the Mitanni were closely related to the Iranians and Indo-Aryans in religion and in language. The exact nature of this relation, however, is difficult to determine for several reasons. In the first place the evidence of the language and religion of the Mitanni rulers is closer to Indo-Aryan than to the earliest specimens of Iranian. This, however, might be misleading, as the oldest Iranian documents we have, namely the Old Persian inscriptions of the Achemenid kings (sixty to fourth centuries BCE) and the verses of the religious reformer Zoroaster (Zarathushtra, seventh century BCE?) in the book called the *Avesta,* are not nearly as old as the *Rig Veda.* Thus we do not know the earliest form of the Iranian languages, nor the exact nature of the religion before Zoroaster had reformed it. Only a handful of phonetic transformations separated the language of the *Avesta* from that of the *Rig Veda.* For example, as we saw in Chapter 1, Iranian reduced "s" to "h," so that Sanskrit *Sindhu* (stream, the Indus River) becomes Iranian *Hindush* (applied to the Indus region and its inhabitants), from which we get "Hindu" and, via Greek, "Indus" and "India." This sound shift has not yet occurred in the Mitanni documents, which could mean that Iranian and Indo-Aryan had not at that time split apart, and that the Iranian shift of "s" to "h" was still in the future. Again, Zoroastrian religion, although it retains the sacrifice, the fire, and the fire priest (*zaotar,* Sanskrit *hotar*), has reformed the old Indo-Iranian worship of the *daevas* (Sanskrit *devas*), so that its religious conceptions are somewhat distant from those of the *Rig Veda,* which itself has diverged from prehistoric Indo-Iranian religion.

Mitanni	***Iran***	***India***
Arunashshil	Ahura Mazda	Asura Varuna
Mitrashshil	Mithra	Mitra
Indara	Verethraghna	Indra Vritrahan
Nashattiyanna	Naonhaitya	The Two Nasatyas

Thus in Zoroastrianism the high god of light, Ahura Mazda, corresponds to the Vedic Varuna, whereas in Vedic religion, Varuna's designation, Asura, comes to mean a class of demons hostile to the devas. On the other hand the Indo-Iranian tribal hero Indra Vritrahan ("dragon-slayer") is reduced to the demon Verethraghna in

Zoroastrianism, whereas he retains his original respectability among the Mitanni and the Indians.

It is reasonable to think, but far from certain, then, that the Mitanni evidence belongs to the stage before the characteristic Iranian sound shifts had occurred, before the separation of Iranian and Indo-Aryan. In any case the migration of Indo-Iranian across the Iranian Plateau, the splitting off of the Indo-Aryan group and its migration to the upper Indus region where the *Rig Veda* was composed, must have occurred near the time of the Mitanni kingdom. The entry of Indo-Aryan speakers into India and the composition of the *Rig Veda* can reasonably be put between 1500 and 1200 BCE.

The Later Veda

This Vedic Civilization developed in India from antecedents in Western and Central Asia. Although in many respects a simpler, more rural, and even tribal civilization when contrasted with that of the now ruined Indus cities, it was destined to penetrate much more deeply into the Indian subcontinent, establishing its languages over North India, Bangladesh, and Sri Lanka, and leaving the impress of its religious and intellectual life on the entire region. As it did so, it absorbed and melded with the fragmentary cultural remains of the Indus Civilization, changing as it did so.

The Aryan tribes, constantly warring against the native Indians (among whom they must have encountered the descendants of the Indus city dwellers) as well as against each other, gradually spread eastward from the home of the *Rig Veda* in the Punjab. As they did so the priests and princes of the Kuru and Panchala tribes came to be regarded as the very model of orthodox behavior, and their territory, the Delhi region between the Indus and the Ganga basins, became the "Middle Country" of Vedic or brahminical religion. Aryan tribes continued to spread eastward down the Ganga to Bengal, which they had reached before 500 BCE, and others pressed southwestward from the middle Ganga to the western coast of Gujarat by the same date.

As the Aryan tribes expanded over North India, the sacrifice, which was the center of their religious life, also expanded in scope and complexity, so that a large liturgical and scientific literature arose. This literature as a whole is called "the Veda." The *Rig Veda,* as we have seen, is the oldest work of Vedic literature. It is technically a *Samhita* or "collection" of hymns (*rich*) in praise of the gods, chanted by the priest (*hotar*), whose functions derive from Indo-Iranian times. The development of other priestly specialties called forth the creation of new Samhitas: the *Yajur Veda Samhita* for the use of the *adhvaryu* priest, concerned with the manual operations of the sacrifice (*yajus*), and the *Sama Veda Samhita* for the *udgatar* priest who rendered the hymns in song (*saman*). The fourth collection of Vedic hymns, the *Atharva Veda,* is the latest and quite different from the other four, being a miscellaneous collection of medicinal incantations, love spells, philosophical speculations, and the like.

Each of these Samhitas acquired several distinct schools of priests to perpetuate the hymns and the priestly functions associated with them. In time each of these schools composed a prose text called a *Brahmana* that expounded the ritual context and significance of the collection of hymns to which it was attached. All the major Brahmanas show signs of having been composed in the Middle Country of the Kuru and Panchala tribes. Further scholarly study of the sacred lore developed in two divergent directions: the mystical and speculative on the one hand, and the technical and scientific on the other. The first trend is embodied in the works called *Aranyakas* ("forest treatises") and *Upanishads* (approximately, "esoteric teachings"). These were often put in the form of dialogues between *brahmin* priests and the kings of the recently established Aryan kingdoms of the middle Ganga, further east of the Kuru–Panchala land. The major works of this group had been completed by 600 BCE, prior to the emergence of Jainism and Buddhism, non-Vedic religions whose teachings take as axiomatic certain doctrines first advanced in the Upanishads.

On the technical side, the multiplication of sacrifices and their increasing complexity caused the creation of a more systematic science of ritual, *kalpa,* written down in the form of a series of cryptic prose rules called *sutras.* In time the science of kalpa acquires four divisions with their own texts: *Grihya Sutra* (rules for domestic ritual), *Shrauta Sutra* (rules for the higher ritual), *Shulva Sutra* (rules for the construction of the fire altar and other ritual accessories, in effect a kind of geometry), and *Dharma Sutra* (rules for Aryan behavior, the first law books). Other scientific specialties—phonetics, etymology, grammar, metrics, and astronomy—arise over the concern for the exact utterance of the sacred Vedic verse (*mantra*), on which the efficacy of the sacrifice depends, and the correct specification of the appropriate time of sacrifice. This technical literature as a whole is called *Vedanga,* the "limbs" of the Veda.

Thus each priestly tradition had its own special function in the sacrifice, and its own Samhita, Brahmana, Aranyaka, Upanishad, and Sutra literature. A significant amount of this literature has survived to the present. The sacrifice brought into being the entire range of ancient Indian sciences, and only when the Vedic impulse had run its course did the sciences detach themselves from the old Vedic priestly schools and their dependence on the sacrifice, and acquire a life of their own.

The Vedic Sacrifice

The intricacies of the sacrificial ritual that called forth this extensive literature known as the Veda can be reduced to three simple movements: the consecration of the sacrificer, the ritual feast, and the deconsecration. The sacrificer must be an adult married Aryan, initiated into Vedic religion. The preliminaries of the sacrifice include the marking off of a sacred space, within which an altar is constructed and fires are kindled. Sacrificer and priest, who become mystically one person, are purified for entry into the sacred sphere. The sacrifice proper is modeled on the feast offered to an Aryan guest. Offerings such as clarified butter, milk, *soma,* rice balls, or the flesh of goat, a cow, a horse, or a sheep are offered to the fire, and the gods or ancestors who sit invisibly on the sacred grass that has been spread on the ground nearby partake of the offering transformed by fire. Various acts of deconsecration, including a bath, penance for ritual errors inadvertently committed, and fees to the priests, disconnect the sacrificers from the priests and permit them to reenter mundane life as separate persons without danger.

The sacrifice is divided into two broad types, the domestic (*Grihya*) and the higher (*Shrauta*) sacrifice, each, as we have seen, with its own sutra manuals. The domestic sacrifice is much simpler and probably more archaic. It requires only one fire, the sacred fire of the household kindled on the occasion of the householder's marriage and kept perpetually alive by his care, whereas the higher sacrifice requires three. Furthermore, the higher sacrifice involves several priests, whereas in the domestic sacrifice the householder acts as his own priest, and brahmins appear only as stand-ins for the gods, if at all.

The higher sacrifice includes three major categories, along with a host of special rites. There are, first, the calendrical rites of the Vedic lunar calendar: rites of the new and the full moon, rites to usher in the three Indian seasons (spring, the rains, autumn), and offerings of first fruits at the ends of the two growing seasons. Next there are the Soma sacrifices, at which the inebriating juice of the soma plant is pressed, diluted with water, strained, and drunk. Finally there is a series of sacrifices primarily intended for kings: the Royal Consecration (*Rajyasuya*) establishes his rule; the Drink of Strength (*Vajapeya*) strengthens him against his subordinates and enemies, as does the Horse Sacrifice (*Ashvamedha*), by requiring all in whose territory the consecrated stallion wanders to fight or recognize the sacrificer's overlordship.

The higher sacrifice became of such high importance to its priestly custodians that they invented forms so demanding they can never have been performed, such as the sacrifice that takes one thousand years to complete, or another that needs 609 animal victims from an elephant to a bee, or yet another requiring a fire altar of 10,800 bricks. The sacrifice outgrew its original model of the feast, and became a cosmic principle. Where in earlier belief the Sky Father and Earth Mother had united to procreate the world, now the creation was understood in terms of the Cosmic Man (Purusha or Prajapati or Brahma) who sacrificed himself to himself. The dismembered fragments of his body became the various aspects of the phenomenal world, including the social orders of priest, warrior, herdsman-farmer, and serf, which sprung from his mouth, arms, thighs, and feet, respectively. From this it was but a short step to the philosophy of the Upanishads, in which all phenomena are reducible to a single—now impersonal—principle, inherent in sacred speech: the monistic doctrine of Brahman, the Absolute, from which all things derive their being.

The Family and Its Ancestors

The increasing elaborations of the higher sacrifice and its theory lead us to the beginnings of Indian philosophy, and the more archaic and conservative domestic ritual gives us a perspective on the organization of the Aryan family, which had not greatly changed since Proto-Indo-European times. The legacy of these ideas about the family is very long-lasting, and we give further detail on this important topic in Chapter 6.

The family was an extended family, consisting of a householder, his unmarried daughters, his sons and son's sons, and their wives. The family was a corporation, owning property as a unit, with the householder as its presiding officer and executor; only he was capable of offering its worship, all others being minors in law and religion until his death or retirement, whereupon its property might be partitioned among the surviving sons.

Assisted by his wife, the householder made offerings to the sacred fire of the hearth for the benefit of the household as a whole. The Five Great Sacrifices daily honored the creator Brahma, the Fathers (ancestors), the Gods, Creatures, and Men with recitation of the Veda, offerings of food and water, burnt offerings, scattered grain, and hospitality to an Aryan guest, preferably a learned brahmin priest. However, the domestic ritual was especially concerned with the nourishment of its deceased patrilineal ancestors, the Fathers, who although dead were still very much part of the family, depending on it for continued sustenance and bestowing on it their blessings. These rites, called *Shraddha,* were offered monthly, and their essential element consisted in offering a ball of rice (*pinda*) to the householder's father, grandfather, and great-grandfather, with other offerings to the remoter Fathers. The dead depended absolutely on the offerings of the family, and required its unbroken perpetuation through the birth of sons for their felicity in the next life, whereas the living required the boons of health and fertility that the Fathers held in their gift.

The Shraddha was the endpoint in a series of life-cycle rites beginning with birth, continuing with initiation into the religious life and marriage, and ending with the funeral ceremonies of cremation and the special rite that ushered the soul of the deceased into the World of the Fathers. Of this series, initiation was particularly important, in that it marked the end of infancy and fitted the Aryan boy to learn the religious lore. Initiation was thought of as a second, spiritual birth; only brahmins, *kshatriyas,* and *vaishyas* could be initiated, and were called "Twice-Born," as distinct from the "Once-Born" *shudra* to whom knowledge of the Veda was denied (see Chapter 6), these being the four varnas or castes that made up Vedic society.

Marriage was also particularly important, as it was essential to the perpetuation of the ancestral cult and at the same time was fraught with danger. One could not marry a girl who was a *sapinda,* that is, one whose family offered the rice ball (pinda) to any of the several patrilineal ancestors to whom the boy's family made offering. The bride, then, must not be closely related. On the other hand, she must be of good Aryan family, orthodox in its religious practices, for her to become religiously competent to assist in the rites and to raise legitimate heirs. Finally, having determined the excellence of the family into which she had been born, she must through the wedding ritual be mystically disengaged from it and its ancestral cult, and initiated into the family and ancestral cult of the bridegroom. Thus for the girl marriage is the initiation into the religious life, and after death she participates in the offerings made to her deceased husband. For the boy it signifies ritual adulthood and completeness, for only a married man can become a householder and a sacrificer, because a wife must assist in the ritual, and should his wife predecease him he must retire. Marriage has a threefold character: It is the irrevocable gift of a daughter by one family to another, the initiation of the bride into the rites and family of the groom, and a sacrament entered into for the fulfillment of religious obligations, which cannot be cancelled in divorce.

After the death of the householder the sons could continue to live jointly under the authority of the eldest, but at some point the property would be divided more or less equally between them, and each would become a householder in his own right with obligations to make offerings to the Fathers. Daughters could not inherit land because they could not make offerings to the deceased but would marry into the families of strangers (although they would continue to be maintained by their brothers while they remained unmarried); the "women's wealth" they carried with them from the family of birth to the family of marriage was generally in the nature of utensils and jewelry—dowry in the form of moveable wealth rather than land. To ensure the unbroken continuity of offerings to the Fathers various devices were available whereby a sonless man could acquire a legal heir. If he had a daughter, she could be appointed to beget an heir who then would not be the heir of his own father; if he had no daughters, a younger brother could cohabit with his widow to beget an heir; or he could adopt an heir under conditions that bear the characteristics of marriage, namely gift, initiation, and sacrament. Because the adoptive son was destined to offer the pinda to his adoptive father, it was essential that he come from an orthodox family (hence, one could not adopt an orphan, as his parentage was doubtful), that his natural father have other sons to be his own heirs, and that he be irrevocably and sacramentally given to his adoptive father.

The Tribe and Its Organization

The Vedic tribes were assemblages of such patrilineal extended families, grouped into lineages by common descent from the remoter patrilineal ancestors, and loosely allied to each other by the ties of marriage, common culture, and the solidarity that warfare against external enemies evokes. Among the brahmin priestly families at least, there was a system of patrilineal clans called *gotras,* each consisting of families descended from the same group of sages (*rishis*) who had been, they believed, those who first "heard" the hymns of the Veda by divine inspiration, and transmitted them to ordinary men. Brahmins of the same *gotra* were united by common descent and, in the earliest period, shared a particular hairstyle, dress, and rituals; the gotras were linked to one another by the obligation to marry a person of another gotra.

All Aryans had not been created equal. They had sprung from the body of the Purusha already differentiated by function. The priestly brahmin, specializing in the sacred utterance, came from his mouth; the kshatriya or warrior whose duty is to protect came from his arms; the vaishya, engaging in herding, agriculture, and trade, coming from his thighs, is the economic support of society; and the shudra, coming from the feet, is the servant caste.

Thus the Vedic tribes were by no means egalitarian, but were divided into four orders by function, united by their interdependence, and ranked hierarchically. Political power rested with the kshatriya order; in some tribes power was broadly diffused among the heads of great warrior families, to be concentrated in the office of a chief (*rajan*) only temporarily, in times of war. In others a hereditary chiefdom increasingly concentrated political power in a single warrior lineage. This was preeminently true of the Kuru and Panchala tribes of the Delhi region. Such chiefdoms can indeed be called kingdoms, so long as we remember that they were tribal in nature, their authority extending over a tribe and its clients in whatever territory they happened to hold, rather than the inhabitants of a demarcated territory whatever their tribal origin. Far from being despotic, the power of the king was consecrated by submission to the higher authority of the priest. Although the brahmin was subject to the king, he was at the same time the source of the royal authority. What made the Kurus and Panchalas the paragons of kingship for a later age was not only their striking success in the strengthening of monarchy in the tribal state, but their patronage of brahmin priests and the Vedic sacrifice.

The Vedic age was a heroic age in which warfare was the privilege and predominant occupation of the chariot warriors and their retinues, guided by the ideals of seeking death in battle, honorable conduct during war, mercy to the one who submits, and princely generosity to all in the disposition of spoils. Although warfare was endemic, the nature of Aryan society put limits on its scope. Aryan tribes did not unite against non-Aryan, for there was no political basis on which such unity could be fashioned; indeed Aryan tribes fought each other as often as they fought non-Aryans. The scale of warfare, therefore, remained small. The aims of war were also limited, chiefly to movable wealth (cattle, gold, women), and occasionally to territory into which the tribe could expand. The ability of the kingdom to absorb foreign populations was limited by its tribal constitution. On one hand, the laws of adoption were so stringent as to exclude one means of absorbing captives into the body politic very often found in simpler societies. On the other hand because the kingdom was tribal, conquered peoples could not enter into direct relations with political authority. They could only be integrated into the tribe by becoming domestic slaves or the clients (*shudras*) of individual households, and the means for so dealing with large numbers of enemies did not exist. Thus the tribal state rarely aimed to conquer and rule over its neighbors, and the formation of larger states, other than through confederation of related tribes, had to await the development of new principles of statecraft.

The spread of Indo-Aryan language and Vedic culture across North India, and the decline of the non-Aryan languages and religions of the indigenous inhabitants, proceeded partly through warfare, enslavement, and clientage. The word for slave (*dasa*) also means "barbarian" in the early part of this period after the name of an indigenous people and the term for the servile order (shudra) is probably also taken from the name of a non-Aryan tribe. The transformation also proceeded voluntarily, however. Non-Aryan kings are in evidence, sometimes in alliance with Aryan kings; and non-Aryan kings sought with their patronage the supernatural benefits conferred by the Vedic royal sacrifices through the brahmins. As the Vedic age drew to a close, few parts of North India had not been touched, however lightly, by Vedic civilization, and Vedic civilization took into itself features of the people over whom its kings ruled, and those with whom they were allied.

CHAPTER 4

New Religions, New Empires

Religions of Renunciation
The Rise of Magadha
The Mauryas

Vedic civilization, spreading gradually eastward down the Ganga, became weaker and more dilute the further one went from its upper Gangetic source. The political and religious forms that arose in the middle Gangetic basin of the sixth century BCE had been quickened by the touch of this civilization, but struck out in fundamentally new directions.

The late Vedic texts, called Aranyakas and Upanishads, which direct the theory of the sacrifice away from the ritual itself toward the beginnings of philosophy, found their setting not in the Kuru-Panchala kingdom, but in the eastern kingdoms of Kosala, Kashi, and Videha, along the middle region of the Ganga. There the wealthy kings of newly founded states competed in attracting brahmin philosophers from the more prestigious western centers of learning to adorn their courts, engaging them in philosophical discourse and putting up handsome prizes for the victors in debate. A fourth eastern state, Magadha, later to emerge the strongest of them all and absorb them into its growing empire, was the least brahminized. The brahmins of the Middle Country showed nothing but contempt for them; a medicinal spell preserved in the *Atharva Veda* wishes fever away to the peoples of Magadha and their eastern neighbors of Anga (Bengal) along with other undesirables.

Although some of these eastern peoples eagerly sought out Vedic civilization in its most current forms, others turned to the new anti-Vedic religions—*Jainism, Buddhism,* and *Ajivikism*—that developed in their midst. This was not merely a reflex of their distance from the Middle Country, or of the influence of non-Aryan populations, but it had to do as well with the crisis Vedic civilization itself was undergoing, and the new forms of society and state arising in the eastern lands, to which Vedic religion was no longer adequate.

We have only hints of the scope and content of this crisis, but it included the decline of the Kuru-Panchala kingdom and the extinction of its ancient dynasty, which in the times of the Upanishads was no more than a memory. The cohesion of the tribal state and the political power of its warrior elite were challenged by the rise of upstart kings of a sort most commonly found in the eastern kingdoms. The new style of kingship aimed at the creation of armies more professional in nature and hence more dependent on the king; at the acquisition of territories rich in natural resources and docile, tax-paying peasants rather than booty or territory for tribal expansion; and at keeping the peace between the diverse tribal groups drawn together in the new supratribal territorial state.

The heterogeneity of the population of such states posed novel problems for their statesmen to solve and fresh support for the concentration of power in the hands of the king. Newly conquered peoples, not bound in clientage to individual warriors, now entered into direct relationship to the throne through the taxation of their produce, which yielded large revenues by which mercenary armies could be raised. Within such groups custom continues to regulate behavior, but the relations among them, once wholly regulated by clientage, increasingly came under royal supervision and arbitration. A body of contract and criminal law grew up side by side with the literature of the new statecraft that had made it necessary.

This new statecraft calculated its advantages dispassionately and pursued them ruthlessly; gradually but inexorably it gobbled up the Vedic tribal states by the superior power that its organizing principles were able to harness in the service of a state whose nature it was to expand it to the limits of its abilities. The old heroic ideals languished. To the earlier age, society had seemed an extension of the cosmic order, both natural and divine at the same time, and moral life was that which did not stray from immemorial custom. Now individuals emerged from the crumbling social matrix and found themselves isolated. They saw the world in a new light, and some, like one of the kings in the Upanishads, lamented their isolation: "The great kings and heroes of the past," he said, "have abandoned their glory and passed to the next world.... The oceans dry up, the mountain-tops fall, the Pole Star trembles, the stars are loosened from their moorings, the earth founders, the gods leave their stations.... In this flux, I am like a frog in a dry well."[16] Others, now perceiving society as a mere human artifact rather than an element of the divine order, renounced the obligations of the householder and sought salvation through quietism and meditation.

Some who shared this new perspective, however, reacted differently. For if society is essentially of human making, it can be refashioned and manipulated by humans as well. These were the new statesmen, advisors to the king. Interestingly, they were more often brahmins than not. Whereas the Vedic king was merely the most powerful among the kshatriya mobility, relying on the cooperation of the supernatural aids of his brahmin chaplain (*purohita*), the stereotype of the new statesman is a brahmin who is neither priest nor warrior, famous more for his political cunning than for his piety, religious scholarship, or moral sensitivity.

Religions of Renunciation

The Vedic sacrificer believed that the ritual act would bless him in this world—with long life, wealth, and the birth of sons—as well as in the next. After death he hoped to dwell forever in the World of the Fathers, presided over by King Yama, the first man to die, and nourished by the pious offerings of pindas tendered by his descendants. But speculation on the meaning of the sacrifice soon transformed it from a simple act of reciprocity between man on one hand and the gods and fathers on the other, into a cosmogonic principle. During this evolution of ideas it came to be believed that one must again suffer death in the next life, and imperceptibly this belief was elaborated into the doctrine of Rebirth (*samsara*) or the endless wheel of redeath and rebirth into other bodies, to which the soul is subject. The closely related doctrine of Moral Causation asserted that the deed (*karma*) caused this endless transmigration of the soul from one body to another, the moral value of one's acts determining whether one was reborn as a higher being, such as a brahmin or a god, or a lower one, such as an animal or a plant. The vast cycles of time that suffused the new cosmology were probably shaped by astronomical knowledge spreading from Mesopotamia.

These doctrines together attribute to the universe a structure that is comprehensible, moral, impartial, and strictly just, in which virtue always gets its reward and evil its punishment, if not in this life, then in another. All living beings are subject to these inexorable laws, even the gods themselves, who can escape neither death nor the consequences of their deeds. The doctrines of Rebirth and Moral Causation, then, served to undermine the preeminence of the gods, and the sacrificial act (karma) in religious thought, which, however exalted in themselves, could confer only temporary salvation. These doctrines pointed toward a new conception of salvation, that of permanent Release (*moksha, nirvana*) from the endless turnings of the wheel of Rebirth. Finally, the Vedic belief in a past golden age when religious knowledge was complete, and men naturally long-lived and virtuous—a view of time quite general in the ancient world—crystallized into the doctrine of the Four Ages (*yugas*) of cyclical time through which the world passes. The Four Ages, named after the throws in the Vedic game of dice, are *Krita* (the winning throw, a four), *Treta* (trey), *Dvapara* (deuce), and *Kali* (a one, the losing throw). In each succeeding age *dharma* (religion, morality) declines by a quarter from the pristine perfection of the Krita age, the length of human life diminishes, and the struggle for existence grows more brutish. At the end of the present Kali age in which it is our misfortune to live, the world will be destroyed and reconstituted and the cycle will recommence in a new golden age, and so endlessly.

The doctrines of Rebirth, Moral Causation, Release, and the Four Ages become the axioms of all subsequent philosophy in ancient India. We find them in embryo in the Aranyakas and Upanishads, side by side with a multitude of competing speculations. Although no single philosophy can be extracted from the creative ferment of ideas that these Vedic works record, later ages selected certain of these ideas as their permanent contribution to philosophical thought. Their ideas are expressed in the "Great Utterances" (*maha-vakya*), memorable sayings that sum up the deepest truths of the theory of the sacrifice, which have a distinctly monistic tendency; that is, toward the idea that a single impersonal principle underlies the multiplicity of the world (somewhat different from monotheism, the idea that there is only one God, who is a person). The great utterances such as "I am *brahman*," and "That art thou," signify the identity of the individual soul with the impersonal World-soul (*Brahman*, the absolute, neuter, and therefore nonpersonal, not to be confused with the creator Brahma, the Vedic text called Brahmana, or the brahmin caste), whereas "Not this, not that" implies that the World-soul is not to be mistaken for any object of the senses. Knowledge of the Vedic verses (*mantra*), closely guarded from profane ears, had once sufficed to confer the highest bliss upon the Aryan; now it was rather the secret knowledge of the identity of the individual soul with the World-soul that held out the hope of salvation in the form of escape from Rebirth, and the merger of the one in the other. The significance attached to this new knowledge tended to throw the actual performance of the sacrifice in the shade, or rather to concentrate attention on its inner meaning at the expense of its outward performance. By stages the theory of the sacrifice abandoned ritual performance and tended toward meditation and ascetic withdrawal from society.

The Renouncers

The origins of asceticism in India go at least as far back as the *Rig Veda,* in which we hear of the *muni,* the silent visionary who has let his hair grow long and goes about naked or in orange rags. In the eastern kingdoms of the sixth century BCE there were large numbers of ascetics. Renouncing social ties, some ascetics passed a celibate existence as forest hermits living off the fruits they could gather for themselves; some became wandering beggars and teachers; some submitted themselves to harsh penances, lying between fires in the summer and wearing wet clothes in winter; and some sat plunged in meditation.

The brahmin and kshatriya philosophers of the Aranyakas and Upanishads had retained their allegiance to the Vedic lore, but these *shramanas* or renouncers of life in society were entirely hostile to the Veda. The Vedic obligation to procreate a son for the perpetuation of the ancestral cult confronted in the doctrines of the renouncers the new ideal of lifelong celibacy in the interests of escaping transmigration, and the two ideals could not but find themselves at odds. As a later maxim had it, brahmin and shramana are like snake and mongoose, natural enemies.

The problem of Rebirth and the hope of Release were by now the unquestioned terms within which the new doctrines unfolded, and the various renouncers offered dozens of different ways to escape the one and achieve the other, each teacher competing for a following. We know little of the many philosophies that did not survive this competition, but history was kind to three of them: Ajivikism, Jainism, and Buddhism. The Ajivika religion survived some two thousand years; we last hear of it in South India, about 1400 CE. Jainism spread all over India and reached Sri Lanka, although today it is confined to certain castes principally in Gujarat on the west coast and Karnataka in the south. Buddhism, on the other hand, although it ultimately disappeared from all but the mountainous fringes of the subcontinent, spread to Afghanistan, Central Asia, the East Asia, Sri Lanka, and Southeast Asia.

Each of these three religions of renunciation offered different solutions to the problem of Rebirth. For the Ajivikas, the course of the soul from one life to the next was guided by an inscrutable destiny (*niyati*) that appears to have been beyond human influence. The Jains believe in an irreducible plurality of living souls whose pristine brilliance is clouded and weighted down by matter. Any deed (karma), however good, perpetuates this bondage, by causing fresh accretions of matter to the soul, but at the same time the effects of previous deeds are waning and previous accumulations of matter are being sloughed off. The prescription, therefore, is to cease to act altogether. Noninjury (*ahimsa*) to other living beings is a doctrine that probably originated with the Jains and then spread to Buddhism and Hinduism, promoting vegetarian diet and the sanctity of animal life. Jain quietism assumes a radical form among the most spiritually advanced monks, who renounce action to the point of deliberate self-starvation. Buddhism, on the other hand, teaches that what binds us to the wheel of Rebirth is neither fate, nor the deed in and of itself, but rather the selfish cravings (*trishna,* "thirst") that motivate our deeds. If desire is renounced, deeds can continue to be performed without continuing to affect one's perpetual rebirth. Buddhism offers itself as a middle way between the extremes of ascetic self-mortification that Jainism represents and the sensual, self-indulgent life of the ordinary man in society, and perhaps of the Ajivikas, who had a reputation for sensuality (perhaps undeserved).

The founders of these three religions were contemporaries, and the sixth-century middle Gangetic kingdoms of Kosala, Kashi, Videha, Magadha, and Anga comprised the geographical horizon of their early teaching and their first conversions. We know little of Maskarin Goshala, the Ajivika teacher, but Vardhamana the Mahavira (Great Hero) and teacher of Jainism was born of the princely class in Videha, and Gautama the Buddha (Enlightened One) was also a prince by birth, of the Shakya tribe, in the foothills of Nepal, which was under the hegemony of Kosala. The rapid success of these teachers in the lightly brahminized eastern kingdoms checked the spread of Vedic religion, and they, together with merchant venturers and conquering kings, extended a newer version of Indian Civilization to the limits of the subcontinent and beyond. The new importance of trade and coined money is nicely captured in the story of the rich merchant Anathapindaka, who wanted to purchase a piece of land from Prince Jeta to give to the Buddhist order of monks. Prince Jeta did not wish to sell, so he named an impossible price: Cover the piece of land with coins. Anathapindaka did so. In the depiction of this story carved on the Barhut Stupa (Figure 4), we see servants unloading the squarish coins of the time from a bullock cart and spreading them on the ground like tiles.

FIGURE 4 The merchant Anathapindaka buys a grove from Prince Jeta for the Buddhist order of monks, Barhut Stupa, 2nd century BCE

The Rise of Magadha

At the commencement of the fifth century BCE the most powerful state of north India was Kosala, occupying the territory at the confluence of the Ganga (Ganges) and Yamuna rivers. King Prasenajit had absorbed Kashi and held several tribal states on his northern borders under his hegemony, including the Shakyas, the tribe of the Buddha. To the east, on the north bank of the Ganga, lay Videha, now held by a confederacy of tribes, of which the Vrijjis and Licchavis were most prominent. These tribes had no monarchs; political authority was diffused among a warrior nobility, among which the Mahavira had been born. On the south bank of the Ganga lay Magadha, a small state with sway that extended over Anga further eastward. Magadha was overshadowed by the strength of Kosala and Videha, but it was destined to absorb them and spread its power across the face of India.

How exactly this came about is obscure. We do know that Magadha's king, Ajatashatru, was both ambitious and ruthless. Having gained the throne by killing his father, he engaged in a series of lengthy wars with Kosala and Videha in which he conquered the latter. Legends might contain a kernel of historical truth when they state that Ajatashatru's minister employed the stratagems of the new statecraft to undermine the Vrijjian confederacy: Pretending to have fallen out with his master, he was given refuge by the Vrijjians, and proceeded to set them against one another by fomenting false rumors and suspicions among them.

The capture of Videha gave Magadha control of the Gangetic waterway, and in time the capital was shifted from a defensive inland fortress (Rajagriha) to a site on the Ganga called Pataliputra (modern Patna). This site, which Ajatashatru had earlier fortified against Vrijjian attack, now became a command center of an expanding empire as well as an emporium of riverine trade. Magadha's rapid growth devoured all the Gangetic states under a series of rulers remembered in ancient texts for their patricidal inclinations, unscrupulousness in pursuing expansion of their empires, wealth, and the obscurity of their origins.

Three concepts that become standard in later ages seem to belong to this period and these developments: the *four means*, the *circle of states*, and the *four-limbed army*. The first two doctrines presume a king who wishes to expand his kingdom in a field of like-minded expansionist kings, and is discussed in Chapter 6. The four-limbed army conceptualizes the army as having four limbs like a four-legged animal: foot soldiers, cavalry, chariots, and elephants. The army appears now to be a unified force having functional parts, rather than a congeries of personal armies serving the great warriors, as in the Vedic period. The four-limbed army (*chaturanga*) gave its name to the game of chess, invented in India, with the addition of the king and the minister (corresponding to the queen in modern chess, significantly the most powerful piece on the board). Thus we have what amounts to a new statecraft in this period, connected with the new statesman, the royal minister.

By 326 BCE the Nanda dynasty was ruling a Magadha that now included the greater part of North India to the east of the Indus basin. In that year Alexander of Macedon, who had extinguished the rule of the Persian emperors and replaced it with his own, led his troops across the Indus (having crossed the Hindu Kush the previous year) into Taxila (Takshashila), where in good Vedic fashion the king of that place feasted Alexander's men on three hundred oxen. Taxila had been and was to remain a center of Vedic learning to which brahmins and princes of the east came for instruction, as well as being a crossroads for international trade, and for invasion. The states of this northwestern region fit more into the mold of the Vedic tribal state than the more centralized empire of the Nandas and their successors the Mauryas. For although some of the states Alexander encountered in the Punjab were monarchical, others were tribal republics, and in all the ownership of the sinews of ancient warfare—elephants, horse, weapons—was distributed among a warrior elite rather than, as in Magadha, falling under royal monopoly.

Alexander's engagement with the elephant corps of the Indian king whom the Western sources call Porus (probably connected with the old Vedic name Puru), although successful, took a heavy toll in manpower and troop morale. When he reached the Beas River in eastern Punjab, his war-weary veterans refused to advance further at reports of the many war elephants owned by the oligarchic tribal states that lay beyond. The mutiny of his troops forced Alexander to retreat. He descended the Indus and crossed the Makran desert on his way to Mesopotamia, dying in Babylon in 324. His Indian conquests quickly melted away.

The Mauryas

Shortly after Alexander's death, in about 321 BCE, an adventurer named Chandragupta Maurya, of whose origins there are many conflicting legends, wrested Magadha from the last of the Nanda dynasty. Mauryan rule quickly expanded into the political vacuum in the Punjab created by Alexander's retreat, his untimely death, and the struggle for his empire that broke out among his generals. Magadha shortly reached a common frontier with the kingdom of Seleucus, who successfully seized Alexander's eastern conquests. Seleucid–Mauryan relations were consistently amicable. Seleucus abandoned a vast tract of territory to Chandragupta, largely including modern Afghanistan, in exchange for five hundred elephants, sometime after he had captured Babylon in 312 BCE. The Mauryas appear to have continued to supply the Seleucids with war elephants for several generations, for we know of another such transfer to Antiochus III approximately a century later, and elephants became so highly sought after by the Hellenistic kingdoms of this period that the Ptolemies of Egypt, cut off from Indian sources of supply of the Seleucids, whose empire stood between Egypt and India, captured and domesticated the elephants of sub-Saharan Africa. Ambassadors of both the Seleucids and the Ptolemies were sent to Pataliputra under Chandragupta and his successor Bindusara, and considerable fragments of a memoir of Chandragupta's India written by the Seleucid ambassador Megasthenes have survived. Megasthenes took a great deal of interest in the methods of elephant capture and training, and his embassy must have been instrumental in the transmission of elephants and the techniques of training to the Hellenistic world.

Megasthenes' book, the *Indika,* paints a picture of a society in which the mass of men are an unarmed peasantry peacefully tilling the soil unmolested by the clash of armies nearby. Horses, elephants, and weapons are a royal monopoly, and are returned to royal keeping when not in use. The army, a large professional class more numerous than any other except the peasantry, had personal servants, and was utterly idle in times of peace. The landed warrior elite of Vedic times is nowhere in evidence; what we have instead is a paid army detached from land ownership, and a farming class detached from military service. Megasthenes gives us the outlines of a fairly extensive bureaucracy. He notes the existence of a system of hereditary occupational castes, and describes seven of them. His is a very rosy picture of India. He praises the frugality of the Indians, and asserts that they keep no slaves, although he was certainly mistaken in saying so. Theft is rare, and punishment mild. He also repeats stories of fantastic races of India from the fifth-century book of India by Ctesias, such as those with ears so large they wrapped themselves up in them for blankets when they went to sleep, or the mouthless folk who nourished themselves by breathing the vapors of cooked food but would become violently ill from the stench of an army camp. These stories became permanent fixtures in Greek and medieval European ideas of India, right down to voyages of discovery that put Europeans once more into direct contact with India.

Under the third Mauryan king, Ashoka (reigned c. 268–231 BCE), the Mauryan empire reached its greatest extent, containing in its boundaries all of the India subcontinent except its southernmost tip, and the western territories ceded by Seleucus; Ashoka himself added Orissa to his patrimony in a campaign of his eighth regnal year (Map 5).

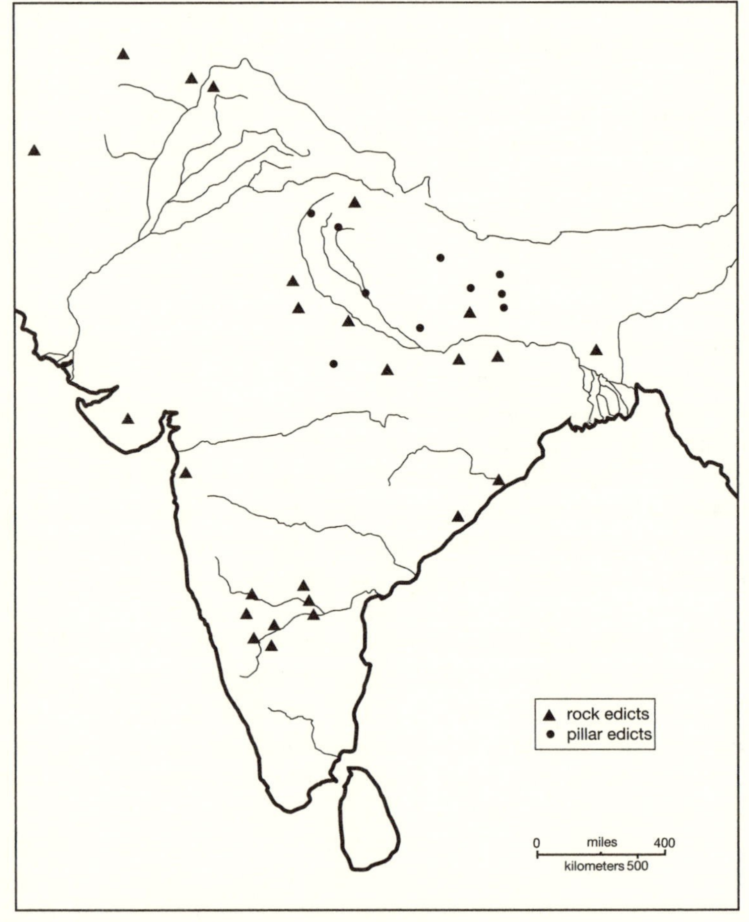

MAP 5 The Mauryan empire at the time of Ashoka

Ashoka has left us a magnificent record of edicts addressed to his people inscribed on rock faces and stone pillars from which we get a detailed understanding of his reign (Figure 5). This empire was divided into at least four provinces under viceroys for the most part chosen from the royal family, in addition to the region around the capital, Pataliputra, probably directly ruled by the emperor. Royal highways connected some, at least, of the provincial capitals to the center. Its massive army had no equal, although tribal pockets in the hills and jungles remained beyond the reach of the Mauryan state. A large bureaucracy administered the land revenues and adjudicated disputes. It was the very incarnation of the new statecraft.

The Mauryan kings had a preference for the nonbrahminical religions of renunciation, as had the earlier kings of Magadha. Chandragupta is especially remembered among the Jains as their patron, two of the Mauryans are known to have been benefactors of the Ajivikas, and Ashoka was personally a Buddhist. The unmerited suffering the Kalinga war had inflicted on innocent noncombatants brought about a spiritual crisis in Ashoka's life, which led him to turn his back on the ruthless statecraft that had achieved such brilliant success in the expansion of the Mauryan state. Ashoka chose to devote his policy instead to the paternal guidance of his subjects' welfare both in this world and the next.

This new policy, which Ashoka calls his *dharma,* is recorded in the edicts inscribed in stone throughout the realm. Most are in the North Indian languages of the period (called Prakrits), but a few, in the region of the Indus and beyond, are in Greek and in Aramaic, which had been one of the languages of government in the old Persian empire. Ashoka's edicts tell us that he henceforth abandoned wars of annexation, and urged his descendants to do likewise, to the end of the world cycle. In its stead he sought the conversion of neighboring states to dharma, and he claimed to have achieved this victory of dharma among the Hellenistic kings to whom he had sent ambassadors. In its practical aspect, Ashoka's dharma includes the planting of shade trees and the digging of wells along the highways for the refreshment of man and beast, and the planting of medicinal herbs for the cure of men and animals, which, he tells us, he has done not only throughout the realm, but among his neighbors in South India, Ceylon, and the Hellenistic kingdoms. He promoted the sanctity of animal life, prohibiting animal sacrifice in certain places and protecting certain species against slaughter; for his own part he put an end to the daily slaughter of animals in the royal kitchen, which had

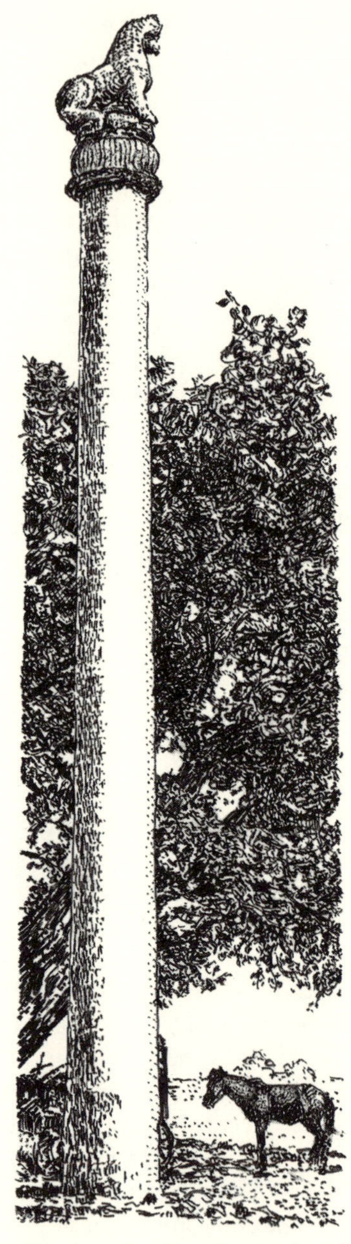

FIGURE 5 Ashokan pillar, Lauriya Nandangarh, 3rd century BCE

totaled hundreds of thousands, save only two peacocks and a deer, and promised to eventually eliminate even these from the royal menu! Whatever the limits of his commitment, Ashoka certainly promoted the spread of vegetarianism among laypeople. In social relations, Ashoka's dharma consists of respect for brahmins, shramanas, parents, friends, and inferiors, and an end to bitterness between the sects. He states his preference to persuasion rather than coercion, but reserves the power of the state in the background, warning the refractory forest tribes to repent lest they be killed.

Ever since the times of Goshala, the Mahavira, and the Buddha, the religions of renunciation, by abandoning society to its own devices, aided the growth of royal power; even as the perception of society as subject to human will and manipulation had provided the basis on which new techniques of statecraft, more powerful than those of the Vedic age, could be developed. Ashoka, at once the head of a powerful state and a Buddhist, directed the state once again toward a transcendent object, and attempted to bring the principles of the religions of renunciation to bear on its policies. The principle of noninjury toward living beings (*ahimsa*), born of the renouncer's need to escape the consequences of Moral Causation (karma), now became the active principle of compassion, and for once in human history it became the guiding spirit of political life. It was a remarkable historical moment, in which a remarkable king tried to put nonviolence at the center of the state as far as he could. Whether it is possible to reconcile nonviolence and state power is a question, because the state monopolizes power, and wields it, to create an internal peace and protect the people from external powers. Ashoka tried to apply nonviolence both internally and in his relations with other kings, but within limits, as we have seen. His reign was a lived experiment that addressed the very nature of state violence and the limits to which it can be mitigated by its opposite, ahimsa.

CHAPTER 5

Classical India

The Formation of Classical Indian Civilization
(187 BCE–320 CE)
The Classical Age (320–600 CE)
Late Classical Indian Civilization (600–1000 CE)

Classic forms of kingship, fine arts, and religion—classic in the sense that they become durable models for generations to come—take shape and find their culmination in the age of the Gupta Empire. These models are formed in the period before the Guptas and after the collapse of the Mauryan Empire. It is a paradox that the formative period for these models is a period of foreign incursions and contending smaller kingdoms, not of imperial unity, until the Guptas reconstitute a large empire, although on a plan different from that of the Mauryan Empire. After the Gupta Empire unraveled, there developed a stable pattern of large regional kingdoms ruled by dynasties that were very long-lived.

The Formation of Classical Indian Civilization (187 BCE–320 CE)

In the post-Mauryan period the political and religious life of North India set out in a different direction. The high degree of centralization and bureaucratization with which the Mauryas had run their state was never again achieved; instead looser, more indirect forms of overlordship served, from time to time, to knit together regional empires. Vedic brahminism was revived, but joined with a popular, devotional form of religion that we may now call Hinduism, and monkish Buddhism underwent a parallel evolution that resulted in the Great Vehicle (Mahayana) form of that religion. Indian Civilization was taking what we recognize to be its classical form.

Ironically, the formation of classical Indian Civilization occurred in an age of nomadic invasion in the northwest, the rise of indigenous kingdoms in the South and the growth, in the first century CE, of Roman luxury trade with India. Indian Civilization redefined itself in terms much broader than Vedic civilization had been capable of, spread across the subcontinent, and implanted its religions in Central Asia, China, and the Indo-China Peninsula.

The Shungas and the Indo-Greeks

The Mauryan Empire survived the death of its greatest ruler by scarcely fifty years. In c. 187 BCE Pushyamitra Shunga, brahmin general of the Mauryas, assumed power by a military coup d'état. The empire over which he and his line presided for a hundred years was much smaller than that of Ashoka, being essentially confined to the middle Gangetic basin and parts of Central India. It was also much less centralized in structure. The Shungas exercised military overlordship over a number of local rulers, some of whom appear to have issued coinages of their own.

Pushyamitra revived the Vedic horse sacrifice, and in fact performed it twice. He also was cordially disliked by later Buddhist writers, who accused him of destroying as many Buddhist monuments as Ashoka had built, on the theory that any kind of fame, good or bad, is fame. This bad reputation among the Buddhists is undeserved, for we know that Buddhism continued to be patronized under the Shungas and by Shunga feudatories. Nevertheless, royal favor now inclined toward brahminism, and the Shunga kings revived the Vedic royal sacrifices but also lent their patronage and prestige to the emerging worship of the Hindu god Vishnu. Ultimately the brahminical tradition accommodated itself to the theistic, devotional religions of this sort, and gained greater popularity in so doing.

In 250 BCE, Diodotus, Greek satrap of Bactria in what is now Afghanistan, revolted against his Seleucid overlord. Remoteness from the center of Seleucid power (whose rulers were more preoccupied with the control of Syria, Palestine, Asia Minor, and Mesopotamia) and the invasions of Parthian nomads from the north a few years later served to guarantee Bactrian Greek independence. By the death of Antiochus III in 187 BCE, Seleucid power had gone into steep decline in approximately the same year as Pushyamitra's coup ended Mauryan rule. Under King Demetrius the Greeks of Bactria invaded India and, according to Indian legend, reached the very walls of Pataliputra before they retreated to the Punjab. The cause of this retreat appears to have been the revolt, in Bactria, of Demetrius's general Eucratides; in any case by about the mid-second century BCE, Demetrius's kingdom had split into two, the Eastern Greek kingdom occupying the Punjab under Menander, and the Western Greek kingdom of Bactria and the Kabul Valley. Further nomadic incursions into Iran served to force the Western kingdom into the Punjab, at the expense of the other, which now was confined to its eastern edge. Ultimately these nomadic invaders entered India itself. The two Indo-Greek kingdoms, hostile to one another to the end, succumbed to the nomads, the Western by about 90 BCE and the Eastern by about the year 30.

During the brief existence of Greek rule in the Indian northwest, Greek kings were obliged to come to terms with the culture of the Indians they ruled. Menander of the Eastern kingdom issued coins bearing the symbols of Buddhism, and represented himself to his subjects as their "savior" on the inscriptions they bore in Greek and Prakrit. Buddhist literature remembers king "Milinda" as a philosopher king whose ashes, after his death, were honored in the way appropriate to a saintly ruler, by being buried in a memorial mound or *stupa*, like the remains of a Buddha. The hostile Western kingdom preferred Hindu symbolism, and sent to the Shunga court as ambassador a Greek native of Taxila, who, like the Shungas, was a devotee of Vishnu. An inscribed pillar in Central India bearing the image of the Garuda bird on which Vishnu rides commemorates the embassy of Heliodorus to the Shunga king Bhagabhadra. The common religious preferences that united the Western Greek kingdom with the Shungas against the intervening Eastern Greek kingdom with its Buddhist leanings reinforced the mutual benefits of political alliance against the common enemy. Reasons of state caused the Greeks to patronize the religions of India, rather than impose their own. Hellenistic sculpture did establish itself in the northwest, but its themes were Indian, and usually Buddhist. The hybrid Greco-Indian art of Gandhara is one of the few expressions of Hellenistic culture in the Indian culture area.

The Nomads

The last decades of Greek rule in the Punjab brought India outsiders of a different sort, descendants of the mounted nomadic herdsmen of Central Asia. In the first century BCE, two Iranian-speaking peoples, the Scythians and the Parthians (whom the Indians called Shakas and Pahlavas) made their appearance in the northwest. Parthian rule extinguished Greek at Taxila before midcentury, initially perhaps as an extension of the larger Parthian or Arsacid Empire of Iran, but if so it soon became an independent entity in itself, and endured for over a hundred years.

In the second century BCE Chinese annals inform us that warfare among the tribes of Central Asia had driven a people called the Yuezhi to the borders of Bactria, from which they expelled the Scythians by the end of the century. In the first century CE, a clan of this people, the Kushanas, established its hegemony over the rest and expanded into India. By the end of the first century or the beginning of the second century CE, Kanishka, greatest of the Kushana kings, was lord of an empire that straddled the Hindu Kush, holding large territories both in Iran and India, well into the Gangetic basin. When Kanishka's line vanished a century later, with the advent of the Sassanian empire in third-century Iran, India had not yet seen the last representatives of the period of nomad invasions, for in western India dynasties of Scythian extraction, who had established their rule in the first century CE, ruled under the Iranian title of *kshatrapa* (satrap) till the end of the fourth century.

These events were in fact the first revolution in a cycle of military invasions of India by peoples who had been mounted nomads in Central Asia before they became military predators on the sedentary agriculturalists first of Iran, then in India. This cycle is repeated every five hundred years or so. The first wave, composed of Iranian-speaking peoples just described, had broken upon Indian shores in the first century BCE. In the fifth century CE, the Hunas, probably speaking a Turkic language and related to the Huns of Europe, made their appearance in the northwest. By 1000, Muslim Turks who had established themselves in Afghanistan began a series of Indian raids that, over the next two centuries, led to the creation of the Sultanate of Delhi. In the 1500s, the Mughals, related to the Mongols, acquired a foothold in the subcontinent that became the basis of the largest Indian empire prior to European imperialism.

Because the nomadic herdsman of Central Asia must carry everything he owns, he cannot accumulate goods and still remain a nomad.[17] His nomadic life therefore allows very little margin against hard times, and plundering agricultural settlements is one of the ways he might seek to relieve hardship. Possession of abundant horses and mastery of the techniques of mounted bowmanship can give a decisive edge over the larger, more ponderous armies of the sedentary kingdoms. The nomadic tribe embarking on a career of plunder soon finds it cannot maintain its flocks and herds and prosecute wars at the same time. Military success soon extinguishes its nomadic economy. Its military leadership is at first purely personal; the chief depends for the perpetuation of his authority over his followers on his continuing ability to extract large amounts of ready wealth from the peasants on whom he preys. Plunder quickly exhausts its possibilities, and when it does so personal leadership is undermined. If military hordes often have achieved great success with astonishing rapidity, their collapse into small, squabbling bands is often equally precipitous.

The nomad states of early India, above all the Kushanas and Western Kshatrapas, had passed beyond this stage to more stable political forms, turning personal leadership into hereditary monarchy, and replacing the indiscriminate plunder of hostage kingdoms with taxation of the peasantry. Because they lacked previous experience of the bureaucratic skills necessary for the administration of a land tax that would provide a ready flow of revenue without ruining the peasantry who supplied it, they must have been obliged to reach an accommodation with the Iranian and Indian elites who had developed such skills over the centuries.

The patronage of local religions could only facilitate such collaboration, and the transition from military to bureaucratic rule as the rulers were increasingly seen by the ruled as supporters of their religions rather than its enemies.

We do not see the details of this process in the fragmentary evidence of Kushana and Western Kshatrapa rule, only the results. The coinage of the Kushanas shows that they patronized rival Indian cults, including that of the Hindu god Shiva and the Buddha, but because their territory fell in both India and Iran, numerous Iranian deities (not to mention Mesopotamian and Roman) also appear. Kanishka is warmly remembered by Buddhist legend as its benefactor, especially of the popular form called Mahayana, which now begins to emerge into the light of history. The Kushanas, however, long retained the symbols of their Central Asian identity, especially in their pointed caps, cutaway riding coats, baggy pants, and felt boots so well adapted to their ancestral environment, and so inappropriate in the hot plains of North India, where their coins and portrait statues have been found (Figure 6).

FIGURE 6 Kushana torso, Mathura, 2nd century

The Western Kshatrapas, on the other hand, ruled for some three centuries a territory entirely cut off from Iran and Central Asia, and accordingly seem to have Indianized themselves much more completely. The first extensive Sanskrit inscription (150 CE) occurs in the reign of one of their kings, Rudradaman, in which his protégé praises not his lord's horsemanship and archery, but his mastery of music, logic, poetry, and Sanskrit grammar. This is a significant development, showing an emerging engagement of kingship with the fine arts.

Indian Civilization borrowed very little from the Central Asian intruders, beyond their cavalry techniques, which effectively ended the history of chariot warfare; whereas the Vedic deities had ridden aerial chariots, the Hindu gods in this period mount the backs of their chosen animals. Through their patronage of the nascent popular religions, the sciences, and courtly poetry, however, they made a significant contribution to the formation of classical Indian culture. In addition they provided the means of communication by which Indian culture, and Buddhism in particular, reached the oasis states of the arid Tarim basin and thence to China where, legend tells us, it arrived in the first century CE.

The Indian Peninsula

Classical Indian Civilization, at the time it acquired its characteristic form, spread over the whole Indian subcontinent and found a footing in the royal courts of Southeast Asia as well. Its evolution and spread within India were simultaneous and reciprocal. The peoples of the Indian Peninsula were doubly connected with classical India. First, because the Dravidian languages had once been widely spoken in the north, aspects of culture had been absorbed into the cultures of North India since Vedic times. Second, royal families and warrior classes of the Deccan and the South were intimately engaged in the formation and promotion of the new forms of poetry and the other arts. The principal states of this period were those of the Satavahanas, based in what is now the state of Maharashtra on the western side of the peninsula, and the three Tamil kingdoms of the extreme southern tip.

In the course of a long history, the Satavahanas at times held large portions of western India in their control, and frequently clashed with their rivals to the north, the Western Kshatrapas. Their inscriptions and the rock-cut monasteries built under their patronage show considerable favor toward Buddhism but, like most Indian monarchs, they extended their support to the different religions, and in fact they performed Vedic sacrifices as well. The caves at Karle and other places are among the most appealing monuments of the formative period. Living in a region where Indo-Aryan and Dravidian languages come together, the Satavahana kings are associated with the development of the *Katantra,* a Sanskrit grammar for nonnative speakers, and the cultivation of courtly poetry in Prakrit. Hala, one of their kings, composed a canonical anthology of courtly poetry, the *Saptashati* or *Seven hundreds,* in a Prakrit language called Maharashtri. Because of the excellence of his anthology, Maharashtri came to be regarded as the ideal Prakrit language for classical poetry, especially poetry of love. In sum, the Satavahana kings were, like other Indian kings of the formative period, actively promoting new styles in art and architecture, religion, and kingship.

In the Tamil country the three kingdoms of the Cheras (or Keralas), Pandyas, and Cholas, from west to east, had been in existence since the time of Ashoka, who did not annex their territories but sent ambassadors of the dharma to them. The kings of these ancient lineages, and other smaller kingdoms, contributed through their patronage to the development of a third classical literature, that of Tamil, contemporary with Sanskrit and Prakrit courtly poetry. This is called the Sangam literature, which refers to anthologies compiled by a *sangam* or gathering of literary connoisseurs, of Tamil poetry, in the Pandya kingdom of Madurai, in the second to fourth centuries CE. A grammar of Tamil, called *Tolkappiyam,* somewhat along the lines of the *Katantra,* was composed at about the same time as the compilation of the anthologies, and it includes a formal theory of poetics that established the conventions of the Sangam literature—a body of knowledge and conventions that was shared by poets, patrons, critics, and the refined ladies and gentlemen of the warrior class. The classical Tamil *ars poetica* recognized two main types of poetry, that of the private (*aham*) and the public (*puram*) realms, or, poems of love and heroic poetry, the poetry of war. This social-literary formation was contemporary with the beginning of an international luxury trade by which Greek sailors, making use of monsoon winds, sailed merchant ships from Egypt and the Mediterranean to the Tamil kingdoms, bringing Italian wine in amphoras, red coral jewelry, and other rarities to the south Indian royal courts. Tamil was the first of the Dravidian languages to develop a courtly literature; Telugu, Kannada, and Malayalam followed later.

In the island of Sri Lanka (Ceylon) the immigration of Indo-Aryan speakers (the Sinhalese) and the conversion of their kings to Buddhism as early as the times of Ashoka drew it within the orbit of ancient Indian Civilization at an early date. By the first century CE we begin to hear of royal courts in Southeast Asia that adopted Indian arts, religions, and ideas of kingship, beginning with Funan in what is now Cambodia and South Vietnam.

Devotional Religion

In the post-Mauryan period the history of Indian religion underwent another fundamental shift of direction. The Vedic religion had centered on sacrifice to the gods and Fathers by the Aryan householder, whereas the anti-Vedic religions of Jainism, Buddhism, and the like had stressed renunciation of society, withdrawal into a life of ascetic quietism, and meditation. Neither movement could be described as popular, open to the full participation of the masses. Now new varieties of the religious life, emphasizing devotion to a supreme deity, rose to meet that need. The adoration of images of the gods in shrines and temples with offerings of fruits, flowers, and prayers of praise and petition are consequences of the belief that the grace of God is superior to the automatic justice of the scheme of Rebirth and Moral Causation. Under those doctrines individuals gets exactly the reward or punishment to which the ethical quality of their deeds entitle them. But heaven help us if we get what we really deserve! By the grace of a god—Vishnu, Shiva, or a deified Buddha—who transcends the scheme of Rebirth, we might get better than we deserve, freedom from the binding effects of our deeds, in a word, release. Devotion to God is the warrant for that unearned gift.

The *Bhagavad Gita,* a classic of devotional Hinduism, presents its doctrines as the higher path in comparison to Vedic and ascetic religion. The *Gita* is in the form of a dialogue between Arjuna, a hero of the great Indian epic (the *Mahabharata*) of which the *Gita* is a section, and his charioteer Krishna, who is in reality a human incarnation or avatar of the high god Vishnu. Krishna analyzes the various religious disciplines in terms of the deed (*karman*): The Vedic priest seeks salvation through the deed of sacrifice, little knowing that it binds him to the wheel of Rebirth. The ascetic who renounces the deed in favor of the higher knowledge follows a superior way, indeed, but he deludes himself if he thinks he can completely cease to act, for he still must breath, eat, and so forth. A way of escaping the consequences of the deed nevertheless exists: It is to renounce desire for the fruits of the deed, while continuing to perform one's religiously appointed duty in society. This teaching is very near that of Buddhism, which also prescribes suppression of desire behind action rather than suppression of action itself, but the *Gita* differs in urging men not to renounce society but on the contrary to meet their social obligations with inward detachment. Krishna goes on to show how, through devotion to God, even the lowliest humans receive unearned grace by which they may be saved.

Formulated in this way, devotionalism appears as a third stage in the evolution of Indian religious ideas, following Vedic sacrifice and the anti-Vedic religions of renunciation, which emerges at a determinate period in history. It is more likely, however, that the worship of images, petitionary and propitiatory prayer, devotional acts, and the idea of grace have roots in India that go back at least as far as the Indus Civilization, and have long been practiced by the humbler orders of society. Devotionalism is not an invention of the post-Mauryan age; what has happened is that devotionalism has achieved respectability among the literate elites, especially brahmins, acquired literary expression in Sanskrit, and thus left documents by which we can trace the later stages of its growth.

Hinduism represents the result of this new partnership between brahmin learning and popular devotionalism. It is in this period that Vishnu and Shiva become the twin foci of Hinduism, as they remain today. Vishnu, through the doctrine of his "descents" or incarnations (*avatars*) by means of which he descends into the world from age to age to punish the wicked and aid the good, draws to himself many sects that were certainly non-Vedic and probably purely local in extent. Vishnu in the forms of the Fish, the Tortoise, the Boar, the Man-Lion, the Dwarf, Rama of the Axe, Rama king of Ayodhya, Krishna the Dark, the Horse, even the Buddha, surpasses older sects not by suppressing them but by absorbing and universalizing them. Shiva in the form of the phallic image (*linga*), or as Lord of Yogis or Lord of Beasts, or the members of his household, the Mother Goddess (Devi, Durga) his spouse, and his sons the warrior Skanda (with whom the Tamil Murugan is identified) and the elephant-headed Ganesha, show a similar ability to absorb and universalize local religious practices.

The growing popularity of devotional Hindu sects posed a grave challenge to the austere religions of renunciation, and provoked the growth of devotionalism within them. The Buddhist sects of the Great Vehicle (Mahayana) introduce the idea of grace in the doctrine of Buddhas-to-be (Bodhisattvas), who, out of compassion, bestow their surplus merit on those who pray to them. Even in the sects of the stricter persuasion (pejoratively called Hinayana or Little Vehicle by their opponents, but usually referred to as Theravada or Doctrine of the Elders in current scholarship, following Sri Lankan usage), however, the devotional impulse leaves its mark in the adoration of images and sacred places of pilgrimage.

The Classical Age (320–600 CE)

In 320 CE Gangetic Magadha again became the center of a growing empire under the Gupta dynasty. The name of its founder, Chandra Gupta I, recalled that of the Mauryan adventurer who had seized the throne of Pataliputra more than six centuries before. However, the Gupta age was by no means a revival of the Mauryan. Political power was much less centralized under the Guptas than it had been in Mauryan times, but in their age the refinement of art, letters, and manners achieved classic definition. Kingship took on a remoter, more god-like aspect and its overlordship more indirect forms. The king of classical India was urged to submit his power to the higher authority of the brahmin, and to intervene less in the customs of his subjects than Ashoka had.

The Guptas (320–550 CE)

Chandra Gupta, Great King over Kings, had created a mid-Gangetic empire centered on Magadha, much as Ajatashatru had, and the year one (319–320 CE) of the Gupta era used in the inscriptions of his successors probably marks the commencement of his reign. His son Samudra Gupta greatly expanded this patrimony through war. Virtually all the petty states along the Ganga and Yamuna rivers were annexed, and the border kingdoms of Bengal, Assam, and Nepal, and the tribal oligarchies to the west, were forced to pay tribute. An expedition down the eastern coast reached as far as the Pallava kingdom of Kanchi (Kanchipuram) in Tamil Nadu. The Guptas showed no intention of permanently dominating the southern kingdoms; according to the court poet, Samudra "conquered and then released" the kings of the South, winning thereby much glory (and doubtless much plunder as well), but nothing more lasting. Even the distant kings of Sri Lanka and the Indo-Iranian borderland offered their personal submission, made presents of maidens, and begged for Gupta charters confirming them in the possession of their own territories as Gupta vassals. If we can believe an inscription of

Samudra Gupta, there is evidence that the poet is exaggerating the significance of the gifts and flattering speeches of foreign ambassadors to the imperial court. Kings now display their patronage of and participation in courtly poetry, music, and other fine arts. Gold coins of Samudra Gupta represent him embodying a balance of the warrior virtues (killing a lion with bow and arrow) and artistic refinement (playing a stringed instrument), which, together with support of religion and the practice of dharma, constitutes the classical ideal of kingship (Figure 7).

In the next generation Samudra's son Chandra Gupta II rounded out the Gupta realm by putting an end to three centuries of Shaka (Western Kshatrapa) rule in western India. Most of North India was under Gupta suzerainty by the year 400, which falls in the middle of his long reign. Although Gupta rule did not extend southward into the peninsula, it achieved considerable influence in the Vakataka kingdom of the upper peninsula, whose prince married Chandra Gupta's daughter. This princess, Prabhavati Gupta, became regent of the Vakataka kingdom when her husband died during the minority of her sons.

Faxian, a Buddhist monk from China who at the beginning of the fifth century journeyed across Central Asia to India to collect accurate copies of the scriptures, has left a memoir of his travels. In it he paints a picture of India in the times of Chandra Gupta II that is very close to his own ideals. The people are prosperous and happy, he assures us, and the state does not register them or hinder their movement. It does not inflict corporal punishment on criminals, or at most chops off the right hand of a rebel for a second offense. Vegetarianism has made such progress that if animals were slaughtered for food the monkish traveler did not know of it, and only low-caste hunters sold meat. He even claims that the people did not eat onions or garlic, or drink wine, statements that can only be true of some of the higher classes. On the other hand, he notes the existence of an untouchable caste whose dwellings are segregated from the rest of society, and who beat a piece of wood when they approach a city or market to announce their presence so that others can avoid coming into contact with them. The wealthy have built and endowed Buddhist monasteries and free hospitals for the care of orphans, widows, and cripples.

During the reigns of Chandra Gupta II (376–415) and his son Kumara Gupta I (415–455), India enjoyed an age of prosperity and order while the other great civilizations faced the grave menace of Central Asian invaders. The Xiongnu in China, the Huns in Rome, and the

FIGURE 7 Gold coins of Samudra Gupta, 4th century

Ephthalites or Hephthalites in Sassanian Iran are likely to have been culturally related peoples speaking Turkic languages. India was not to be spared for long; Skanda Gupta (455–470) takes credit for having rescued the fortunes of his dynasty by victory over the Hunas, probably also related to the foregoing peoples, who appeared in the northwest at the beginning of his reign. A second Huna wave from about 500 CE established a nomad empire in the northwest but it reached deeply into Central India as well. Gupta vassals in its path transferred their allegiances to the invaders, and other areas asserted their independence of Gupta overlordship. Although some form of Gupta suzerainty continued to be recognized in the eastern provinces in Bengal and Orissa as late as 570, the breakup of the empire was in large part caused by the effects, direct and indirect, of the second Huna invasion. Huna rule lasted in various areas of the west and northwest at least to 600, and much later they seem to have been fully integrated into the military stratum of Hindu society as Rajputs.

Unlike the ideal of a modern nation-state, central authority in the Gupta Empire did not intervene with the same intensity everywhere within its boundaries. The relations of the provinces to the throne varied. The Gangetic lands formed a core of directly ruled territories, whose indigenous kings had been deposed by Samudra Gupta. Encircling this core was a belt of states that were obliged to pay tribute, heed the imperial command, and renew their loyalty from time to time by personal attendance at the imperial court. Heavy as these obligations might have been, the internal affairs of these states remained in the hands of the existing rulers, whether kings in the case of the northern and eastern states, or tribal elders in the case of the tribal states of the west and southwest. Gupta suzerainty over the tribal states might have contributed to the growth of monarchy within them by strengthening the authority of the chief with whom they dealt, and as Gupta rule recedes eastwards in the sixth century, ambitious independent kings suddenly arise in areas previously under tribal forms of government. In the Kathiawar peninsula and Bengal, the extreme western and eastern provinces, on the other hand, the Guptas appointed their own governors to administer them and, presumably, to remit taxes to the throne. By virtue of their remoteness and the fact that governorships tended to become hereditary, however, these two provinces came to approximate semiautonomous tributary states. The generals of Kathiawar became kings as Gupta power failed, although the governors of Bengal continued to recognize their overlords until late in the sixth century. Compared to the Mauryan Empire, all of whose provinces appear to have been governed by royal princes, the structure of the Gupta Empire is less centralized and less homogeneous, although its style is grander.

Classical Indian State and Society

The economic basis of the classical Indian state was the king's share in the productivity of the realm. The king's duty was to protect, and in return he had a claim to a fraction of the peasant's crop, usually put at one sixth in the law books, but variable according to local conditions and needs of state. Throughout the ancient period, cultivators were in short supply, and not land. The wise king, therefore, would encourage immigration from neighboring kingdoms, and encourage peasants to bring virgin land under cultivation by granting life ownership of fields; remitting taxes; and providing seed, draft animals, and irrigation. Although Indian kingship was subject only to supernatural review for its misdeeds, that the peasant might "vote with his feet" was an inducement to mild treatment.

Although the king could not tax the ascetic meditating in the forest, the protection he afforded entitled him to the sixth share in the ascetic's religious merit. The invisible rewards to be gained prompted kings and private persons alike to grant lands and whole peasant villages to learned brahmins or Jain or Buddhist monks, or to endow religious institutions such as temples, monasteries, and colleges. Royal grants in effect transferred the king's share to the religious grantee, whereas private citizens who wished to make gifts of land to religious institutions would have to buy out the king's interest. The state was naturally reluctant to allow tax-paying fields to leave the tax rolls, and therefore tended to limit religious grants to virgin lands, and forbid the migration of peasantry to them. Religious institutions therefore played an important role in the extension of agriculture by turning virgin land to the plough.

Religious grants differed from grants to nonreligious officials in that they yielded no revenue to the king and were irrevocable. Because of the permanence of religious grants, the deeds were inscribed on copper plates, many of which have survived. Among the clauses of these deeds we find lists of the immunities the grantees enjoyed from interference by the king's officials, and the privileges that amount to considerable internal sovereignty over the lives of the cultivators of the grant, such as the right to administer criminal justice and collect the fines imposed.

Thus religious grants continued to enjoy royal protection while they were immune from intervention in the administration of the granted fields and villages and their peasant cultivators, yielding only spiritual returns to the state and not taxes. Many temples and monasteries over the centuries became wealthy objects of Turkish plunderers. So favorable were the terms of religious grants that copperplate charters were sometimes forged.

We know little about the terms of nonreligious grants, which were written on perishable materials such as palm leaf or birch bark. That fact in itself shows that although they might pass from father to son for generations, these grants were nevertheless held only so long as the king did not revoke them, and not, as in the case of religious grants, "as long as the moon and the sun endure." Nor were they, in every case at least, tax-free. Indeed the collection of revenue became intimately connected with rights over land and cultivators. Royal governors and revenue officials might be assigned the revenue of certain villages in their provinces as their salary, remitting the revenue of the rest of the province to the throne. The administrative simplicity of such an arrangement, as opposed to collecting all revenue into the royal treasury from which salaries would then be disbursed to remote provincial officials, suited the governmental capacities of the age. Thus a large class of intermediaries interposed themselves between the king and the peasant with considerable rights to administer justice and collect revenue from tillers of the soil. Rural collector, governor, and landlord tended to approximate the tributary king, enjoying increasingly the elements of sovereignty within their jurisdiction and deriving their incomes directly from it, so long as they continued to supply revenue to the imperial treasury.

The great bulk of revenue came from the produce of the land, but the king extracted his share of the productivity of other classes of subjects as well, whether fishers, herders, artisans, or merchants. The right to exact tolls and excise taxes also derived from the king's duty to protect, and took certain characteristic forms in the marketplace. Royal agents established standard weights and measures and rooted out fraud. Interest rates and contracts were subject to local custom, but were enforced by the king when disputes were referred to him for settlement. When prices went far astray of prevailing standards of fairness the king would intervene to restore them, creating royal markets for such commodities and forbidding private trade, in the interests of protecting the people against shortage, or the merchant community against market gluts.

To a large degree Indians regulated their behavior not by the state but by the *caste system.* Each caste had its occupational specialty, and its place in a hierarchy of ritual purity. The impure occupations, such as barber, washerman, and sweeper, were strictly necessary to the purer orders of society, such as the brahmin priest, because besides performing services that were important economically, they also removed uncleanness, which the brahmin could not do for himself without jeopardizing his purity. The castes, then, were interdependent, but were also held separate from one another by rules limiting their contact. These rules tended to forbid different castes to intermarry, dine together, or even come into physical proximity, for fear the less pure should defile the purer. Within each caste a local council of elders would see that its members followed its customs as regards food and drink, marriage, inheritance, and ritual, and could punish offenders with sanctions ranging from fines and penances to permanent expulsion from the caste.

It is often thought that the castes of India are unchanging, but that is mistaken. Castes are continually coming into being or splitting into smaller castes, improving or losing their position in the hierarchy, as an effect of migration, population growth, new occupational specialties, the entrance of tribal groups into Hindu society, and other causes. The castes themselves are constantly, although slowly, changing their boundaries and their position vis-à-vis other castes; what is relatively unchanging over the centuries is the caste *system,* which defines and redefines the positions of the castes in its hierarchy according to a graded scale of purity.

The Sanskrit law books (*Dharmashastras*) have contributed to the erroneous notion of unchanging castes. According to them, the four orders (*varnas,* literally "colors") of Vedic society, the brahmin priest, the kshatriya warrior, the vaishya cultivator, herder, or trader, and the shudra serf, are the four original castes sprung from the body of the Primeval Man at the Creation, and all other castes are the result of improper sexual connections between these original social orders. Thus the occupational duties of the castes were fixed at the beginning of the world and transmitted hereditarily for all time, whereas the new castes derive their duties from the combined heredity of their mixed parentage. The origin, nature, and capacity of the caste system to impose order on changing relations of social groups is much more complex than this simple theory of the law book admits, as we see in Chapter 6 when we return to this important topic.

The Indian king was the caretaker of a social order that he did not create.[18] He did not legislate for society, in the modern sense of the term, although his edicts commanded obedience, and he was the supreme arbitrator of disputes between individuals or groups. His judgment in a dispute, or that of the brahmin judges to whom he delegated his judicial authority, might rest on one of four sources: the sacred law (dharma), the immemorial customs of clans and castes, the usages of the marketplace, or the royal edict reflecting the needs of state. Of these, dharma carried the highest prestige, and an extensive literature was devoted to the science of the sacred law (Dharmashastra). Its earliest and most authoritative works were the *Dharma Sutras* of the Veda, essentially complete in Mauryan times, followed by the more systematic and extensive treatises called *Dharma Smritis* beginning with the *Laws of Manu.* The composition of smritis ceased by about 600 CE, followed by a period in which commentaries on and digests of the sutras and smritis were composed, a scholarly industry that persisted well into nineteenth-century British India.

The purpose of this literature was not to create law, but to determine the religious duty (dharma) that was eternal, unchanging, and transcendent. Dharma might be discovered through four ways: by consulting revelation (*shruti,* in effect the Vedic literature proper) or tradition (smriti; i.e., the Dharma Smritis such as that of Manu); should these sources fail to give guidance on a particular point, the behavior of virtuous men or the prompting of one's own conscience would imply the existence of a sacred injunction even without explicit authority in the Veda.

It was the duty of the king to see that men performed the duties appropriate to their caste and station of life (*varnashrama-dharma*) and in general to conform to his policies and judicial decisions in such a way that dharma was advanced. Nevertheless local custom was not to be abrogated unless it was greatly offensive to dharma. In fact, where dharma and custom were in conflict in a judicial decision, the king was supposed to decide on the basis of custom; the usages of the marketplace overrode dharma and the customs of castes and regions; and all three could be set aside in favor of the king's edict, that is, reason of state.

Thus the king was completely free to conduct the affairs of state as he saw fit. He was subject to no constitution limiting his powers; he could issue edicts or revoke them on his sole authority and without courting the assent of any other person or group, and expect obedience. His rule was thus theoretically unchecked, and over time divinity was increasingly attributed to him. Where a European king might claim mere divine right, the Indian king was, in a certain sense, himself a god. The inscriptions of Samudra Gupta, for example, describe him as the equal of Kubera, god of wealth; Varuna, dispenser of justice; Indra, god of war; and Yama, god of death, mortal only in that he conforms to the usages of society, but in truth a very god on earth.

This otherwise despotic power, however, was limited in two ways: by supernatural sanctions and practical limitations. The brahmin priests and scholars of dharma were themselves gods on earth who, although powerless themselves, incarnated that sacred principal (*brahma*) from which the royal power (*kshatra*) had sprung, and by which it was legitimized. Royal power should therefore join brahmin authority in submission to it, as wife to husband, to make it procreative of good. In practice that would have meant conducting the affairs of the realm within the framework of the holy law, and heeding the advice of learned brahmins, insofar as the needs of state permitted.

On the other hand, tradition and practical considerations limited the degree to which the king could effectively interfere in men's lives. The king's recognized duty was to punish the wicked, protect the good, direct men to their appropriate duties (*varnashrama-dharma*), and prevent the intermixture of the various castes. However, the classical Indian king was not to reform society or improve human nature, as Ashoka had attempted to do. Caste law was decided by custom, not created by the king, and he could modify it by edict only within narrow limits. Disputes between individuals were properly settled by caste, village, or guild assemblies, and the king could not intervene unless the dispute was referred to him by the parties concerned. The king could initiate judicial proceedings only where the interests of the state were directly concerned. Society, through the system of castes, was largely capable of regulating itself, with minimal interference by the state to restore the balance from time to time.

Late Classical Indian Civilization (600–1000 CE)

States and Empires

In the first half of the seventh century CE, Harsha, prince of the small state of Thaneswar near Delhi, knit together an empire that included the whole of the Gangetic Valley from the eastern Punjab to Bengal and Orissa, with subordinate allies in Kathiawar to the west and Assam to the east. The entire political fabric unraveled after his death in 647. Although this short-lived imperial venture had few lasting consequences for the political history of India, Harsha attracted to him a distinguished poet, Bana, who wrote a biography called *The deeds of Harsha,* and a Chinese

Buddhist monk, Xuanzang, who wrote a memoir of his *Travels to the Western world,* and from these works we have a more detailed knowledge of this ancient Indian kingdom than of any other.

Harsha's empire was a loose assemblage of conquered kings who were obliged to pay tribute, give military aid, and render personal homage by attendance at court. The "feudal" character of the empire was reflected in the imperial army, which was really a collection of smaller armies, each owing their loyalties to their particular prince, and not directly to the emperor. The whole was a heterogeneous affair in which noncombatants, such as personal servants, storekeepers, grooms, courtesans, and wives, must have greatly outnumbered the effective fighting force. Such an army moved slowly—scarcely 10 kilometers per day in times of peace—but grandly. The glitter and pomp of this army, made audible with golden drums, trumpets, horns, and conch shells, must have had an awesome effect on an enemy force, offsetting its inability to act swiftly. It must also have had a salutary effect on the loyalties of Harsha's subjects as he passed on tour of the realm.

Because of the inherent weakness of Harsha's newly created empire—a small bureaucracy and large numbers of tributaries always eager to establish their independence—it could only be held together by his constant personal attention and presence. Xuanzang tells us that except during the rainy season Harsha was constantly on tour, never remaining long in one place and living in temporary grass shelters that were burned after his departure. Daily he distributed alms to Buddhists and brahmins, heard the grievances of the people against his officials, and dispensed justice. The fissiparous tendencies within the empire were held in check by his personal intervention and awe-inspiring presence, and when he died his empire proved unable to live without him.

The middle Ganga, with its large concentrations of cultivators, thriving agriculture, riverine trade, access to copper and iron deposits, and its rich cities such as Harsha's Kanyakubja (Kanauj) continued to be the prize for which the Hindu princes of North India competed, and the Turkish Muslims after them. In 647 Wang Xuance, ambassador of the Chinese emperor Tang Taizong, reached Harsha's domain only to find that a minister named Arunashva had usurped the throne. Wang assembled an army from friendly kings in Assam and Kashmir and attempted unsuccessfully to control this region and build an empire on its wealth.

In the middle of the eighth century two major powers emerged, the Gurjara-Pratiharas from the western desert of Rajasthan and the Palas of the eastern Ganga, who for two centuries contested the control of the middle Ganga and in effect divided it between them. The Palas lost control of Kanyakubja to their rivals in about 800 CE, and were essentially confined to Bihar and Bengal, where their rule continued until the end of the eleventh century. The Palas were great patrons of Buddhism that, in a Tantric form (discussed later), flourished in eastern India during their rule, and was transmitted to Tibet. Pala sculpture has also left its mark on the Southeast Asian countries with which this kingdom had commercial and diplomatic relations.

From as early as 550 CE we can begin to trace the rise in western India, especially the Rajasthan desert, of dynasties that call themselves *Rajput* (Sanskrit Rajaputra, "king's son") which remains the dominant martial and land-owning elite of the region to this day. The fact that they appear just about the time Huna rule vanished, and that the name Huna later appears in lists of Rajput clans, suggests that some of these lineages might have been Indianized Central Asians, but others were certainly indigenous. In any case the Rajput patrilineages show a propensity toward the fragmentation of political authority along kinship lines as they ramify, a tendency that could have its roots in nomadic social organization. Of the three early Rajput lines of which we have records, the Gurjaras were divided into four branches by 650, and the Chahamanas into eight or nine by 1000. Only one branch of the Gurjaras, calling themselves Pratiharas ("Gatekeeper," a subordinate title) and ruling at the important commercial city of Ujjain, succeeded in overcoming the limitations of early Rajput political organization based on kinship, and established an empire through alliance with other, unrelated Rajput chiefs. The Gurjara-Pratiharas created the only Rajput empire, which by capturing Kanauj became essentially a central Gangetic rather than a western power.[19]

This alliance held together for two centuries (c. 750–950), during which the Gurjara-Pratiharas succeeded in developing some of the elements of bureaucracy and a unified military without which a successful confederacy of plunderers cannot develop into a stable state. They contained the growth of Muslim power to the Indus region that Arab generals had reached by 712, but their empire broke up in the tenth century, and the Turkish Muslim invaders from the end of that century found many small successor states ruled by the various Rajput lineages that had previously been the subordinates of the Gurjara-Pratiharas.

In the peninsula during the post-Gupta era, two other centers of power defined themselves, on opposite coasts (Map 6). The upper

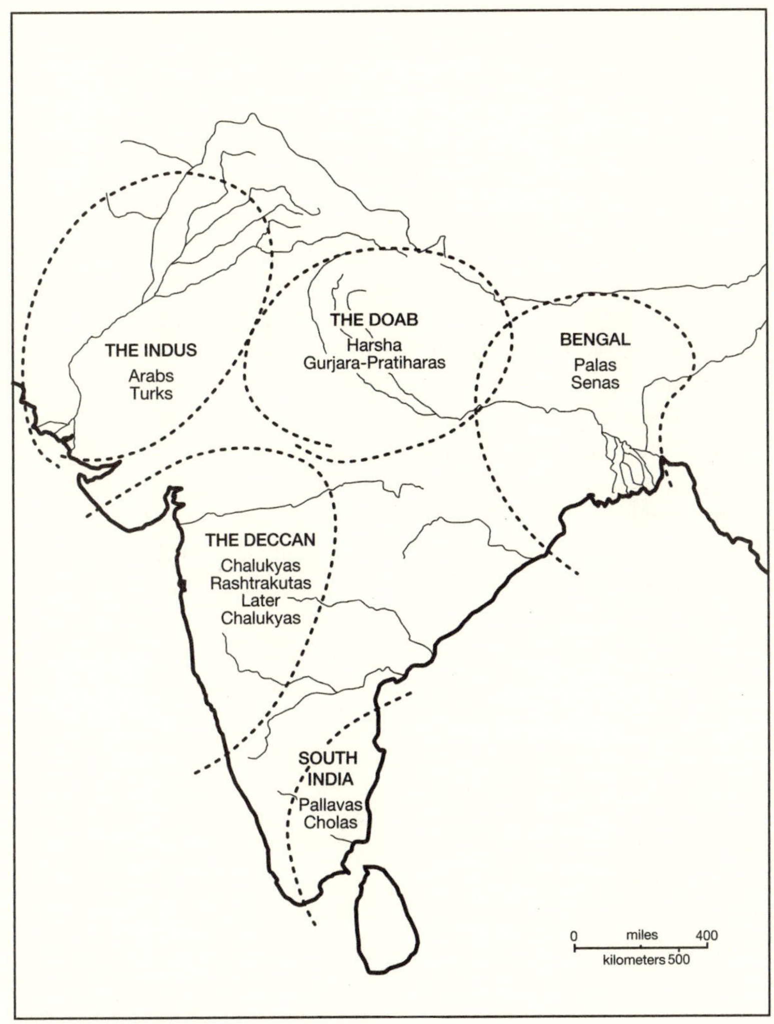

MAP 6 Political centers of late classical India

western Deccan was under the Chalukyas of Badami in Harsha's time, and the contemporary Chalukya king, Pulakeshin II, prevented Harsha from penetrating the peninsula. In the eighth century the Rashtrakutas overthrew the Chalukyas and established a powerful state that, on several occasions, undertook raiding expeditions to the Ganga. They contested Ujjain, an important commercial and trading center midway between the Ganga and the western coast, with the Gurjara-Pratiharas, and also clashed with the Pallava and Chola rulers of the Tamil country. At the end of the tenth century the Rashtrakutas were replaced by a revived Chalukya line, which unified the upper Deccan until the end of the twelfth century when it broke up into a number of successor states.

In the Tamil country on the southeast side of the peninsula, the Pallavas had ruled the Coromandel Coast at least from the times of Samudra Gupta, whose southern expedition reached their capital, Kanchi. They have left for us some of the most beautiful monuments of classical India, in the sculptures of Mahabalipuram and the Shore Temple, south of Chennai. In the ninth century, a vassal lineage bearing the ancient name Chola, which had been held by one of the three ancient Tamil kingdoms, founded an empire that reached its zenith of power in the eleventh century and persisted into the thirteenth. Their two greatest kings were Rajaraja (985–1014) and his son Rajendra I (1014–1042). Under the first, Sri Lanka was invaded and the northern part of the island became a Chola province under military rule; under the second Chola arms reached the eastern Ganga, reversing Samudra Gupta's raid on the south, and, in a naval expedition without precedent in ancient India, sacked the coastal cities of the Malay Peninsula and Sumatra, and held them briefly under Chola overlordship. Chola-period stone temples have survived in abundance and many of them are still under worship.

The overall political structure of the post-Gupta period is one of five or so main regions, each dominated by a single royal family and state apparatus. Although the regional powers were in a more or less continuous competition among themselves, trying to enlarge their kingdoms at the expense of smaller powers and their larger rivals, sometimes invading and plundering the capitol of a regional power, and although new royal families occasionally deposed older ones, on the whole, the five-centered regional pattern was stable. The average length of reign was about 20 years, making for stability, and in many cases the royal families endured for centuries. The Eastern Chalukyas, a buffer state on the east coast between the major powers of the peninsula, continued for over 400 years, the Palas of Bengal for nearly 400 and the Cholas of the south for over 300, and several others lasted two centuries or more. Although the political situation seems always in motion at any given time, in a longer view it had a more or less fixed structure.

CHAPTER 6

Family, Society, Polity

Family
Society
Polity

Ancient Indian structures of family, society, and polity have a deep past and a continuing influence in the present. We need to examine them as long-enduring structures, having a different, slower tempo than the stream of events making up the narrative of history. In this chapter and the next we shift to a different kind of analysis, one that examines social institutions and collective concepts that have a long life and are slow to change, rather than the flow of ever-changing events.

Family

The forms of marriage, kinship, and family in India are highly various, so that it is especially difficult to generalize about Indian society at the family level. Still, there are certain characteristics of family and marriage in India that are striking, and we can make a beginning by describing them, with the caution that they are by no means universal or even typical, but are rather characteristic of family and marriage among *upper caste Hindus*, and continuations of the Vedic pattern described in Chapter 3. Thus they are elite structures rather than average or universal ones, are highly visible and have an exemplary character, and often act as patterns to be emulated by other castes; we then discuss departures from these patterns. We start with these elite ideals because of their wide influence and because we have a rich written record of them in the Dharmashastra. Artistic representations offer other resources. A beautiful Chola bronze sculpture depicts the marriage of Shiva and Parvati, with brother-in-law Vishnu and a female attendant, embodying the perfection of a family scene (Figure 8).

FIGURE 8 The wedding of Shiva and Parvati, Chola bronze sculpture, 12th century

We begin with the two leading features of marriage: It is *arranged*, and it is *indissoluble*. Marriages are arranged by the parents after careful consideration of the various elements that make for a suitable match, principally that the couple are of the same caste, of different clan (*gotra*), and have compatible horoscopes. The concentration on such objective matters does not mean that the couple's feelings are left out of account. But they are not the basis of the marriage, and are subordinated to its main purpose, which is to form a durable relation of alliance between families. Love might blossom between a man and a woman, but after marriage and not as its cause. Very often, especially in the past, these alliances have been formed while the couple were yet children, and it was thought desirable that children be betrothed or even married before puberty (although child marriages were not consummated until after). In modern times, the Republic of India has passed laws to raise the age of marriage, and the practices surrounding marriage are undergoing change in other ways.

Marriage, once arranged, is solemnized by a priest before a sacred fire and with Vedic *mantras;* in fact the marriage ceremony is the most vigorous survivor of Vedic ritual practices. The whole proceeding gives marriage the character of being an indissoluble bond created by sacrament, so that divorce is out of the question. Its purpose is to form a couple who are, so to say, a single person for purposes of carrying out the rituals of the household, of which the oldest married male is the executor and priest. Secondary marriages, without the use of fire and *mantra,* could also be entered into after a primary marriage had been made, and these could be readily dissolved.

We turn now to the leading features of the family in India: It is *extended,* it is *joint,* and it is *patriarchal.*

Extended families are larger than that of the "nuclear" family consisting of the married couple and their children. In India they are generally structured by patrilineal descent (kinship through males), although as explained a bit later, there are prominent examples of matrilineal descent in India. Assuming patrilineal descent as the norm for purposes of constructing a model, the membership of the extended family consists of the married couple, their unmarried daughters, their sons, and their sons' wives and children. We see at once that three generations (or more) are living together in the extended family. We see also that the destinies of boys and girls are dramatically different, as boys remain in the families of their parents, but girls grow up to move away from their parents and into the families of their husbands. This means that the women of the family are of two distinct kinds—the wives (who marry in) and the daughters (who marry out)—whereas the men of the family are of one kind only, to one another, namely patrilineal kin.

Families are extended in membership, and joint in property ownership. That is, the family holds property jointly as a single owner, and the men of the family are the shareholders, so to say, of the property. After the death of the parents the brothers can remain joint, under the headship of the eldest, and can continue so indefinitely, the position of householder passing to the eldest male. Alternatively they might partition the family in equal shares among them. In any case, the family property is not bequeathed by the making of wills (because it is joint, and not the sole property of the father) but by the immemorial custom of equal shares among the brothers. Furthermore, the timing of inheritance might be postponed until long after the death of the householder, with the sons continuing jointly. This delay in partition of inheritance contributes to the extendedness of family membership.

Here again we see that gender differences are strongly marked. All members of the joint family, men and women, have rights to food, shelter, clothing, and the like out of the productivity of the fields and flocks of the family, but it is only the men who are the joint owners of the land. Daughters, because they marry into another family, are not shareholders in the family property in the form of land (although this again has been changed by legislation in the twentieth century). However, they do take a portion of the family property with them at the time of marriage in the form of movable property, especially saris, utensils, and jewelry, which can be very substantial in amount if the family is prosperous. This dowry is called "women's wealth," so that even property is strongly gendered, and follows different trajectories. It will be apparent that, because jointness is about property ownership, only families that have substantial amounts of property will be joint, and that will be a minority of families. Nevertheless the joint family remains an important feature of Indian life, and under the Republic of India on the order of 10 percent of families file income tax as undivided joint families.

Finally, the family is patriarchal in the sense that it is under the authority of the father, or in any case the eldest male to cover the situation of brothers continuing to live jointly. (We call this person the householder.) The family is doubly patriarchal. Feminism has given the word patriarchy the meaning of the institutionalized dominance of women by men; in that sense patriarchy is found in all societies in some degree, and certainly in this one. But the family norm we are describing is also patriarchal in the older, narrower sense of being under the authority of the father, which means that not only all the women of the family, but also the sons, even though grown up, married, and with children of their own, are under his tutelage. In a sense the householder is the only legal adult, with powers to represent all the members of the extended family to the world outside (in a lawsuit, for example), and everyone else is a minor. He is also, in a sense, the family's priest, and makes offerings to the sacred fire on its behalf.

It is worth analyzing this double patriarchy a bit more. The sons, even though grown up, are under the tutelage of their father while he is living, but women are perpetually under the tutelage of men in the Vedic tradition: to the father when young, to the husband when married, and to the son when widowed. At the same time women, as wives, are central to the Vedic ideal that focuses on the married pair as the agent of the sacrifice—or rather, on the married male householder. Because they are subsumed to their husbands, however, they are both essential religiously and not very visible in the written record.[20]

The patriarchal authority with which the householder is endowed is undoubtedly great, but it is not unlimited. He is not the sole owner of the family property but its joint owner with his sons, and as we have seen, in ancient times at least, he had no power to divide the property unequally by a will. In a real sense the family is a corporation that lives on although its members die and are replaced, and the householder is the executive responsible for managing the property for the good of the family as a whole.

This model of "the Indian family" should be understood as an ideal type and not a statistical description of the average Indian family. It is a cultural construction sustained by religious ideas, embodied in mythology, and solemnized by ritual. We have seen that these ideas of the family are already formulated in the Vedic period and were in part shared by other early societies speaking Indo-European languages, such as the ancient Greeks, Romans, and Persians (Chapter 3). In India it remains an important force today among Hindus although, again, aspects of the model have been modified by legislation. The most important source of these ideals is the body of texts called Dharmashastra, the science of the law, which develops and codifies the practices and beliefs of the Vedic peoples. Its many texts have a great deal to say about the two main aspects of family law, marriage and the partition of inheritance. We need to examine ways in which the Dharmashastra tradition sustains this ideal type of the Indian family.

Speaking very broadly, Hindus recognize a great many kinds of personal, superhuman beings, which can be divided into two types: the devas or gods, and "the Fathers" or ancestors. Side by side with the complex rituals of the Veda, with their requirements of three fires and many brahmin priests as intermediaries acting for the householder, there are simpler rituals of the family that involve a single sacred fire of the household and because the householder acts on his own behalf, without a priest or, we could say, as his own priest. The domestic rituals involve feeding supernatural beings of both kinds, but whereas the devas are the same for all families, the Fathers are unique to each, and consist of their deceased patrilineal ancestors (father, father's father, father's father's father, etc.). There is therefore a structural relation between the family and the worship of the ancestors, and between society as a whole and the "national" religion, so to say, of the gods.

Besides the simple daily offerings to gods, ancestors, and other beings made to the household fire, the domestic religion consists of a whole series of rituals called *samskaras,* meaning "polishing" or "perfecting," which helps the person make the transition from one stage of life to the next. These *samskaras* begin even before birth, with rites to promote conception and the safety of the fetus, followed by others through birth and infancy (first sight of the sun, first solid food, and so forth), the initiation of boys into the status of students of the Veda, and marriage. At the end of life various rites are performed, involving cremation of the dead, rites to assist the soul of the recently deceased to successfully make the journey to the World of the Fathers (so that they do not remain wandering about the earth as unhappy ghosts), and periodic rites of feeding the ancestors with balls of rice (pinda) and water. The ancestors return the favor by promoting the health and fertility of the family, its lands, and its animals.

Under this conception the purpose of the family lies outside itself; it exists not simply to care for the living and perpetuate itself, but to feed the ancestors and in so doing provide for their continued residence in the World of the Fathers. Consequently the inheritance of family land goes hand in hand with the obligation to make the offerings to its ancestors.

The ancestors cannot feed themselves, and so their continued happiness requires the unbroken perpetuation of the line of patrilineal descendants. This entails a strong emphasis on the need for the birth of sons, but not every couple has sons, so that the Dharmashastra develops a whole series of legal fictions to create sons where none exist. The twelve kinds of sons the Dharmashastra recognizes begin with the "son of the body" or biological son, and go on to recognize several others. Suppose that the couple have daughters but no sons, for example; it is possible to designate the daughter to marry and raise a son who will be the legal son to her father and mother, but not to his own father and mother. This is the "son of the appointed daughter." Or again, suppose the couple has neither sons nor daughters. By an old custom that anthropologists call the levirate (found also among Greeks and Romans, and in the Bible) and the Indians called *niyoga,* the childless widow should cohabit with her deceased husband's younger brother to beget a son, who will be heir to the deceased and not to his natural father. This is not a marriage, for the younger brother must form his own marriage to beget heirs of his own. In classical times the ancient custom of niyoga passed out of favor, and adoption became more prominent. Adoption again is different from what people in the West might be used to: In ancient India the adoptive child was rarely an orphan and should, rather, come from a family known to be of good standing and of the same caste. Because the adoptive son is irrevocably parted from his natural parents and integrated into the family of his adoptive parents, and after their death gives offerings of pinda and water to the latter and not the former, such a boy must not be the only son of his natural parents, or they would be deprived of offerings after death.

This complex of ideas and practices strongly supports married life as a norm and endows it with transcendental purposes. It combines two different principles in a somewhat unstable mixture: the equal importance of the husband and the wife, and the hierarchical relation of the husband to the wife. This is expressed, for example, in ancient ideas of conception of a child that vary between notions of the equal and complementary biological contributions of the parents, on one hand, to the analogy (found also among the Greeks) of the field (the mother) and seed (the father), on the other, according to which the male element determines the structural properties of the child.

The Dharmashastra norm, as we have said, is an upper caste norm, so that to paint a more adequate picture of the family in India we must now introduce some of the leading complications and exceptions. We might start with the attitude of the non-Vedic religions to the family and to social life. Buddhism and Jainism hold that people find their salvation in the renunciation of family life, in the status of monks and nuns. Although not being against the family, the drift of these religions is to drain away the transcendental significance of family (and caste), and to look at family and social relations as matters of ethical behavior, not religious obligation, and as preparation for the higher state of the renouncer. Hinduism itself embraces the ideal of the renouncer, perhaps in response to the success of the anti-Vedic religions, but accommodates it to the norm of domesticity by making it an optional stage *after* one has discharged the duties of being a householder. The ideal of the renouncer is therefore central to all the Indian religions, Vedic and anti-Vedic, in a certain tension with the ideal of the married life.

That said, let us now look at various axes of deviation from the norm we have just examined.

High Caste/Low Caste

We have seen that the Dharmashastra norm for family life especially pertains to high-caste people. In particular it has a great deal to do with the formation and perpetuation of durable family estates; in a way, property organizes family relations. There is a great deal of variation in family life between high and low castes, or perhaps we should say, between families with a lot of property and families with little or none. The family life of the poor tends to be structured more simply. In the absence of property around which to form extended families, the families of the poor tend to be nuclear, marriages tend to form and break up at the will of the individuals who are party to it rather than being arranged, and they lack the patriarchal character of the Dharmashastra family norm.

Patrilineal/Matrilineal

Although patrilineal descent is very widespread, there are several groups organized on the contrary principle of matrilineal descent, mainly in the South in the state of Kerala and part of Tamil Nadu. These include the royal families and land-owning aristocracy (called *Nayar*) of Kerala, who until recently lived in large matrilineal landed estates, of which the mothers and daughters were the shareholders. The structure of the Nayar family was not exactly a mirror image of the patrilineal family, for the men resided in the family of birth with their mothers and sisters, and visited their wives rather than residing with them. A Nayar lady often had several husbands who would visit on different evenings, the visitor leaving his shield outside as a notice to others. Thus under the historic Nayar system, marriage was attenuated, had little alliance character, and was largely a matter of personal preference. Fatherhood was greatly attenuated, too.[21]

The Nayar were Hindus in good standing and cultivated Sanskrit learning. They are a good illustration of the fact that the Dharmashastra does not lay down its norms as an orthodoxy that must be adhered to by all, but recognizes the validity of regional custom and caste custom.

North India/South India

The Dharmashastra itself explicitly recognizes the marriage of cross cousins as a regional custom of the South and valid for people who live there. Dravidian-speaking South Indians, and the people of Sri Lanka, have a preference for the marriage of cross cousins; that is, the children of a brother–sister pair, or the equivalent among more distant cousins.

Cross-cousin marriage allows marriage alliances between families to be perpetuated generation after generation, an effect that is not possible in North India. One of its effects is to lessen the difference between the family of birth and the family of marriage for a girl. Inscriptions show that the royal families of South India took advantage of the ability of cross-cousin marriage to repeat itself, so to say, to cement political alliances with other royal families through marriages repeated for several generations.

Hindu/Muslim

The coming of Islam did not necessarily change the family life of Indians who became Muslim, and there are Muslims in South India who are matrilineal, for example. However, one of the effects of Islam on South Asia has been to interject a marriage pattern from the Middle East into the practice of some South Asian Muslims, as promoted by the Islamic law (Sharia). That is the preference, not for the cross cousin as in South India, but for the patrilineal cousin, the father's brother's child; putting it another way, the children of two brothers are preferred mates for one another. This is quite against Dharmashastra norms, which forbid marrying close kin and especially patrilineal kin, and is different again from the South Indian pattern, in which such kin would call one another brother and sister, and be unmarriageable. Muslim law, moreover, provides for divorce and remarriage, and a rather different inheritance pattern.

This must suffice as a sample of the great variability of family life in India. We turn now to the larger, suprafamilial structures of lineage, clan, and caste.

Society

A family cannot exist in isolation; it must have relations with other families, and these relations have to do with the rules of marriage.

In the first place, a family is grouped with others into lineages or clans, by virtue of the prevailing form of descent, either patrilineal or matrilineal, and these clans are generally exogamous; that is, their members may not marry one another because they are seen to be too closely related. For example, brahmins are divided into seventeen or so exogamous patrilineal clans called *gotras*. They are supposed to be the patrilineal descendants of the sages (*rishis*) who first heard the Veda and thus acquired knowledge of it for humans at the beginning of time. One may not marry a *sagotra,* a person of the same gotra. Furthermore, the Dharmashastra rules provide that one may not marry a *sapinda,* a relative who offers the *pinda* or rice ball to the same person; that is, a relative with whom one shares a common ancestor. The rule is expressed in terms of a number of degrees or generations separating the two from their common ancestor. Usually, if two people share an ancestral connection that is seven or fewer generations old on the father's side, or five on the mother's side, they are considered *sagotra.*

In the second place, the lineages and clans that forbid marriage within are in relations of marriage alliance or potential marriage alliance with other lineages and clans. Such groups of lineages and clans in relations of marriageability make up a caste or *jati.* A caste is usually endogamous; that is, one must marry within that caste and not into another. However, there is often a tendency toward hypergamy (that is, a woman of lower status marrying a man of higher status), and in some settings this carries over into intercaste marriages. The reverse direction is regarded as wrong. The Dharmashastra texts have a pair of words for these two directions of marriage: "with the hair" (*anuloma*) and "against the hair" (*pratiloma*), as if one were stroking a cat in the right and the wrong direction, respectively. But for the most part, the relations between castes are governed not by marriage but by relations of another kind.

We come, then, to the caste system for which India is well known (although the Republic of India has made caste discrimination illegal and instituted affirmative action measures to overcome past caste disabilities). The castes number in the thousands, and they are generally limited in their extent to a single region of India. Castes have names, and very often people's names give clues to their caste. Each caste is associated with a particular occupation; but the traditional occupation is not obligatory, and members can take up other employments. The caste generally has a local assembly of elders that governs the behavior of members, with powers to impose sanctions for violation of the norms of the caste that include, in the extreme case, the power of outcasting. The norms of the caste typically include restrictions on interactions with persons of other castes, especially marriage and sexual relations, which are generally forbidden, and the sharing of food and drink, which is subject to various restrictions. Generally speaking, a hot meal that includes boiled rice may only be shared with persons of the same caste, whereas uncooked rice and wheat, whole uncut fruits and vegetables, and sweets cooked in clarified butter (*ghee*) and sugar can be bought in the market and accepted from the hands of someone of another caste.

Because the castes are, at least nominally, associated with occupational specialties (farmer, potter, blacksmith, etc.) the relations among them are in part relations of economic exchange. Often, however, they are not relations of market exchange in which goods or labor are exchanged for money. In villages, in the past the dominant land owner families had patron–client relations with particular members of the different service castes that supplied them with pottery, woven cloth, iron tools, and the other craft specialties that an agricultural household did not make for itself. Such ties between the patron, called the *jajman* (whence we speak of the *jajmani* system, meaning the system of patron–client relations), and the worker castes were long-term relations, and payments were generally in the form of shares of the harvest rather than a weekly or monthly money wage. The economic relation was thickened by ceremonial obligations and privileges that humanized it at the same time that it reinforced its inherent inequality.

Intercaste relations are also governed by ideas of impurity and pollution, which provide a scale along which castes are ranked in any given location. Like many societies in the world, the Indians have historically regarded the biological excretions of the body as sources of impurity that have to be properly regulated and removed by bathing and the like, and they avoid the impurities of others. Within the family this involves a certain etiquette of eating, the observance of a condition of temporary pollution by family members at times of births and deaths in the family, and the temporary seclusion of its women during menstruation. With respect to outsiders, one must limit contact with the bodily substances of those in the lower castes because they have a lower relative purity that can be transmitted through cooked food, water, and sexual relations. By contrast it is elevating to accept food from superiors, especially from the god; so that in the temple food is offered to the god and then given to the devotees to eat as *prasad* or sacred food.

So far we have been speaking about the jatis; but there is another word, *varna*, which is used for caste, especially in the Dharmashastras. Where the jatis number in the thousands and are localized to particular regions, there are only four varnas. As early as the *Rig Veda* we encounter a creation story, according to which the world was created by sacrifice, which was the most creative principle in the belief of the

Vedic peoples (see Chapter 3). The primordial being, Purusha (man or spirit), often also called Prajapati, lord of creatures, or Brahma, was created through an act of sacrifice in which he was the sacrificer, the sacrificial victim, and the deity to whom the sacrifice was offered; in short, he dismembered himself, offering himself to himself. In doing so, the parts of his dismembered body became the things of the phenomenal universe (animals, plants, minerals, the divisions of time, and so forth), including human society in its four parts: From his mouth came the brahmin, who is associated with the sacred utterance of the Veda; from his arms, the kshatriya or warrior; from his thighs, the vaishya farmer and tradesman; and from his feet the shudra or servant. The story says in effect that the duties of the four varnas are a part of the design of the world from the beginning of time. Among the four varnas, the first three are called "Twice-Born" because their boys take the initiation, seen as a spiritual birth, by conferral of the sacred thread as they enter the stage of the student; and their common duty is to *study* the Veda, to *offer* sacrifices, and to *give* religious gifts. The special duties of the brahmin are, in addition, to *teach* the Veda to others, to *officiate* at the sacrifices of others, and to *receive* the religious gifts that others give as a merit-making action. The special duty of the kshatriya is to protect, and that of the vaishya is to produce the material means of subsistence through agriculture, trade, and stock breeding. The shudra, because he is excluded from Veda study and sacrifice, cannot take the initiation and is therefore "Once-Born," and his duty is to serve the other castes.

What is the relation of the jatis to the four varnas? The Dharmashastra propounds a theory by which the many jatis are generated by intermarriages among the four varnas, in both directions, with and against the hair, creating new castes through the mixture of the varnas, and the further intermixture of the mixed castes. The theory as we find it cannot be literally true, because the jatis have a great variety of names that suggest quite various origins, many of them having come from tribal societies outside the Vedic religion, others being craft specialties, and still others being regional names of groups that have been turned into castes. For the most part the jatis are thought of as belonging to one or another varna, but the members of the brahmin, kshatriya, and vaishya varnas (i.e., Twice-Born, thread-wearing castes) are a minority of the population, and very much the greater part of Indian society consists of shudra castes of greater or lesser purity. So the Dharmashastra treatment of varna gives us a picture of caste that is quite distant from what exists on the ground.

In modern times caste has changed greatly but it has not gone away. After independence and the creation of the Republic of India and Pakistan, scholars thought that caste would wither away under the conditions of modernity, but that has not happened. In some ways, ballot-box democracy has intensified caste identities. In a society in which every caste is a minority party and the elite, Twice-Born castes constitute little more than 10 percent of the population, tickets have to show some mix of castes to appeal to voters of many castes, who often vote in blocs. In this way castes and modern caste associations act like ethnic associations or other interest groups in other countries, and are by no means an obstacle to democracy as such. Caste is also politically salient in the Republic of India with respect to affirmative action policies. These give privileged access to government employment and university admissions to "scheduled" castes and tribes; that is, those on an official schedule or list of groups regarded as disadvantaged. What has changed is that the caste *system* no longer exists as such, and the castes have become more like competing interest groups.

Polity

In the period in which Buddhism and Jainism arose, it is apparent that political power within the tribe was broadly diffused over the warrior class, who owned the means of warfare. The forms of political organization on this base formed a spectrum of types between two poles, called in Sanskrit *rajya* and *sangha*. Rajya means "kingship" (from *raja*, "king"), and sangha denotes a republican form of government, more or less in the sense of the Roman republic in which the governing class was an aristocracy and the affairs of state were decided through the deliberations of the Senate. We call them tribal republics because they are named peoples, not territories. Such republics were not democracies in that political decision making was limited to the elite class, but neither were they monarchies.

To a considerable extent the polar types are associated with the Vedic and anti-Vedic religions, respectively. It is probably no accident that the Buddha and the Mahavira, founders of Buddhism and Jainism, both came from the warrior class of tribal republics to the east of the Vedic heartland. In a sense, the sangha as a political form is perpetuated in the Buddhist order of monks and nuns, which is called precisely the Sangha, and whose decision-making chapters recall the assemblies of the ancient tribal republics. Of course, both religions flourished under royal patronage as well.

On the other hand, the Vedic religion of the brahmins shows a strong preference for kingship, and, as we saw in Chapter 3, it has a number of rituals the object of which is to strengthen and elevate the king, over both his external enemies and his potential rivals from within, including his own kinsmen. Thus the Vedic religion aligned the brahmins with kingship and promoted the growing concentration of power in the hands of the king and at the expense of the old deliberative assemblies.

Another aspect of this polarity of political forms is that they seem to associate with different social forms. In the Buddhist texts tribal republics are said to consist of "rajas and dasas," whereas the four castes or varnas are associated with the monarchies. These words mean king and slave in classical Sanskrit, but of course if a tribal group has a whole class of rajas it must mean something like warriors or chiefs. We must picture such a society as being similar to that of the ancient Spartans, who had a class of free landholder-warriors and another (the helots) of servile laborers tied to the landholders. Thus the tribal republics were complex societies, but had a largely two-tier social system of classes, whereas the Vedic monarchies were socially more complex, and their classes were the four varnas. It seems that kingship and its progress are associated with the development of the caste system.

The tribal republic as a form of government lasted a very long time, and we continue to hear of examples of them well into the period of the Gupta Empire. The book on statecraft called the *Arthashastra* is written from the point of view that kingship is the normal and desirable form of government, but it devotes a whole chapter to sanghas and how the king is to deal with them. From its account we learn that the great strength of the sanghas, which made them formidable enemies on the battlefield, was their strong solidarity in the face of outsiders, growing from the pronounced fellow feeling and sense of personal engagement with political decision making that their political structure fostered. This being so, the way to overcome them, says the *Arthashastra*, is to divide their counsels and break up their solidarity from within by sending secret agents to sow dissension. Over the long run, monarchy was the winner in its competition with the tribal republic, and the latter disappear from sight after the Gupta period. From time to time, though, we find warrior brotherhoods based on kinship groupings and having a more or less egalitarian structure coming to power in a region, only to evolve into kingdoms of the normal type.

One of the notable aspects of the monarchies that developed after the Vedic period leading up to the formation of the Mauryan Empire was their strongly expansionist tendencies. This perhaps explains their comparative success over the sanghas, for the ability of the latter to absorb territory was strictly limited by the tribal character of their form of polity, and they seem to have been able to absorb conquered populations only as slaves or serfs attached to particular warrior households. Kingship, on the other hand, especially in the case of Magadha and its rivals, showed unlimited tendencies of expansion. Earlier texts speak of states in terms of tribal names—the Kashis, the Kosalas, the Shakyas, the Magadhas—but this gives way to territorial names for kingdoms: Kosala and Magadha become named places rather than peoples.

Different cultures of kingship are found in different kinds of texts, and we can associate them with political forms of different periods. We can take the heroic kingship of the great epic, the *Mahabharata,* the calculating kingship of the *Arthashastra,* and the divine kingship of the Dharmashastra as reflections of the pre-Mauryan, Mauryan, and post-Mauryan periods.

The *Mahabharata* is a growth of ages, so that its text refers to no one period of history, and indeed is a picture of a society of the imagination. Yet in the older core of the epic there are ideas about kingship and society that cohere and that express what we could call an ideal of heroic kingship. This ideal seems to be a distant echo of the warrior-ruled societies of the Vedic age. Under the heroic ideal, the king was first and foremost a leader in battle, and was often chosen by election on the eve of battle, having few powers and prerogatives in peacetime. The warrior king was little more than the first among equals.

The growing success of Magadha seems to have been accompanied by the growth of a new statecraft and a new kind of statesman, the cunning brahmin minister who advises the king and whose new science achieves written form in the text of statecraft called *Arthashastra.* Although the text called the *Arthashastra* that survived, written by Kautilya, was probably not composed until the post-Mauryan period, it summarizes a long tradition of writing on statecraft that probably goes back to the Mauryan period and earlier (see Chapter 4). The new statecraft has a coolly rationalistic attitude that comes through clearly in two of its oldest doctrines: the *Four Means* and the *Circle of States.*

The Four Means by which a king should deal with a problem are conciliation, gifts, sowing dissention, and force. Force is last not because it is thought to be bad, but because it causes losses, and underlying the whole series is what we would call nowadays a cost–benefit analysis.

The Circle of States is a doctrine that analyzes the situation of a king who wishes to expand his territory. This king, called the Conqueror, has a neighbor, which is naturally his Enemy, because when expansionism is assumed to be normal, neighbors must have opposing interests. For the same reason, the Enemy's neighbor is the Conqueror's natural Ally, with whom he can coordinate the destruction of the mutual enemy. One must also take account of the Enemy's Ally, and the Ally's Ally. Then to one's rear there is the neighbor who can strike with deadly force when you are advancing against the Enemy; call him the Heel-Catcher. Beyond him is the one to whom you call for help, the Rescuer; the Heel-Catcher's Ally; and the Rescuer's Ally. There might be a king adjoining both the Conqueror and his Enemy, called the Middle King, whose situation is that he can affect the outcome by the interjection of a very little force of his own, tipping the balance of power one way or another. Finally, there might be a large, distant king, called the Neutral, who has the same ability to manipulate events with very little cost to himself.

After the fall of the Mauryan Empire we find a quite different culture of kingship growing up within the Dharmashastra texts, accompanying the formation of empires of a much less directly centralized kind. The new evelopments are paradoxical in that they promote the idea of the divinity of kinship in the strongest terms—the king is a god in human form, and is to be so regarded even if he is an infant—at the same time that the doctrine of righteous conquest (*dharmavijaya*) promotes a form of kingship whose authority is limited and indirect. Military conquest is regarded as righteous not in relation to its causes, but by the manner in which the conquered are treated. The righteous conqueror reinstates the conquered king, accepting his submission and his tribute; the unrighteous conqueror deprives the conquered king of his goods, wives, family, and life—"uproots" him, as they say—and absorbs his territories into the conqueror's own direct rule. The strong bias away from such extension of centralized rule can only have contributed to the formation of tributary empires of the type we find the Sungas and the Guptas creating, empires formed by a congeries of smaller kingdoms linked by paying tribute to a larger, highly pluralistic, loosely integrated empire. In such empires the relations are of king to king rather than king to people, and they have often to be enforced by war. Thus kingship and a certain kind of loosely integrated empire became the pattern for the classical period.

In the seventeenth century, European travelers to India used the idea of Oriental Despotism to describe Indian political forms. This was an ancient idea developed by Aristotle to explain the difference between the Greeks and the Persians: The Greeks had private property and political liberty, but in Persia everyone was a slave of the Great King, who owned all the land; everyone held land of the king, and the king could take it back at any time. In the Renaissance this idea, linking private property with liberty and weak property with despotism, was revived to describe the empire of the Ottoman Turks, and travelers to India applied it as well to Indians, the Mughal Empire above all. Others extended it to the description of ancient India.

Although the culture of kingship in the classical age certainly exalted the character of kingship, to describe it as despotic is quite wrong. For the king presided over a social order that he did not create and for which he was at best the caretaker and arbitrator of disputes, as we said in Chapter 5. In truth the kingdom was made up of many self-regulating corporations governed by bodies of elders, and in whose affairs the king was not to interfere unless invited. We have already seen that the behavior of members of a caste is governed by a caste assembly, but there were many other such groups, including villages and merchant guilds. In the Chola kingdom, for example, we find a village assembly of peasant landholders deciding village affairs, an assembly of peasants at the district level, one of merchants deciding the affairs of trading towns, a *sabha* of brahmins deciding affairs of the temple, and many other corporate groups. Thus it was normal for local government to be carried on by many small deliberative bodies, in relation to which the king existed as an arbitrator of disputes. Although kingship was answerable only to God, it was limited by ideas of dharma and custom. Only in the modern age did the centralized power of the state reach all corners of the social system.

CHAPTER 7

Mentalities

Religion
Law
Science
Classical Arts and Letters

Having taken a long-perspective look at concepts and norms pertaining to family, society, and state, we need now to survey the structures of formal thought that are characteristic of Indian Civilization in the ancient and classical periods and that continue long after. The most salient of these are religion, law, science (principally mathematics, astronomy, astrology, and linguistics) and the arts. They show great abundance and variety, but have an overall coherence of view that we try to identify.

Religion

We have examined the rise of different religious movements and religious change in different periods of the past; now we need to look at the pattern of religion in the long view and see it as a whole.

It is important to keep in mind that the records on which our knowledge of all the ancient civilizations depends were written by a certain category of people who monopolized the ability to read and write; in the ancient world, literacy was a force for civilization, but not one making for equality. This category in India largely consisted of the brahmins, the monks and nuns of the non-Vedic religions of Buddhism and Jainism, and specialist castes of scribes, plus the personnel of the royal court. We see the past, therefore, largely through their eyes and by means of texts shaped by their interests. They give the written record of ancient India an overwhelmingly religious cast. Few of the surviving records could be called secular, so that there are many aspects of Indian Civilization about which we are relatively poorly informed.

About religion we are very well informed, and the abundance of records testifies to its central importance. This abundance and the complexity of Indian religious history make it difficult to find ways to make meaningful generalizations about it. India is the home of religions that have spread widely, especially Buddhism, which took root in Central, East, and Southeast Asia; Hinduism, which greatly influenced Southeast Asia; and Jainism, which reached Sri Lanka. Thus the story of Indian religion is of great importance for the history of Asia generally, and not confined to India itself. It is probable that at the time of the Guptas there were more Buddhists in the world than adherents of any other religion. Religion created a kind of international community through which monks, priests, and scholars traveled to India from places as distant as China, Korea, and Japan. This partial and earlier globalization of the world gave it a common body of stories, ideas, and artistic images, and spread Indian sciences, ideas of law, and canons of art along with its religions.

One way of forming an overall picture of the history of Indian religion without getting lost in the detail is to focus on finding and examining its structure. It seems to have three "moments" that appeared successively in time, which we can call the religions of sacrifice, world renunciation, and devotion. Each of these moments has its characteristic cosmology, aim, and technique for achieving that aim, and each makes an enduring contribution to Indian Civilization that remains to this day.

Sacrifice

The first moment begins in the Vedic period, with the religion of sacrifice that is preserved in the Vedic literature of the brahmins. Some call this religion brahminism. As we have seen, the cosmology consists of a plethora of divinities mostly associated with the sky, called the devas, and the Fathers or ancestors. Key aims of its adherents are to promote the health and welfare of the family in this life, and, after death, to reach heaven or the World of the Fathers. The means for doing so is the sacrifice in its many kinds, and following the central conception of dharma as the eternal religious law that prescribes the duties of one's social station in terms of the four varnas. It is the elaboration of the dharma that constitutes the enduring contribution of the sacrificial religion. The Vedic sacrifice continues to this day in the central features of the Hindu marriage ritual and some other domestic rituals associated with the life cycle and the care and feeding of the ancestors. The Vedic tradition was further developed and elaborated after the Vedic period and throughout the classical period in the Dharmashastra texts we discussed in the last chapter.

Renunciation

The religions of world renunciation, features of which we looked at in Chapter 4, consist above all of the anti-Vedic religions of Buddhism and Jainism. Some aspects of late Vedic religion, however, belong to this group and in some ways anticipate or lay the groundwork for the anti-Vedic religions, especially the more philosophical and nonritualistic texts called Upanishads and Aranyakas. Yoga seems to originate outside of Vedic religion—it certainly has nothing to do with the sacrifice—and to be reconciled to it later, so that it is not regarded as anti-Vedic. And, in later Hinduism, the religion of world renunciation is absorbed and regularized by reckoning renunciation as an optional stage of life after one has acquitted one's duties as a householder. The central philosophical system of the classical age, the *Vedanta*, is propounded by an order of renouncer monks.

It is sometimes said that these religions are "atheistic" in that they do not recognize God as the highest principle, but that is somewhat misleading because they do not deny the existence of the gods (*devas*) and indeed all manner of superhuman personal beings. The gods, however, are demoted and do not have the saving power for humans that they have in the religion of sacrifice; they are now subject, as are all living beings, to the greater cosmological principle of the Wheel of Rebirth (*samsara*) and the Law of Moral Causation (*karma*). By this new principle one is bound by one's deeds to perpetual birth and death in an endless succession of bodies; and the aim, accordingly, is to achieve release of some kind into a permanent state. This state is described in different ways, positively as liberation or merging, and negatively as isolation or extinction (blowing out, as of an oil lamp). The technique of achieving this aim is renunciation of the world (that is, of family life) and meditation. The enduring contribution of the religions of renunciation is the doctrine of Rebirth and Moral Causation, which becomes axiomatic to all subsequent religious and philosophical systems, redefining the human condition in a way that has proved definitive for Indian Civilization. Although the Dharmashastra sacrificial tradition has been supportive of the caste system, the religions of renunciation have had the effect of calling it into question.

Devotion

The word "devotion" translates the Sanskrit *bhakti*, which in historic Hinduism denominates the attitude the worshipper (*bhakta*) directs to the high god, Vishnu or Shiva, whence Hindus can be described as Vaishnava or Shaiva. Other religions develop a devotionalist character as well, especially the large branch of Buddhism called the Mahayana or Greater Vehicle. The cosmology of these religions is roughly speaking monotheistic, in that a universal high God is the highest principle in Hinduism. In Mahayana Buddhism there are corresponding savior figures, which are the Buddhas of various worlds or heavens, and Bodhisattvas (persons on the path to becoming Buddhas) to whom one can pray as savior figures. Again, though, monotheism is not quite the right word (perhaps simply calling it theism would be better) because the existence of many, many gods and divinities of all kinds is not denied; they are simply of lesser importance. What is different from the religions of renunciation is that the high God is superior to the moral machinery of Rebirth and Moral Causation, and is completely beyond the power of any other being or force, so that his acts are completely free and uncoerced; God is the one truly free agent and prime mover in the universe.

The aim of the religions of devotion is not sharply differentiated from that of the religions of renunciation, and includes nonrebirth, but perhaps we could say that as a highly God-centered religion the emphasis is not so much on escape and extinction as on merging with or, better, dwelling in the presence of God. The technique of achieving this beatific state is contained in the name, devotionalism: throwing oneself upon the mercy of God, and receiving his grace as a wholly unearned and uncompelled gift. Concretely, bhakti takes many forms of worship (*puja*) of God involving the image and the temple. The archaeological record of temple building and image making from the post-Mauryan period onward marks the rapid growth to dominance of this form of religion, which becomes the mainstream form in the classical age. The sculpture of images for worship and the architecture of temples to house images were objects of artistic refinement, raised to the highest level during the classical period, as in the Gupta period image of the Buddha from Sarnath (Figure 9), and the exquisite Kandariya Mahadeva temple from the late classical period (Figure 10). The enduring contribution that devotionalism makes to the stock of Indian

FIGURE 9 The Sarnath Buddha, 5th century

FIGURE 10 Kandariya Mahadeva temple, Khajuraho, 11th century

religious ideas is the idea of God's grace as a power that is untouched by the wheel of samsara. He is able to save his devotees even though they do not deserve it and are continually bound to rebirth by their deeds.

Indian religious history proceeds by *addition* rather than by *revolution*. In that way its structure appears to be quite different from that of countries to which the Biblical religions have spread, for the latter largely conceive themselves to be the negation of preexisting religions and require an exclusive loyalty. The history of religion in Christian Europe and the Muslim Middle East, for example, has a sharp discontinuity between its "pagan" and its Christian or Muslim periods. Of course this is only relatively true, and we can point to many features of

Christianity in Europe, such as Christmas trees and the like, that appear to be survivals of pre-Christian practices. But by and large, the effect of conversion of European peoples to Christianity has been quite dramatic, both in the self-representations of Christianity and, to a large extent, in practice. The same could be said of Islam in the Middle East. In India, on the other hand, there is a notable persistence of older religions side by side with new ones, giving the religious picture a kind of geological character, in which strata of different ages are juxtaposed. The reason is, of course, that the Indian religions do not require exclusive loyalty and they tolerate other religious forms as inferior but valid paths to salvation.

Hinduism as a religion is a complex and loosely structured entity without a central institution defining what orthodoxy is and imposing a degree of uniformity; perhaps we should say that it is a family of religions that have grown up together and therefore have a shared history and a mutual resemblance. One authority, when trying to define orthodoxy, comes up with a negative criterion: nonobstruction of the Veda. It serves to exclude Buddhism and Jainism, which deny the authority of the Veda, but to include Yoga and other movements that, although not derived from Vedic religion, nevertheless do not deny its authority. This definition of dharma defines Hinduism.

Devotional Hinduism is very much a popular religion and it includes popular religious practices of all levels of society. This is not true of the religion of sacrifice, which was a "national" religion for the Aryans and excluded the shudra and the non-Aryan, or of the religions of renunciation, at least in their earliest stages, which although open to all are dominated by the order of monks or renouncers. In the theory of the Vedic sacrifice the spiritual capacity (*adhikara*) to offer sacrifice is possessed only by twice-born male householders, but in several key Hindu texts the capacity to participate in the devotional religion explicitly includes women and low-caste people. It is not an accident that poetry written by women appears in the texts of Hinduism but not in the Vedic literature, and religious poets of low caste are also found among the saints of bhakti Hinduism.

It is worth examining the matter of gender in greater detail, for it has much to tell us. Susie Tharu and K. Lalita had the project of finding where in all of Indian writings from ancient times the voices of women were to be found, not passages that speak about women, but writings from women.[22] For the ancient period they found a significant pattern.

Poems by women were found mainly in three bodies of ancient writings: the courtly poetry of ancient Tamil (the Sangam literature discussed in Chapter 5); a Buddhist collection of hymns by nuns, the *Theri-gatha;* and the poems of bhakti saints who were women. Just as significant is where the voices of women were scarce or absent: the Vedic tradition and its continuation in the Dharmashastra, and Sanskrit courtly poetry. In the Vedic tradition, as we have seen, women have a positive valuation because of the high value of the married couple, but are not agents in their own right, whereas greater agency for women is found among Tamil courtly poets, Buddhist nuns, and bhakti poet-saints. In addition, we note that all three of these spheres had notable contributions by low-caste people as well; in other words, they had a more popular and socially inclusive character than the Vedic tradition. Insofar as the Vedic tradition blends with the newer, devotional forms of religion in the post-Mauryan period, it represents a major widening of the social base for that tradition.

If devotionalism has this deeply popular character we need to ask why it did not emerge before the post-Mauryan period. The answer might lie in the relation of popular religion to the class that monopolized the writing of the texts that survive, namely the brahmins, monks and nuns, and scribes. It seems that the post-Mauryan period sees the creation of a "Hindu synthesis" by this class that reconciles popular religion to the Vedic tradition and gives the new mixture a literature. The ways in which the synthesis was fashioned are apparent in the doctrine of the avatars of Vishnu, and the family members of Shiva, which synthesize what were formerly independent and localized objects of worship.

Vishnu is a god known to the Veda, but he is a minor figure in it, and it is only in the post-Mauryan period that Vishnu develops into a major figure, often depicted reclining on a many-headed cobra with the world creator Brahma issuing from his navel, or as a four-armed standing figure with conch, discus, mace, and lotus, associated with the eagle Garuda. Vishnu has ten avatars or "descents" in which he takes on earthly form to defeat evil and save the good in different world ages: the fish (*matsya*), who saved Manu; the seven sages and the Vedas from the universal flood; the tortoise (*kurma*), who formed the pivot for the churn by which the gods and demons churned the ocean for the treasures that had been carried away by the flood; the boar (*varaha*) who saved Goddess Earth from the flood; the man-lion (*narasimha*) who killed the demon king Hiranyakashipu Prahlada; the dwarf (*vamana*), the Vedic Vishnu;

Parashurama, or Rama of the Axe, who killed the kshatriya oppressors of brahmins, clearing the earth of kshatriyas twenty-one times; Rama, king of Ayodhya, who with the help of the monkey Hanuman rescued his wife Sita from the demon king of Lanka, Ravana; Krishna, charioteer of Arjuna in the great epic, flute-playing lover of the cowgirls in the Middle Ages; the Buddha, whose form Vishnu takes, some texts say, to lead the wicked astray; and Kalkin, the avatar of the future—mounted on a white horse, with flaming sword, he will judge the wicked, reward the good, and restore the golden age. In the Middle Ages, in North India especially, Rama and Krishna are the two most important of the avatars, and Vaishnavas are especially devoted to one or the other.

The stories of these avatars seem to have come from different local sources and were synthesized by being attached to Vishnu through the idea of avatars. Something similar seems to happen to Shiva, although here it is not a question of avatars but of the different aspects or forms of him and his family members. Here again, Shiva seems to originate as a minor divinity of the Veda and to develop greatly in the devotionalist period. Thus we find Shiva Lord of Yoga (Yogeshvara), a renouncer seated cross-legged on a tiger skin, with crescent in his matted locks, a necklace of snakes or skulls, and a trident; Shiva as the handsome husband of the beautiful Parvati, daughter of Himalaya; Shiva Lord of Dance (Nataraja) on the back of a demon, with four arms and hair flying in a fiery halo; and the noniconic form of Shiva as the linga. Shiva's wife has various aspects, including the beautiful bride (Parvati), and ferocious slayer of the buffalo demon (Durga). The son Skanda is a handsome warrior who rides the peacock, identified in South India with the Dravidian god Murugan. The other son, Ganesha, an elephant-headed god who rides the mouse, is the remover of obstacles, and one prays to him when beginning a journey, writing a book, or facing an exam. The stories about Vishnu and his avatars, and the family of Shiva in its many aspects, are fashioned into vast compendia of mythology called Puranas in the classical period, and they are the subject matter of a vast literature of poet-saints in the medieval period, of classical painting and sculpture, music, and dance.

Thus the religious cults out of which the Hindu synthesis was made do not seem to have been invented in the post-Mauryan period but to have been first brought into literary form at that time, and presumably they are much older in origin. This raises the question of the religion of the Indus Civilization, the material remains of which, many scholars have observed, seem to show a resemblance to those of historic Hinduism, especially aspects of the worship of Shiva and Devi. If there are real continuities from that ancient civilization to the Hinduism of the post-Mauryan period it is likely that the elements out of which Hinduism is synthesized have roots running deep into the South Asian Neolithic. The structure of Indian religious history takes on a different aspect when we begin before the Vedic period, with the religion of the Indus Civilization.

The Spectrum of Religions

The religious spectrum of late classical times was extremely broad and varied, so that it becomes impossible to reduce Indian, or even Hindu, thought to a series of generally agreed doctrines. This variety is the outcome of the additive character of religious history in India and the absence of a unitary religious institution defining orthodoxy and punishing deviation. It is generally held in the Indian religions that different individuals have differing spiritual capacities, each requiring specific forms of religious endeavor. Each sect claims its path is better than the others, but concedes that those of other sects are helpful in raising the spiritual level of persons not yet capable of higher things.

This tolerant attitude toward differing religious systems did not prevent sectarian disputes from becoming very bitter at times, but it did permit very ancient religious ideas to survive the appearance of novel ideas that contradicted them, so that a cross-section of the religions of the late classical period is like a geological core in which one can distinguish several layers deposited at different ages. Royal power found it expedient not to try to suppress any sect existing in the kingdom, but on the contrary to support all of them to some degree, so that no ancient Indian kingdom had a single state religion, and all sects were to some degree "established" by royal patronage, whatever the monarch's personal sectarian preferences. A brief survey of religion in the classical period will give a sense of the variety.

The Vedic tradition was perpetuated in late classical India by Dharmashastra, the science of the law, which, as we have seen, elucidated the religious obligations of those upper orders of society (the "twice-born," the brahmins, kshatriyas, and vaishyas who had been spiritually reborn through the initiation rite) that were eternal, unchanging, and not to be tampered with. To be sure, the Dharmashastra was obliged to accommodate itself to changes in religious viewpoint that had overtaken Indian society, as we have already noted. The Dharmashastra had long ago made its peace with the renouncer's ideals of vegetarianism and of the monkish life that had challenged the Vedic obligation of the householder to marry, procreate, and present offerings to the gods and Fathers. This accommodation is the doctrine of the four stages (*ashramas*) of life. After initiation, the Twice-Born youth enters the first stage, that of a student of the Veda or *brahmacharin* at the feet of a preceptor or *guru*. Then he marries and enters the second stage, that of the householder or *grihastha;* upon retirement he may live as a forest hermit (*vanaprastha*), living on the fruits he collects, and meditating at the base of a tree. Finally he may enter the fourth stage, that of the wandering ascetic or *sannyasin*, begging his food and never remaining two nights in one place. Only the first two stages are obligatory for all the Twice-Born, and in the last two we see forms of ascetic renunciation that may be undertaken only after the obligations of the householder stage have been discharged.

Besides the law books in which such obligations are laid out, a science of exegesis of the Vedic Samhitas and Brahmanas, called *Mimamsa*, sought to specify the ritual injunctions in the scriptures by which the twice-born should abide. Thus Vedic religion was far from dead in late classical India; and we continue to hear of kings who performed the horse sacrifice and other higher rituals, although the Hindu rituals of temple and idol were much more popular.

The ascetic tradition of the religions of renunciation is best represented in this period by the great philosopher Shankara, a South Indian brahmin of the eighth century. The philosophical tradition in which Shankara participated is called Vedanta, "End of the Veda," referring to the speculative texts of the Upanishads with which the Vedic literature closes. His teachings are called Advaita or nondualism. Shankara reasserts the unique, nondual being of the absolute (*Brahman*), its identity with the self (*atman*), and the illusion or trickery (*maya*) of the phenomenal world by which the ordinary person mistakenly thinks that the differences between things are real. True knowledge of the oneness of the universe dispels this illusion and brings escape from transmigration. Vedanta complements the Dharmashastra and Mimamsa. Like them its roots are in the Vedic literature, but whereas Dharmashastra and Mimamsa define the Vedic duties of the married householder, Shankara's Advaita Vendanta speaks to the renouncer who is dead to society and has passed beyond those Vedic duties to the higher knowledge. Shankara's philosophy owes much to Buddhism, although he asserted the reality of the inmost self while the Buddhists denied the existence of an enduring soul. In any case Shankara did much to accommodate the renouncer's religion within the brahmin tradition, and contributed in that way to the decline of Buddhist dialectic in India.

Hindu devotionalism (bhakti) was also prominent in South India during this period, in the Pallava and Chola kingdoms. Vaishnava and Shaiva saints, called Alvar and Nayanar, propagated an intensely emotional religion through songs of the love of God sung in Tamil. Many of these saints were nonbrahmin, several were women, and several were of low caste. This movement, therefore, had a broad mass appeal that the exclusive brahminical teachings of dharma or renunciation could not attain, and did not want to attain. After the age of the poet-saints (especially the seventh through ninth centuries), however, the South Indian bhakti movement aligned itself more closely to brahmin orthodoxy by the composition of a Sanskrit text joining its doctrines to the mythology of the epics (the *Bhagavata Purana*), and through the dualistic (Dvaita) Vendanta theology of the brahmin scholar Ramanuja (eleventh and twelfth centuries) who attempted to show that devotionalism was based on the Vedic scriptures. The search for respectability in the eyes of conservative brahmins served to reassert the spiritual basis of the distinctions of caste within the community of the faithful, distinctions that the bhakti poet-saints had tended to regard as merely social and without transcendent significance. But it also served to give a purely regional movement an all-India dimension through its traveling brahmin theologians, and the great age of bhakti poet-saints in North India that begins under Turkish rule is inspired by Southern teachers.

Although the Hindu directs his devotion to Shiva or Vishnu, the worship of the Great Goddess (Devi) becomes increasingly prominent in the late classical age. Perhaps we need to call the Tantracism or Shaktiism that centers on the Goddess a fourth "moment" of Indian religious history. It comes to prominence in the classical and late classical period, after the emergence of devotionalism. It is an esoteric form of Hinduism and Buddhism practiced by initiates of high status. Devi is typically conceived of as Shiva's wife in her various aspects (Parvati, Durga, Kali). Philosophically the Goddess is the *Shakti* or power of Shiva, without which he is a mere lifeless body, so that the sexual union of Shiva and his Shakti becomes the symbol of life and completeness. Something of the demonic clings to this Goddess, and to her worship, which is often conducted in inauspicious places such as cremation grounds or crossroads, in the dead of night and with offerings of wine, animal victims, and even human blood. The worship of the Great Goddess, or Shaktiism, may be continuous with the Indus Valley mother goddess cult. At any event the propitiation of a goddess of smallpox and other calamities is nearly universal in Indian villages, and is doubtless very ancient. Although Devi is typically the spouse of Shiva, any deity's effective force (his Shakti, grammatically and mythologically feminine) can be personified as his spouse. Most branches of Indian religion, Buddhism included, have been influenced by Shaktiism to some degree.

Tantracism denotes those sects, including adherents of the Great Goddess, that seek salvation through the deliberate, ritual contravention of the morality that governs society at large. An example is the rite of the five Ms (*panchamakara*), in which the adepts partake of wine (*madya*), fish (*matsya*), meat (*mamsa*), parched grain (*mudra*), and sexual intercourse (*maithuna*). Such rites were conducted in secret and only by the most advanced members of such sects. Their purpose was not to change the prevailing morality into a more permissive one, but rather to raise the worshipper above the conventional feelings of praise, blame, and pride of family as a means of liberation from the wheel of rebirth by deliberately breaking prevailing taboos, not in daily life but in ritual. They drew their whole force from the fact that the masses of men did not approve wine-bibbing, meat-eating, and sexual intercourse outside of wedlock. Such sects obviously were very small in number and drew heavy censure from the majority. Nevertheless we hear of practices such as these as early as the first century CE, and they exert an increasing fascination in the late classical period. The conviction grows that the debasement of human nature in the Kali age makes the stringent requirements of Vedic sacrifice of renunciation beyond present human capacities, and thus the brahmins concede Tantracism a place as a religion suited to the frailties of man. Tantracists for their part were persuaded that Vedic sacrifice, meditation, and devotionalism were valid religious disciplines, although inferior and suited to novices or those with lower religious capacities. In the long run, however, Tantracism too achieved respectability, and as early as Harsha's time we read of pious princes and princesses engaged in rites that are distinctly Tantric, but not antimoral. The more respectable and more numerous Tantric sects called right-handed sects substituted harmless symbols for the forbidden things, or simply ignored the more offensive rites such as that of the five Ms that the hard-core sects of the left hand continued to practice.

Law

We have spoken of dharma (the religious law), and the body of texts called Dharmashastra, several times. Here we need to consider the various kinds of law in ancient India and the place of dharma among them. The first thing to be said is that we do not find the kind of notion that has become universal in the modern world, the idea of popular sovereignty; that is, the idea that government derives its authority from the people, and that laws are the people's will, as formulated by their representatives in the legislature and revised from time to time. The closest thing to a legislature that creates and extinguishes laws at will as the people's representatives in ancient India are the various kinds of assemblies of local corporate groups and of the tribal republics, which have a democratic cast to them.

Law is pluralistic in Indian Civilization, and the three main forms that it takes are dharma, custom, and royal edict. Dharma refers to the idea of a moral law that is eternal, unchanging, and universal, being limited in neither time nor space. Unlike the religions of the Bible, the moral law is not thought of as the will of a personal deity, but as uncreated and changeless. It is a part of the immutable order of the universe.

The word dharma is also used to denote custom, but in this sense it is capable of being used in the plural. As opposed to the capital-D Dharma, so to speak, which is one and the same everywhere and for all time, the dharmas of lineages (*kulas*), castes (*jatis*), and regions (*deshas*) are many rather than universal, although like dharma the customary laws of these bodies can be thought of as changeless over time. Customary law is binding, but its scope is strictly limited to the people of the lineage, caste, or region to which it pertains.

Royal edict refers to the laws the king enacts, as the expression of his will and for the good of the kingdom. Such laws, again, are authoritative and can overrule dharma or custom. Within the kingdom the scope of royal edicts is unlimited, but they do not accumulate into a permanent body of law. Thus, whereas the dharma is eternal and universal, custom differs in being nonuniversal and edict in being noneternal. Let us look at each of them more closely.

Dharma

How do we know what the dharma is? The first and best source of knowledge is the Veda, or *shruti,* "revelation"—literally "that which is heard" by the ancient *rishis* or sages. In the classical period the Veda is conceived as uncreated and changeless, and it is because dharma is from the Veda that it has these qualities, too. The Veda that is known to humans is but a fragment of the eternal Veda, which the rishis "heard" in a kind of aural revelation, and bits of that revelation have become lost in later ages so that our knowledge of it is gradually shrinking.

Now, in fact, the Veda contains hymns to the gods, stories about the gods, and directions for the performance of rituals, but very little of it consists of moral laws. To derive a body of dharma texts from the Veda there developed a science of interpretation for sifting out the comparatively few genuine injunctions from its textual mass. Only those passages are injunctions that are stated generally (not statements about particular events and persons) and are in the form of "should" statements, as in the model injunction, "Desiring heaven, one should sacrifice." Even such statements are not injunctions of dharma if there is a "seen," that is, a visible or evident, worldly benefit that is causally connected with the act. Only if a Vedic text lacks a "seen" benefit can we presume the existence of an "unseen," nonevident causal connection, through the moral law of karma, with the act prescribed. A standard example contrasts a pair of texts about marriage. A text that says, "A man should marry a woman who is not diseased or ill-tempered" simply states the obvious, and unhappiness will be the result of failing to follow such worldly advice. It cannot qualify as an injunction of dharma, and no bad karma comes of disobeying it. However, if we take a text that says, "A man should marry a woman who is a non-sapinda (not a close relative) and a non-sagotra (not a member of the same patrilineal clan)," because no seen penalty comes about through disregarding the rule, the existence of an unseen connection to a penalty, via the law of karma, must be assumed, and the rule qualifies as an injunction of dharma. Violating it will bring an adverse effect through the law of Moral Causation, one that will be "unseen" in the sense that there is a delay of time between the cause (disobeying the rule) and the effect (for example, rebirth in a lower station).

Because knowledge of the Veda is fragmentary, we might have to resort to other sources where the Veda is silent: smriti, the custom of the good and conscience. Smriti, literally "that which is remembered," covers the post-Vedic texts of the Dharmashastra, which are far more extensive and cohesive dharma texts than the Veda itself. Smriti texts include the brief prose manuals of the Dharmasutras attaching to the Vedic schools, or the later, larger, and versified law books of Manu, Yajnavalkya, and others. Further composition of dharma texts in the classical period took the form of writing commentaries on the basic texts, and digests or compendia of dharma texts from all sources arranged by topic. This literature in its entirety is the Dharmashastra.

The content of the dharma as we find it in these texts, briefly, can be sorted out into a few heads. First and most important there is the dharma of the varnas (castes) and ashramas (stages of life); because Sanskrit can form compounds without limit this becomes the word *varnashramadharma.* This, of course, is the heartland of the brahminical conception of moral duty of the different stations of life, including family life and the relations of the castes to one another, and a very large portion of it is *rajadharma,* the duties of the king. The duties that come under this head are obviously highly particularized according to one's roles in society. As a moral law its sanction is the invisible mechanism of karma, and although the king is supposed to uphold it, much of it is not positive law of the state as such.

A second head of dharma is "dispute," which concerns the contractual aspect of human relations; that is, the agreements people enter into as free agents and about which disputes may arise. Dispute is said to have eighteen "feet," namely, nonpayment of debt, deposit and pledge, sale without ownership, partnerships, taking back gifts, nonpayment of wages, nonperformance of agreements, reneging on sale and purchase, disputes between the owner of cattle and his herders, boundary disputes, assault, slander, theft, robbery and violence, adultery, duties of husband and wife, partition of inheritance, and gambling and betting. A great many of these topics have to do with contracts of various kinds, but they are mixed in with such things as theft and assault that are more like crimes. These matters do indeed come before the courts of the king, but only on the initiative of the aggrieved party, rather than by a prosecutor acting on behalf of the group. Thus these matters are more like lawsuits in which disputes between private parties are arbitrated by the court than they are like criminal cases in which the state brings charges against wrongdoers. Finally, a smallish part of the Dharmashastra concerns what would look to us like a true criminal law that the state prosecutes, called "removal of thorns," mostly having to do with direct dangers to the kingdom.

Because capital-D Dharma presents itself as unchanging and timeless, its self-representations have contributed to unflattering European depictions of Indian society as somehow changeless, as if it stood outside history. However, the rules of interpretation allow a good deal of adjustment of the content of dharma to changing social conditions. One striking means of doing so is the doctrine of *kalivarjya*, "that which is prohibited in the Kali age." By this doctrine, practices that were prescribed in the Veda but have fallen out of favor may be prohibited as kalivarjya, in view of the decline of human virtue in the Four Ages, as described in Chapter 4. The rule against killing and eating cattle in Hinduism is a leading example of this principle. Vedic etiquette required slaughtering and roasting an ox for a guest, and we know from the historians of Alexander that the custom was observed at Taxila as late as the fourth century BCE, as also seen in Chapter 4. The Vedic people prized cattle very highly, which is why this is the prescribed manner of honoring a guest. But when in the wake of Jainism and Buddhism and its ideal of nonviolence (*ahimsa*) a vegetarian diet became the upper caste norm, cattle being highly prized and divinized became especially inviolable, and the rules of interpretation adjusted the changeless dharma to the change in values.

Custom

Lineages, castes, and regions have ancient customs that have the force of law and are to be upheld by the king's courts in cases of dispute brought before them. The king is not to interfere with custom by way of reforming society into conformity with dharma. Custom is not recorded in a book; the Dharmashastra takes note of its existence and respects its authority but takes no interest in making a record of its content, because of its contingent, localized nature. It resides in the consensus and the memories of the groups of which it is the custom, and it acquires force through the various assemblies that govern behavior at the local level. Leading examples would be the matrilineal descent of the Nayars of Kerala, and the practice by all castes in South India of cross-cousin marriage.

Edict

As we saw in Chapters 5 and 6, the king's ability to legislate at will is not formally under any constitutional restraint, although of course the king is answerable to the law of Moral Causation (karma) in the making of laws and the giving of judgments, and may be punished by its means in another life. Examples of royal edicts that have survived by being inscribed on rocks and stone pillars are the edicts of Ashoka, in which the king both engages in moral exhortation but also lays down laws that specify, for example, what animals may not be slaughtered and sold as food on what days of the month. By and large, however, we do not have a large record of royal edicts from ancient times, and most of the largish body of inscriptions made on imperishable materials like stone and copper are gifts of land to religious institutions, not edicts as such. Here again the Dharmashastra made no attempt to form a record of this kind of law, because of its impermanence, and we have but a sketchy idea of what it amounted to in practice.

The king's relation to the law was paradoxical. He was completely free to make law, and subjects were to obey king-made law without demur. Furthermore the royal edict took precedence over custom and dharma, because the survival of the state depended on it, without which custom and dharma would be meaningless, and anarchy would prevail. That anarchic, kingless state is described by the "analogy of the fishes" (*matsyanyaya*); that is, big fish eats little fish, and mere power reigns instead of dharma. Finally, the king also has the executive and the judicial authority, for he is the font of justice, and disputes that cannot be resolved locally go to him or the judges he has appointed for resolution or arbitration. Thus the king has unlimited power to act as expediency requires to secure the continued survival of the kingdom. Yet his power vanishes with him and leaves little or no trace to affect subsequent generations. Moreover, his seemingly limitless authority is in fact severely limited by customary law and the high prestige of the dharma, both of which he should uphold and neither of which is his creation. Modern states with their powers and programs of social reform are more powerful by far.

Thus the nature of law in Indian Civilization is pluralistic and various, allowing for a great deal of localized control and loosely held together by the arbitrating and judicial powers of the king's courts.

Science

At the end of the Vedic period manuals were written in the form of very brief prose rules suitable for memorization, called *sutras*. These highly compact formal treatments of different subjects that are of importance to the Vedic ritual are the first "sciences," using the word broadly to indicate systematized bodies of knowledge. The Vedic sciences (called Vedangas, "limbs" of the Veda) are six in number:

1. Ritual (*kalpa*)
2. Phonetics (*shiksha*)
3. Meter (*chandas*)
4. Etymology (*nirukta*)
5. Grammar (*vyakarana*)
6. Astronomy (*jyotisha*)

One feature of Vedic sacrifice is the great importance of controlling the language of the Vedic mantra, because the efficacy of the ritual depended on the exactness with which the mantra was uttered. Accordingly, no less than four of the Vedic sciences are concerned with linguistic issues (phonetics, meter, etymology, and grammar), and linguistic analysis was the subject in which ancient Indian Civilization was more advanced than any other. The other area of special distinction in science lies in the related sciences of astronomy, astrology, and mathematics, which we treat as a single complex, represented among the Vedic sciences by astronomy, whose ritual function is to fix the proper times for sacrifices. A third "science" that develops greatly in classical India is that of the law, the Dharmashastra of which we have already spoken. It is represented among the Vedangas by the Kalpasutra, or ritual science, which has four branches, each with sutra texts: domestic (*grihya*) ritual, elaborate (*shrauta*) ritual, geometry (*shulva*, having to do with the layout of the brick fire altars), and *dharma*. The *dharmasutras* are the first layer of the Dharmashastra body of literature on the law. A fourth science of considerable importance is not represented in the Vedangas: medicine, called Ayurveda or the Veda of life, which has roots in some of the curative mantras in the fourth Veda (Atharvaveda) and develops a literature of its own.

Thus all of the sciences of ancient India develop out of the preoccupations of the Vedic ritual. As the actual practice of the Vedic ritual fades in importance, the sciences develop on their own and without reference to the old schools of Vedic learning, but they remain guided by the general pattern of formalized religious learning as controlled by the literate classes of brahmins and monks.

In the classical period, Hindus recognize six world theories or philosophical systems (called *darshanas*) as orthodox, and the Buddhists and Jains have their own theories of the world that are comparable. The six darshanas are:

1. *Nyaya* (logic)
2. *Vaisheshika* (atomism)
3. *Sankhya* (evolutionism)
4. *Yoga* (meditation)
5. *Mimamsa* (theory of the ritual and of dharma)
6. *Vedanta* (monism)

All of them are directed toward the salvation of the soul, so that all formal philosophy has a strongly practical purpose and religious bent to it in the classical period. In other words, the six darshanas are not systems of knowledge for its own sake, and neither are they directed toward technology and human interventions in nature. Nevertheless the content of some of the systems would seem to be congenial to the formation of scientific knowledge of modern kind.

The Vaisheshika teaches that the ultimate constituents of nature are atoms. Each of the four elements—earth, air, fire, and water—has its own characteristics (*visheshas*), and when two or three atoms combine into molecules, the characteristics of the result combine those of its constituents. For example, wax melts (water) and burns (fire), so that it is compounded of the two elements. There are four nonatomic substances, which are without characteristics: time, space, soul, and mind. The atoms are eternal, but when the world dissolves they become separated from one another, and they are reunited to form compounds when the Creator makes the world anew. The atoms are points without magnitude, having no extension in space. Some schools of Buddhism also have an atomic theory in which the atoms are points without magnitude in time as well, and exist only for an instant; the world process is a flow of instants in which succeeding constellations of atoms come into and pass out of existence instantaneously. Consistent with the Buddhist doctrine of the impermanent (*anitya*) character of the world, this theory does not include any enduring substance. The Sankhya contains a theory of how the parts of the world evolve out of the amorphous initial state, a theory of cosmic evolution.

Let us look at the classical sciences in greater detail (leaving aside law, of which we have spoken earlier in the chapter).

Astronomy/Astrology/Mathematics

The Vedic astronomy was based on a series of twenty-seven or twenty-eight constellations (called *nakshatras*) through which the moon passes in its orbit of twenty-seven solar days and seven and three-quarters hours. This system, composed early in the first millennium BCE, shows a striking resemblance to Mesopotamian constellations. It is different from and earlier than the system of twelve signs of the zodiac through which the sun appears to travel in the course of the year, first conceived of by the ancient Babylonians and adopted by the Indians. Indian intellectuals evidently participated in an international exchange of ideas about astrology, astronomy, and mathematics in very ancient times, centering on Mesopotamia, as did the Greeks, so that the signs of the zodiac, the weekdays named after the visible planes and the sun and moon, and the astrological art connected with them including the casting of horoscopes, became the common intellectual property of a large region of Eurasia including India.[23] Gupta age astronomy is preserved in treatises called *siddhantas,* two of which have names indicating connection with the Mediterranean: the *Romaka* and the *Paulisha* Siddhantas (the latter named after Paul of Alexandria). Some Greek technical terms were absorbed into Sanskrit, including words for hour (*hora*), center (*kendra*), and angle (*kona*).

Indians made good use of the influx of astronomical and astrological ideas, and the result was largely felt in mathematics. The greatest Indian astronomer of the ancient period was Aryabhata (fl. 499 CE), who assumed a spherical earth and an earth-centered movement of the planets and the sun. In his work we find the following achievements: use of nine symbols and zero, that is, a decimal place-notation for numbers that rendered calculation much easier; ways of calculating square and cube roots of numbers; algebra—such things as areas of figures and volumes of solids, and solving for unknowns; the sine—first of the trigonometrical functions (further developed by Islamic scholars); and the discovery of pi. Indian mathematics returned to the Middle East through Muslims, who transmitted it to Europe. This gave a Muslim name to algebra, which Muslims themselves called "the Indian reckoning," and gave us as well what we still call the Arabic numerals. Europeans continued to use the clumsy Roman numerals for calculations as late as the fourteenth century, when they adopted the Arabic, or, really, Indian numerals.

Linguistics

The linguistic analysis of the Indians has purely indigenous origins as far as we know and, unlike astronomy, it has no evident inputs of influence from other of the ancient civilizations. The greatest sage of grammatical science is Panini, who lived in the seventh century BCE in a region of the upper Indus Valley in what is now Pakistan. Panini's work clearly presupposes many generations of prior analytical work, and indeed language analysis was one of the earliest preoccupations of the Vedic teachers. Two features of Panini's grammar are the very acute phonetic analysis of the language, and the analysis of words into roots plus rules of derivation, which Panini specifies. The work is written in the cryptic sutra form, giving it the elegant precision of a computer program.

Although the grammatical science of ancient India is highly technical and forbidding to anyone but a specialist, one of its effects can be appreciated in the alphabetical order of the scripts in which Sanskrit and other languages of India are written, which follow a rational order that shows obvious prior analysis of phonology. The result is a script called Brahmi, which we first find in the inscriptions of Ashoka, or possibly a bit earlier. Brahmi is the ancestor of most of the modern Indian scripts including the Devanagari script in which Sanskrit and Hindi are written. In this script there is a one-to-one correspondence between the signs and the sounds of Sanskrit language (Figure 11).[24]

Indian writing systems spread with Buddhism and Hinduism to Tibet and Central Asia, to Korea and Japan, and to various countries of Southeast Asia, notably Burma and Thailand—all of which have scripts based on Indian ones. Indian grammars formed the models for grammars of indigenous languages in countries to which Buddhism and Hinduism spread, and Indian phonology was a resource for Chinese philologists to recover the sounds of their ancient classics through the construction of rhyming dictionaries.

In the eighteenth and nineteenth centuries European scholars became familiar with Indian grammatical science, at the same time that the recognition that Sanskrit is similar to Greek and Latin led to the concept of historical linguistics. The formation of modern linguistics owes a great deal to that conjuncture.

Medicine

The Indian system of Ayurveda has some similarities to the humoral system of the Greeks, with its three humors or fluids—wind, bile, and

VOWELS

a	ā	i	ī
u	ū	ṛ	ḷ
e	ai	o	au

CONSONANTS

ka	kha	ga	gha	ṅa
ca	cha	ja	jha	ña
ṭa	ṭha	ḍa	ḍha	ṇa
ta	tha	da	dha	na
pa	pha	ba	bha	ma
ya	ra	la	va	
śa	ṣa	sa	ha	

CONSONANT + VOWEL SIGN

ka	kā	ki	kī	ku
kū	ke	kai	ko	kau

FIGURE 11 The Brahmi script

phlegm—and the Indian system adding a fourth, blood. The various imbalances of the humors are the cause of disease. Indian medicine was much sought after in the Asian world as Greek was in the Mediterranean. It makes much use of diet in its cures. There is no dissection of corpses for the study of anatomy, and its physiology is philosophical rather than observational, being linked to theories of meditation and self-realization.

When we try to summarize the overall character of scientific endeavor in Indian Civilization (again, taking "scientific" broadly to mean formalized, systematic knowledge), we see that what is distinctive about it is not that it is "otherworldly" or "nonempirical," but that it is oriented toward improving life in the world through a technology of ritual rather than a technology of machines. Thus the ideas that are assimilated from Mesopotamia and the Mediterranean are concerned mostly with horoscopes and the construction of almanacs that fix the times of calendrical rituals and assist in the determination of auspicious and inauspicious times. Linkages with machinery in the form of instrumentation are limited. The overall religious character of scientific knowledge has to do with the fact that literacy is largely controlled by religious specialists. The Indian contribution to international science was substantial, especially in mathematics and language analysis, in ways that are very much in use today.

Religious sponsorship directly fostered the development of science, but it also channeled it in certain ways. A good illustration of this comes from the work of the Hellenistic scholar Ptolemy, who wrote on astronomy, astrology, and geography, drawing on several thousand years of astronomical observations and astrological ideas in Mesopotamia. The construction of maps by means of the Ptolemaic grid of longitude and latitude were well known in India and the Islamic world, and European map-makers revived the Ptolemaic system of geography in Europe (with Muslim help) during the Renaissance, along with his astrology and astronomy. Indians used his grid to fix hundreds of locations for astrological purposes and for the construction of almanacs, that is, for the control of time as an aspect of ritual technology. However, there are very few maps from ancient India, and none of them are constructed within this grid. Although such maps would have been useful for the state and its land-revenue apparatus, if they existed they did not last and leave a cumulative deposit on Indian practice. What maps we do have are cosmological in character, or maps of pilgrim routes, roughly comparable to the maps of medieval Europe and having a markedly religious aspect.

Classical Arts and Letters

Post-Vedic Sanskrit literature joins the poetry of the royal court to the mythology and religious inspiration of Hinduism and other forms of devotional religion. The Puranas (Antiquities), large compendia of Hindu myth and doctrine, take their origin in heroic tales of ancient kings. The *Mahabharata,* the world's longest epic poem at about one hundred thousand verses, also begins from bardic tales, of the old Kuru kingdom of Vedic times and the fratricidal war of its princes, into which brahmin compilers have assimilated large chunks of didactic religious material. Both the *Mahabharata* and the major Puranas had completed their development by the first century of Gupta rule. Rather later is the shorter epic, the *Ramayana,* which in twenty thousand verses tells the story of King Rama of Ayodhya, the very model of a virtuous prince, and considered an avatar of Vishnu.

The more characteristic works of classical Sanskrit literature are humanistic, in the sense that although its themes, often drawn from the Puranas and epics, are religious, it aims at aesthetic effects rather than religious instruction. This literature is called *kavya,* which we might define as classical court poetry. Kavya typically takes familiar legends for its themes. The beauty toward which it strives is in the telling rather than novelty of plot, because the story is already well known. Kavya therefore aims at an elaborate, ornamental language, in which simile, metaphor, punning, alliteration, intricate meters, allusion, and other tricks of sound and sense at the poet's disposal combine to convey the flavor (*rasa*) of the emotions experienced by the characters of the story to a highly refined audience. The major genres of kavya are courtly epics, drama, anthologies, royal eulogies, and "messenger poems" in which the lover invokes a force of nature, such as a cloud, to bear a message to his beloved.

The kavya style developed in the pre-Gupta age, from as early as the first century CE. Court literature in the Prakrit languages was widely developed in this period, and a famous anthology of love poems in Prakrit is attributed to a Satavahana king (Hala's *Seven hundreds*). The Sangam literature of Tamil develops at the same time. The Kushana king Kanishka is said to have been the patron of Ashvaghosha, whose *Deeds of the Buddha* is the earliest extant kavya in Sanskrit. Royal eulogies in stone inscriptions in kavya style also predate the Guptas. The greatest master of kavya in the estimation of the ancient Indians themselves was Kalidasa, who graced the court of Chandra Gupta II. The Gupta example of using Sanskrit in inscriptions and legal documents, and the Sanskrit kavya of the poets they patronized, was imitated by their vassals and neighbors, so that by the time their rule came to an end Sanskrit was the courtly language par excellence, as it has long been the language of brahmin learning.

Sculpture, painting, and architecture also reached classical form in the Gupta age, as can be seen in the gold coins of Samudra Gupta (Figure 7), the Sarnath Buddha (Figure 9), and the paintings preserved at the Buddhist caves of Ajanta, built under the patronage of the Vakatakas.

All the fine arts of classical India have formal, written bodies of theory, and indeed the aesthetic theory of ancient India, especially poetics (Alamkara Shastra in Sanskrit, Porul in Tamil), is highly developed. The fine arts have been especially appealing to kingdoms beyond India and were highly exportable and adaptable to other environments, as we shall see.

Formal bodies of knowledge in classical India developed within a cosmology that considered the world in time as subject to change of various kinds, and that placed eternity and truth outside of time and time-bound phenomena. Insofar as the object of contemplation was in the world, it was conceptualized as a *process* of some kind (evolution, decay, or cyclic repetition, for example). The extreme of this tendency is found in Buddhism, which insists on the radical nonpermanence of the world, so that even the transmigrating self is resolved into a succession of instantaneous states. What is highly valued, on the other hand, tends to get removed from the world process and located outside it, in eternity, the realm of truth. Thus the Sanskrit language is removed from history and change, and deemed eternal and changeless, whence the analysis of Sanskrit grammar has a structural character, rather than a historical one. The same may be said of the concept of dharma (capital-D dharma, that is, unlike the time-bound dharmas of regions, lineages, and castes). The special acuteness of intellectual analysis in ancient and classical India comes, often, from taking a structuralist approach and pursuing it in great depth.

CHAPTER 8

The World That India Made

Central Asia
East Asia
Southeast Asia
The Middle East and Europe

We could say that civilizations cast a *penumbra* beyond them, like the half-shadow around an eclipsed moon or sun. It is a useful metaphor by which to think about the wider world, beyond India proper, that was affected by India and that bears durable marks of its influences. In this chapter we make an inventory of these.

As we do so we must take care that we do not become victims of the unintended effects of the metaphors we adopt. In the first place, Indian Civilization occupied a definite space, called India or Bharata, in the deeper past, but the boundaries of this space were fuzzy, not sharply drawn like today's nation-state boundaries. Second, Indian Civilization did not occupy that space in a homogeneous way from edge to edge, but in a lumpy way, so to say, with centers and frontier zones within India. Finally, Indian Civilization in the past was not so much a *thing* as a *process*, a process of cultural invention and dissemination of cultural forms from centers such as religious institutions and royal courts and aristocracies. These inaugurated practices of belief and refinement that invited emulation by neighboring populations, and became centers of networks of influence within India and beyond. So by the penumbra metaphor we should not imagine Indian Civilization as homogeneous within, like the dark shadow of the eclipse.

At the same time, the penumbra of cultural influence around India was not a simple phenomenon, either. We need to understand India's influence, the wider world that India created around it, as a two-way process in which Indians interacted with others, who were not passive recipients of Indian influence but active partners in its spread. What can we say about these processes?

The striking thing about the penumbra of Indian Civilization is that for the most part it was not spread by war or migration. The main processes by which Indian Civilization spread were trade and the adoption of Indian religions and court cultures by foreign countries and their kings. Even that statement, however, is too simple to catch the complexities of Indian Civilization beyond India proper, which had very different natures in different places, depending on the local cultural and political circumstances. To understand this properly we need to survey the different regions beyond India and the different aspects of Indian Civilization that they adopted. For this purpose it is useful to divide the zone of this penumbra into four parts and examine each separately: Central Asia, East Asia, Southeast Asia, and the Middle East and Europe.

Central Asia

As we saw in Chapter 5, Central Asia has played an important role in Indian history through the ages, being a source from which four waves of military invasions, each separated by about five hundred years, have come about and created conquest states in India. The first of these waves involved Shakas, Pahlavas, and Kushanas, former nomadic peoples of Central Asia speaking Iranian languages; the second was that of the Hunas or Huns, Turkic-speaking ex-nomads. The last two were Central Asian peoples who had adopted Islam: the Turkish sultans of Delhi and the Mughals who succeeded them and created a long-lived empire that covered much of India. The effects of these invasions on Indian life have been various, but we can single out the supply of horses and the techniques of mounted warfare as the most salient.

In terms of the extension of Indian Civilization, the role of Central Asia has been crucial, both as a destination and as a stepping-stone to China and the Far East generally. The Kushanas of the first wave were crucial in this respect, for their empire, half in Central Asia and half in India, was exposed to and drew on cultural influences of the many literate civilizations with which they were in contact, but especially that of India. By means of the Kushana patronage of Mahayana Buddhism, that religion spread widely in Central Asia. This region is largely a dry grassland supporting nomadic pastoralists, the source of conquering armies of horsemen that from time to time troubled the settled agrarian civilizations of China, India, Iran, and Europe. However, it also contains small oases watered well enough to support agriculture. In the small agrarian city-states that sprang up in these places there soon were Buddhist monasteries established by missionary monks from India. The spread of Indian Buddhism carried with it Indian artistic renderings of the Buddhas and Bodhisattvas, Indian astronomy and calendar making, Indian linguistics, Indian medicine, and Indian cultures of kingship.

East Asia

Buddhist monasteries in Central Asian city-states became way stations for Indian Buddhist missionaries advancing eastward to China, which according to tradition Buddhism reached in the first century CE, when the Indian monks Dharmaraksha and Kashyapa Matanga came to China at the invitation of the emperor Mingdi. With it came a number of other influences from India. Buddhist monasteries of Central Asia now became way stations for a reverse flow of Buddhist monks from China, Korea, and Japan to places of pilgrimage and Buddhist learning in India. The memoirs of three of these monks, Faxian, Xuanzang, and Yi Jing, are especially illuminating regarding this traffic in pilgrim scholars. What the pilgrim monks mostly sought were correct versions of the Buddhist scriptures and drawings of the various Buddhas and Bodhisattvas to take home where they would serve as models for paintings and sculptures. Other aspects of Indian learning and culture accompanied the religion. Of course, China constituted a civilization in its own right, with a long-established and complex intellectual culture and its own cultural penumbra, so that the nature of the Indian Civilizational penumbra was quite different there than it was in Central Asia.

The high tide of Buddhism in China came in the Tang and Sung periods, when it enjoyed the patronage of the emperors and assumed a place next to Taoism and Confucianism as one of the three great religions of China. But India's effects on China extended well beyond Buddhism. China, being a complex and ancient civilization with a well-established culture of kingship, had no need of Indian ideas of kingship and courtly culture, unlike the Central Asian city-states and the kingdoms of Southeast Asia. Its own sciences, though, were at such a state of complexity that it was able to benefit from the considerable sophistication of Indian sciences. This was especially noticeable in the two areas in which India excelled: astronomy-astrology-mathematics, and linguistics.

As to the first, through the agency of Buddhism, Indian experts in astronomy and calendar making were sought out by the Chinese state and presided over the work of the Astronomical Bureau. We know the names of three of these—Gautama, Kashyapa, and Kumara—from Chinese works, and we know further that Indian works of astronomy by such authorities as Varahamihira and Brahmagupta were propagated in China in translation.

The dissemination of Buddhism in China also involved the dissemination of Sanskrit and perhaps other Indian languages, and a vast industry of translation into Chinese of Indian Buddhist texts. Xuanzang, in particular, presided over a large team of translators when he returned to China from his visit to Harsha's India. In this process of collecting, studying, and translating Indian texts of Buddhism into Chinese, Chinese scholars became exposed not only to the Sanskrit language but also the scripts of India (Brahmi and its derivatives) and the grammar of Sanskrit. Both the scripts and the grammar of Sanskrit were shaped by an acute understanding of linguistics, including especially a highly sophisticated understanding of phonology. Chinese scholars of the classic poems of ancient times had special use for Indian phonological analysis. The Chinese writing system has the virtue that it is intelligible to people speaking widely different dialects, but at the expense of being able to convey the sounds of the words. Over time, as pronunciations of words changed, the rhyming words of the ancient Chinese classic poems no longer rhymed and their original pronunciation became lost. Using Indian phonological analysis, Chinese scholars composed rhyming dictionaries of the ancient classics that helped them recover the pronunciation of ancient Chinese. Today these dictionaries remain useful to scholars investigating the phonology of the Chinese language in the deep past.[25] Although the Chinese did not exchange their excellent script for a phonological script on the Indian pattern, other languages of East Asia acquired Indian-based scripts and grammars, largely through the intermediacy of Buddhist scholars.

We know far less about intellectual effects of China on India, but we know a fair amount about trade and trade goods. Above all we know that Chinese silk reached India at an early point, for it is called "China cloth" (*chinapatta*) in the *Arthashastra* of Kautilya. Silk came overland both via Central Asia, along the famous Silk Road by which it also traveled to the Middle East and Europe, and by sea around Southeast Asia. Indians learned the techniques of silk making, as we know from the famous Mandasor Inscription of central India in which a guild of silk weavers commemorates the building of a temple, an elaborate poem into which the poet weaves several references to their cloth. We also find ancient Indian sources that speak of other Chinese imports—camphor, fennel, vermillion, a high-quality kind of leather, pears, and peaches—in Sanskrit names beginning with *china.*[26] Here again the high refinement of Chinese civilization is such that it is a source, for India, of rare items of luxury.

Southeast Asia

Most long-distance trade in ancient times was in luxuries because the costs of transport were very high; only the most costly goods fetched prices in distant markets that would yield a profit. Indian traders were involved in long-distance trade in ancient times, and we have many representations of seagoing Indian vessels that carried them. There are also many literary references to seaborne trade, such as in the Jataka tales of Buddhism; an example is the Baveru Jataka, which appears to refer to the name Babylon, to which Indian merchants bring a peacock, native to India but considered exotic and highly desirable in Baveru. Southeast Asia had a commodity highly desirable to Indians, it would seem, from the fact that they gave the name Suvarnabhumi, meaning "Land of gold," to the peninsula, or some part of it, perhaps Burma. The Indian demand for gold has always been high, and still is; it is especially important as women's wealth in a society in which land has been transmitted to sons and daughters were given instead a dowry of jewelry and other objects.

The trade of India with the Southeast Asian peninsula goes back, perhaps, to Mauryan times, and trade with the islands begins somewhat later. From the first century CE, Greek traders from the Mediterranean learned the periodic nature of the monsoon winds and how to use them to sail to India and beyond, and at about the same time the Chinese built enormous junks that plied international waters for trade. All in all, there was a quantum leap in seaborne trade in luxury goods that connected the ports of the Hellenized Middle East, India, the Bay of Bengal, Southeast Asia, and China. Because the content of this trade largely involved luxury goods rather than the cheaper necessities of daily life, it had strong political effects, by providing rare and desirable goods around which aristocracies could form, not only as military groups but also as models of refinement for the emulation or envy of others.

Southeast Asia was massively affected by Indian Civilization from about the first century, in ways that are still visible today. From the first century we begin to find signs of the rapid emergence of what Georges Coedès calls Indianized states, both in peninsular and island Southeast Asia.[27] These Indianized states were the main consumers, so to speak, of Indian Civilization, in the form of Indian trade goods, but also in cultural goods such as religions, patterns of kingship, arts and sciences, and Sanskrit and Pali languages.

What was the process of Indianization? How did it work? To these questions we cannot give definitive answers due to the limited amount of evidence we have. However, we can give some tentative answers that have high levels of probability. It seems clear that the Indianization of Southeast Asia was not the result of a large-scale movement of populations from India to Southeast Asia, for the languages spoken in Southeast Asia are not of the two largest language families of India, Indo-Aryan and Dravidian, but of the Austroasiatic and Tibeto-Burman families. It is true that the third language family of India, the Austroasiatic, is largely spread in the peninsula, including Cambodian (or Mon Khmer) and Vietnamese, but it appears that speakers of that family moved from Southeast Asia westward into India in prehistoric times, not eastward from India to Southeast Asia in historic times; that is, the period of the Indianized states of Southeast Asia. The Indians who did move to Southeast Asia, then, were a small number of people concerned with trade, religion, and the state: merchants, Buddhist monks and brahmin priests, and political officials. These would have been the agents of the Indianization of states in Southeast Asia. Were any of them Indian royal families, or were they indigenous Southeast Asian chiefly lineages motivated by ambitions to form powerful kingdoms on the Indian pattern? It seems likely that these kings were mostly indigenous, but the evidence is rather ambiguous in some cases, because Indianization involved getting royal genealogies drawn up in Indian style, deriving royal families from India. Thus one of the early Indianized kingdoms was said to have been founded by a brahmin named Kaundinya, who married a local woman. It is not evident how we should evaluate such a claim, and it is doubtful that many of the Indianized states were founded by Indians. Thus the Indianization process seems largely to have been a matter of indigenous political leaders drawing on Indian luxury goods and civilizational patterns to create strong states; a demand-driven Indianization, so to say.

Coèdes proposes that we think of the formation of Indianized states in Southeast Asia as being an extension into Southeast Asia of the process by which North Indian high culture spread to South India and Sri Lanka, namely, by a combination of luxury trade and the formation of Buddhist (and Jain) monasteries, brahmin settlements, and Hindu temples; the adoption of the North Indian royal style; and the importation of artistic and scientific culture of an emerging classical courtly culture. We might add that this is also like the manner by which city-states of Central Asia became Indianized, through the formation of Buddhist monasteries by indigenous kings and the adoption of Indian royal culture. The appeal of this picture is that it explains how Indian high culture spread without massive migration and without displacing indigenous languages, at the same time injecting large numbers of Indian (especially Sanskrit or Pali) loan words into those languages.

Southeast Asia, of course, was exposed to the influence of China as well as India in the period in question; we could say that it was in the penumbra of both civilizations. Although the peninsula, which Europeans called Indo-China in recognition of this mutual influence, is a kind of crossroads of Indian and Chinese culture, it is striking how much more successful were the Indian patterns than the Chinese ones in taking root in Southeast Asia. The one exception is Vietnam, where Chinese civilization profoundly affected state culture through Confucianism, adoption of the Chinese script to represent an Austroasiatic language, and in many other ways. This was largely a result of Chinese military conquest. Earlier, Vietnam was an Indianized state with an Indian name, Champa, and an Indianized form of monumental architecture and sculpture that can still be seen in an otherwise much-Sinified society. By contrast it appears that Indianization was not extended by Indian military expansion, although there are a few exceptions to this statement, especially involving the Cholas of South India and their military involvement with overseas states in Sri Lanka and the kingdom of Srivijaya in Indonesia and Malaya.

Indianized states were formed by elites on both sides of the transaction. Indianization was at all times selective, and impelled by the demand side of the relation. For example, an indigenous culture of identifying high places such as mountain tops with divinity was given an Indian dress by these Southeast Asian states. Thus Indian Civilization was consumed in Southeast Asia in a selective way, one that involved construing indigenous patterns of culture within imported Indian frameworks. Here again the same may be said of the way in which South Indian gods (e.g., Murugan) get identified with the Hindu divinities of the Puranas (as Kumara, son of Shiva).

FIGURE 12 Devata, Angkor Wat, Cambodia, 12th century

What was imported? Especially Buddhism and Hinduism, notably the Theravada Buddhism of Sri Lanka in Burma and Thailand, Mahayana forms elsewhere, and Tantric forms of both in some places, expressed in the sculptures that adorn Indianate architecture, such as the

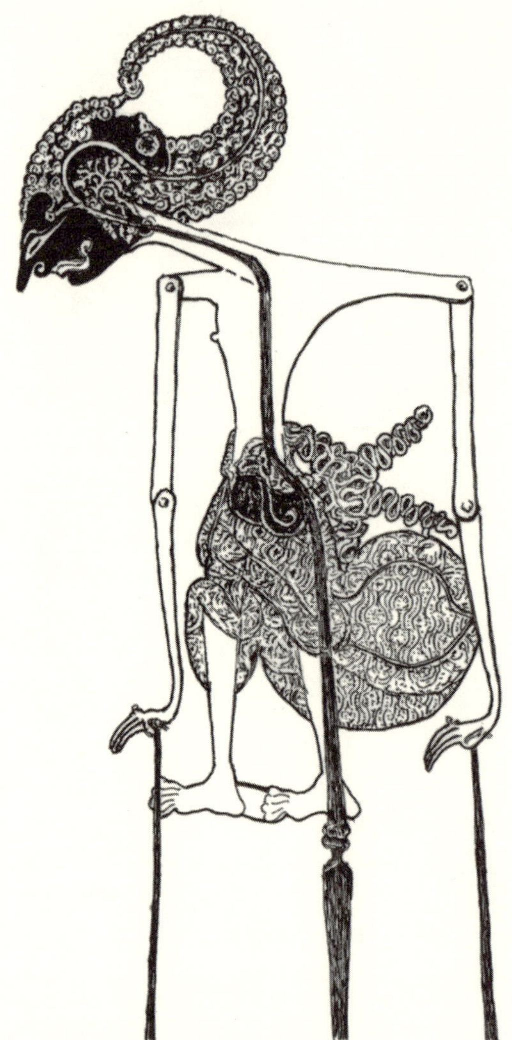

FIGURE 13 Javanese shadow puppet of Arjuna, from the Mahabharata, 19th century

image of the Devata at Angkor Wat, the styling of which is both Indian and non-Indian at once (Figure 12). With Indian religions came the study of Sanskrit and Pali and the formation of scripts based on Indian ones, scripts that continue today in Burma, Thailand, and Cambodia. Also evident are

Indian forms of astronomy, calendar making and time reckoning, astrology, the story literature of the Indian epics and the Buddhist Jataka tales, which suffuse sculpture, painting, the shadow-puppet performances of Indonesia (Figure 13), courtly dance, and courtly forms of poetry. Especially noticeable is monumental architecture, in such spectacular constructions as Angkor Wat in Cambodia and the Buddhist stupa of Borobudur in Indonesia.

Although the great age of Indianized states began to wane in the fourteenth century, after nearly a millennium and a half, a substantial afterglow of Indian-influenced arts remains in living cultural practices of Southeast Asian countries.

The Middle East and Europe

The luxury trade of the Indian Ocean, connecting India with the Middle East and Europe, became highly active from the first century CE. Before that time, sailing voyages were coasting voyages, made with the land always in sight, which made for a very long journey between India and Arabia and the Mediterranean. The discovery by Greek sailors that the monsoon winds blew eastward in the summer and westward in the winter allowed for sailing directly between the Arabian Peninsula and India, gathering one's courage and sailing across the open sea, out of sight of land. Because the monsoon changed direction between seasons, it became possible to complete a round trip in one year. This increased the tempo of the Indian Ocean trade greatly. One effect of this is found at Arikamedu, on the southeast coast of South India, where archaeologists have excavated a Greco-Roman trading station. It was a location at which Greek sailors brought wares from the Mediterranean, including Arretine pottery from Italy and amphorae of wine, for trade in India, and collected Indian trade goods in a warehouse against the arrival of their ships. Many Roman coins have been found in South India and Sri Lanka, giving further testimony to the wide reach of this trade. Arab and Jewish merchants also had trading stations in India, and the reverse might also be true. Indians are mentioned at Alexandria in Hellenistic times. India and the Middle East were also connected by land routes, from the times of Alexander if not earlier.

India's trade with countries to the west goes way back. In the Bible it is said that Hiram, king of Tyre, sent ships of Tarshish to Ophir for "apes, ivory and peacocks," to decorate the palaces and temple of King

Solomon. All three are indigenous to India, and peacocks are found nowhere else. Ophir is thought to be Sopara, in the vicinity of present-day Mumbai on the west coast. This Biblical passage illustrates for us the connection of long-distance trade with luxury goods, and of luxury goods with high politics and religion, and the maintenance of elites.

From the first century, if not earlier, a pattern took shape that governed the terms of trade between India and the Mediterranean. From the Mediterranean, India sought gold above all, and the red coral that grows in that region and nowhere else, which is used for jewelry in India to this day, plus other luxury goods such as wine. From India and Sri Lanka peoples of the Mediterranean sought gemstones (beryl, rubies, and later diamonds), pearls, ivory, sword blades of steel, vessels of bronze, and fine textiles of many kinds including printed cotton (Figure 14),[28] among other things. These terms of trade remained in force for a very long time, and for peoples to the west India was a land of fabulous luxury and manufactured items of a high quality. It was not until the Industrial Revolution that these terms of trade were changed, around 1815. After that time India became a source of raw materials such as cotton, and Europe, specifically Britain, was the place in which cotton from America and Syria (and briefly, during the American Civil War when the Union blockaded the export of cotton from the South, from India itself) was turned into cheap cloth by machinery, which could be shipped to India and sold there more cheaply than the indigenous handloom cotton cloth. The ancient luxury trade changed into a modern trade in machine-made mass consumables that was to India's disadvantage, in which India became a source of raw materials and a market for cheap manufactured goods from Europe.

One other pattern of the ancient trade should be added to this sketch: the trade in horses and elephants. They are critical elements for the military in India, and hence for the entire political system. Horses and elephants are in complementary distribution in relation to India. Elephants are indigenous to India, and within India they are concentrated in the elephant forests of the wet zone (Map 3), east, and the south; they are scarce in the Indus Valley. Horses, on the other hand, are not indigenous to India; that is, there are no populations of wild horses that can be captured and trained for human use, and they do better in the arid zone. Consequently, ancient Indian kings always took a great interest in the control of elephant forests, and the horse trade from Central Asia and the west, and were willing to pay a premium

FIGURE 14 Indian block-print cotton fabric from Gujarat, found in Egypt, c. 11th century

for horses. For example, kings of Vijayanagara promised a handsome price to Portuguese traders who brought horses by sea, for which the Indians paid whether horses arrived dead or alive, so anxious were they to secure their supply for the army. Later, under British rule, the Indian Army acquired horses from breeding grounds in Australia (New South Wales; such horses were called "Walers"). On the elephant side of the ledger, where India was at an advantage, Greek kings of the Hellenistic states who succeeded Alexander went to great lengths to acquire elephants to use in their armies against one another. They appear also to have imported Indian elephant drivers, for the word *Indios* came to mean an elephant driver in Greek, and with the drivers came knowledge of elephant techniques. The Seleucids in the Middle East secured considerable numbers of elephants from the Mauryans, and we hear of at least three large consignments of elephants from the Mauryas to the Seleucids at three different times, whereas the Seleucids' rivals, the Ptolemies of Egypt, caught and trained African elephants, probably with the aid of Indian elephant men. The elephant trade finally fizzled out due to the huge costs and great distances involved, and because Greeks and Romans devised effective countermeasures to address the limited numbers of elephants in western armies. However, elephant warfare continued within India until modern times, as did the Indian dependence on the horse trade.

The trade between India and the peoples to the west, Iranian, Arab, Greek, and Roman, then, grew to large proportions. It was a luxury trade, but we should not think of it as a trade in frivolities, in things that people can do without, for these very expensive items were important in maintaining social hierarchies and political structures. The volume could be great. Romans deplored the large drain of gold to India in exchange for luxuries, which, they feared, could ruin the state.

Although the quantum leap in trade that began in the first century bound India closer to the lands to the west of it, and made for an appealing image of India as a land of wealth and desirable luxury goods, the westward spread of Indian religion was not so extensive. Buddhism, which proved to be India's most exportable religion, spread over most of East Asia and Southeast Asia, as we have seen. It reached westward through Afghanistan, as the recent destruction of the colossal standing Buddha of Bamiyan reminds us, but little further. At the same time Christianity was spreading across the Mediterranean and Middle East, as far eastward as Iran. It was in the Greek-influenced world of Afghanistan and the Indus Valley that we find Greek-influenced sculptures of the Buddha and other Indian religious figures. On the whole, though, trade, not religion, was the greater vehicle of communication between India and the lands to the west in ancient times.

Intellectual exchanges with western lands are especially found in the astronomy-astrology-math complex in which ancient India made such notable achievements. India was both a borrower and a lender in these matters. Astronomy and astrology and the math that goes with them, arising in Mesopotamia (Iraq) among the Sumerians and others, initiated an international exchange of ideas that took in all of the ancient peoples from Greece and Rome to India, and it is because of this exchange that the twelve signs of the zodiac and the seven weekdays presided over by the sun, moon, and five planets are found throughout this large region, as we saw in Chapter 7. India contributed to this exchange the invention of algebra, the beginnings of trigonometry, the place-notation for numbers, and using the zero as a placeholder, among other things. These are not just events that happened long ago; they are living forms of knowledge that are a part of the everyday workings of modernity throughout the world. We could not function without them.

The other area in which Indian science was especially well developed is language analysis (linguistics, especially phonology and grammar), applied first to Sanskrit in the Vedic period, and then to other languages within India and in Central Asia, East Asia, and Southeast Asia. Here India's contribution seems to be entirely homegrown. Although it greatly influenced the study of language and the making of scripts in wide parts of Asia, it was only in the eighteenth century that it was absorbed into European ideas of language analysis. At that time the study of Sanskrit by Europeans contributed greatly to the formation of modern linguistics.

The world that India made, casting its half-shadow well beyond the homeland of Indian civilization into most of the adjacent lands of Eurasia, had substantial effects. It is striking that the vehicles of this partial Indianization of other countries and civilizations were religion and trade rather than warfare and empire building, in the way that Hellenism, for example, was spread by the empire building of Alexander. The world India made was not put together at the point of a spear but through the appeal of its products, its religions, and its sciences.

CHAPTER 9

Turks and Mughals

Islam and India
Turks
Mughals

Indian Civilization has a long but intermittent relation to Central Asia. The Aryans and their horse-drawn chariots came from Central Asia and established the Vedic religion in India in the second millennium BCE. The Shakas, Pahlavas, and Kusanas around the beginning of the common era were speakers of Iranian languages, whereas the Hunas from about 450 were Turkic in language. Although of different language families, both waves had similar profiles, being nomads from Central Asia who had mastered a manner of warfare based on unlimited supplies of horses and using techniques of mounted archery. Ultimately many of them were absorbed into the warrior class of the Indian population. Turks of Central Asia established their rule in Delhi from 1206, and Mughals of Central Asia, also Turkic in language and ethnic affiliation, from 1526, both having armies very much based on cavalry and therefore on the continuing importation of horses from Central Asia. Thus the Turks and Mughals were continuing an ages-old pattern of at least five major intermittent invasions from Central Asia leading to the formation of conquest states in India. The Turks and Mughals differed from the previous invaders in being Muslims, and, as such, participants in a far-flung, cosmopolitan community (*umma*) of Islam. A signal effect of the community-making capacity of the religion of Islam was to bring Iranian scholars, scribes, artists, and fighters into the formation of cosmopolitan Turkish and Mughal states in India, giving the enterprise a composite, Indo-Persian cultural character. Iran and India, of course, had an ancient cultural connection, and Iranian Islam took form within the penumbra of Indian Civilization, so in a sense this development was also a reiteration of past patterns. It is important to hold in mind that the Turk and Mughal states were not Muslim states; they were Indian states with components that were Central Asian, Iranian, and Islamic, as well as Indian.

There is, to be sure, no mistaking the importance of Islam as a religion in the history of India, as we can see by looking at a map of the world. Up to the creation of nation-states in 1947 undivided India contained the largest Muslim population of any country in the world; much greater, it should be noted, than the Middle Eastern countries in which Islam had its beginnings. Religious identity acquired great significance for the politics of nation making in the twentieth century, and when the British brought colonial rule to an end and left India they divided the territory they had ruled into two independent states, Pakistan and India, along religious lines. Pakistan was a Muslim-majority state and the Republic of India a Hindu-majority state, although many Muslims remained in India, together with adherents of other religions. Pakistan had two wings, on either side of the Republic of India: East Pakistan, which broke away from Pakistan in 1971 and renamed itself Bangladesh, and West Pakistan, which with the formation of Bangladesh is now simply Pakistan. These three parts of the modern map—Bangladesh, Pakistan, and India—constitute the countries with the second, third, and fourth largest Muslim populations in the world (the first is Indonesia). Islam, which grew up in a dry and relatively sparsely populated part of the world, acquired a huge number of adherents in the much more populous lands of India and Indonesia.

Because of the way in which religion has combined with the politics of nation-state formation and ballot-box democracy in the twentieth century, religious identity has a greater salience and political weight than ever before. We are likely to project that salience back in time and overestimate the role of religious identity in the deeper past of India and to miss the other regional and ethnic factors at play in the formation of the Turkish and Mughal states.

Islam and India

Before the Turks or Mughals, Arabs brought Islam to India by trade and military expeditions. Indians and Arabs had long been engaged in trade with the Red Sea regions, and Arab traders resident on the western coast of India were probably the first Muslims of India, becoming Muslim soon after Islam arose in Arabia. At the same time, Islam propelled the formation of an Arab empire that expanded rapidly, reaching Sindh in 711 CE in its easternmost military venture, about the same time as it reached Spain in the west, less than a hundred years since its beginnings. As it expanded through trade and conquest, the Muslim community evolved from an Arab community into a multiethnic one. The mercantile and imperial expansion of Muslims beginning in the seventh century was replicated by the mercantile and imperial expansion of Christian Europe beginning with Columbus and Vasco da Gama in the fifteenth and sixteenth centuries. India (and indeed Asia as a whole) was deeply affected by both these waves of expansion, which are the topic of this and the next chapter.

The tremendous outward expansion of Islam is an outstanding example of the community-making power of ideas in history. Islam began through the revelations received by Muhammad in Mecca where he was born and Medina to which he and his following, the beginnings of the Muslim community, fled. The "flight" or *hijra* from Mecca to Medina in 622 CE was a central event in the Prophet's life, and was the starting point of the Muslim era for the rendering of dates; thus the year 2000 CE is the year 1378 AH, "after the hijra." The Prophet had been forced out of Mecca because the leading merchant families feared his growing following constituted a threat to their power, an early expression of that community-making power.

Muhammad represented his message as the revelation of God through the Archangel Gabriel, and he situated himself in the series of biblical prophets beginning with Abraham and continuing with Jesus. Gabriel commanded Muhammad to *recite* (*iqra,* whence *Quran,* the recitation), which he did, to a small but growing band of followers in Mecca: a message of God's power and goodness, his oneness and uniqueness, of the day of judgment when souls of the dead would be judged and sent to paradise or to hell; a message, too, of the obligation to *submit* (Islam is submission; a Muslim is one who submits) to God's will and respond with gratitude to God's goodness, by leading a moral life, providing food and alms for orphans and the poor.

When he fled to Medina it was in a state of war among the eleven or so tribes to which its population belonged, each tribe having a fort on the oasis. Muhammad did not flee to Medina at random; he was invited to come in, as an arbitrator among the feuding tribes. In doing so he drew up a kind of a constitution for Medina, laying down relations between his own followers and the Medinans, between Muslim believers of Medina and the nonbelievers in the new religion of the Prophet, and between the Arabs and the Jews (three of the warring tribes were Jewish), confirming the Jews in the exercise of their religion and the possession of their goods. Muhammad became the arbitrator of disputes among the tribes, a kind of super-tribal leader. At the same time he was the leader of his own community, which followed him not because of blood relation as in the tribes, but in recognition of his prophethood. Thus to the tribal idea was superadded the idea of the community of the faithful (umma), and for Muslims tribal ties were superseded by the authority of Muhammad, before whom disputes among the faithful must be brought.

The Prophet lived for only ten years after the flight to Medina, but in that short time he laid the foundations of the community of believers that grew and spread at a remarkable rate in the first century of Islam. The first step was the Islamization of Mecca, accomplished through a series of battles that achieved final success eight years after the flight. By taking Mecca, Muhammad became the leader of a state, appointed by God, who gave it laws, with a treasury, an army, and a number of tribal allies, not all of them yet adherents of the new religion that was about to sweep through the Arabian Peninsula. What had been created was an idea, centering around Islamic monotheism, of a community of the faithful demanding a higher loyalty that replaced or supplemented loyalty to the tribe, and with it, a universalist ethic.

The death of Muhammad threw the Islamic community into a constitutional crisis, because no one could succeed him as prophet. The solution was the office of *caliph* (*khalifa*) or "successor" to the Prophet, who became the central political leader of the growing state. The first four caliphs were drawn from the companions and relatives of the Prophet, and are called the "rightly guided caliphs": Abu Bakr, Umar, Uthman, and Ali. They were followed by the Umayya family of Mecca, and then the Abbasid family ruling from Baghdad, in the following periods:

The rightly guided caliphs	632–661
Umayyads	661–750
Abbasids	750–1258

Each of these periods involved important stages in the evolution of the Islamic community.

Immediately after the death of the Prophet the tribes that had been allied to him went their separate ways, and the state might have disappeared completely. What is more, many tribal leaders posed as prophets, not of the old tribal deities, but of God (Allah), in succession to Muhammad. The Muslim historians call this "the apostasy" (*ridda*). It was the urgent task of the first caliph to counter this danger, and to insist that Muhammad was the "seal of the prophets"; that is, that there would be no more prophets after him; and also to regain the submission of the apostate tribes by conquering them. The "Wars of the Apostasy" were successful, and the success swelled the army with new allies, creating a momentum that continued to expand until the entire Arabian Peninsula was taken, and continued into countries beyond. Within ten years of the death of Muhammad, Arabia was secured, and the rich and densely populated river valleys of the ancient agrarian civilizations of Iraq and Egypt were in Arab control. Under the early caliphate, then, was created an Arab empire, held in trust for the Muslim community by the caliph.

Thus the community remained at this time an Arab one, but not for long. What historians call the first Arab Empire had spread into ancient countries that had, by comparison, huge populations and that depended on agriculture and governments supported by the tax on land, surveyed and collected by cadres of administrators. Under the empire, Arabs could buy land subject to slight tax, but non-Muslims had to pay a poll tax (*jizya*) and land tax (*kharaj*), and so long as they did so their religions were tolerated—they were *dhimmis* or adherents of the tolerated religions, Judaism and Christianity. But an unanticipated consequence of the success of the first Arab empire was that non-Arabs embraced Islam and became Muslims. At first the only way of attaching them to the new community was for them to become clients (*mawali*) under the protection of one of the Arab tribes, having a second-class status with heavier taxes and fewer privileges than the Arab Muslims. This two-tiered effect within the community could not last forever, because of the vast number of non-Arabs in the conquered countries, and the tension between the two main parties pushed the community toward a more cosmopolitan and less ethnically Arab self-definition. This paradoxical effect of Arab success was completed under the fourth caliph, when he left the Arabian Peninsula on a military campaign and made his capital in Iraq, at Kufa. The caliphate never returned to Arabia, and generally resided in Damascus, and later in Baghdad, which was built by the Abbasids. Arabia itself lost its political importance, but it remained the center of pilgrimage for Muslims, and is so today.

The selection of the third caliph, Uthman of the Umayya family of Mecca, was a victory for the Meccan oligarchy, now within Islam, and their families now filled high offices, leading to a virtual civil war in which the first wave of Arab conquest was spent and the rapid expansion of the empire came to a sudden halt. The caliph was assassinated, and the fourth caliph, Ali, clashed with the nephew of Uthman, Muawiya, governor of Syria, who charged Ali with complicity and demanded vengeance. The split widened after Ali's death when the empire fell to Muawiya and his heirs, the Umayyad caliphs, for the embittered followers of Ali did not recognize the subsequent caliphs and formed a political and religious opposition that became the Shias.

Under the Umayyad caliphs the state was restabilized and the conquests resumed. The second Arab conquest reached beyond Egypt across North Africa to Gibraltar and Spain; it put Constantinople, the capitol of the Byzantine Greeks, under attack; it reached into Central Asia, to places that soon became centers of Muslim learning and devotion, Bukhara and Samarkand, in Uzbekistan; and it reached Sindh, in India by 711 CE, in the first Muslim century. Sindh was the first state in India with a Muslim head. The governors of Sindh, very far from the caliph, ruled virtually independent of him. Islam sank deep roots in Sindhi society, and as Sindhi society became Islamic it became a conduit through which those elements of Indian culture and learning—mathematics, astronomy, fable literature, medicinal practices—were absorbed into the Islamic world and, in part, transmitted to Europe.

The governorship of Sindh split into two states with Arab rulers that held the lower Indus Valley. However, the Arab Empire could not spread further into India, held in check by the empire of the Gurjara-Pratiharas, whose army was immense. In the end, the rule of Muslims came to north India not through the Arabs, but through different ethnic groups, the Turks and the Mughals, from Central Asia.

Umayyad control of the caliphate came to an end in 750 CE with a coup by the Abbasid family. Although the Abbasid family was Arab, its coming to power represented the victory for the cause of the non-Arab mawalis or clients, that submerged, second-class citizenry of the empire who were in fact vastly more numerous than the Arab component. In the regions of the older civilizations of Persia and Iraq and Egypt, the mawali class included the old nobility and the various learned and skilled groups under the pre-Islamic governments that fell under the control of a network of Arab military men spread ever more thinly across an ever larger surface as the empire grew. So we may say that the Abbasid revolution resolved the growing contradiction in the Muslim community between the Arab minority elite and the mawali majority. By the mid-800s Abbasid power was in disarray and local power centers, often under Turkish rule, were dividing up the eastern Islamic world.

The outcome of these processes, in the eastern wing of the empire, was the flowering of a new Perso-Islamic culture, including a literature in the Persian language, now written in a modified form of the Arabic script. This was very portentous for India, because it was this Persianized form of Islamic culture, and its Iranian personnel, that would come to North India in the train of the Turkish invaders.

Turks

People often suppose that Turks must come from Turkey, but it is the other way around: The name Turkey comes from the Turks. The homeland of the languages of the Turkic family is Central Asia, and the Ottoman Turks of Turkey came from there and created an empire, as part of a broad process of Turkish expansion from Central Asia. Even today the northwestern provinces of China and the countries along the southern border of Russia as well as northern parts of Iran, have large populations of peoples speaking languages of this family, such as the Azeris, the Kazakhs, the Kyrgyz, the Turkmen, and the Uzbeks, who give their names to the countries of Azerbaijan, Kazakhstan, Kyrgyzstan, Turkmenistan, and Uzbekistan.

The Turkification of Islam came about through the practice of employing Turkish military slaves as elite guards by the caliph and the other political leaders of Islamic countries where the taking of Turkish slaves through trade and war was underway. The institution of the military slave (*mamluk*) is important for India, because the first dynasty of Sultans was called the Slave Dynasty. But to understand it, one has to put to one side most of the connotations of the word slave, because the Turkish military slave was often very well off, and could be the general of an army or the governor of a province, and could own property, including slaves, himself. Raised from boyhood to be the elite of the military, the mamluk troops were often in a position to take power by military coup; by the fourteenth century there were mamluk kings in many parts of Islamic civilization, from Cairo to Delhi. The rise of Turkish powers took place during the fragmentation of the caliphate in the mid-ninth century, during which Islam lost its political direction, long before the Abbasid caliphate was extinguished completely by the Mongols in 1258.

The Turkish conquest of north India began in about 1000 CE under Mahmud of Ghazna, a Turkish ruler of Central Asian origin settled in Afghanistan, who created a large empire by expansion westward into Iran and eastward into India. His armies made many raids deep into the valley of the Ganga, and down the Indus Valley to Gujarat, bringing back huge amounts of plunder and ransom from the wealthy kingdoms and richly endowed temples of North India. For the most part Mahmud and his successors, called the Ghaznavids, extended their permanent rule only across the upper Indus Valley, to the region of Lahore, replacing the earlier Muslim rulers. Lahore became an outpost of Perso-Islamic culture in the territory of Indian Civilization.

The Ghaznavids were replaced by another family, the Ghurids, who resumed the conquest of North India toward the end of the twelfth century, and fielded large armies led by Turkish slave generals. The Ghurid king was assassinated while his troops were off in North India in the midst of a successful invasion, and, their master having died, the generals raised one of their number, Qutb-ud-din Aybak, to be their sultan, and the first of the sultans of Delhi, in 1206 (Figure 15).

The Turkish Sultanate is best thought of as a conglomerate of three groups: Turks, Iranians, and Indians. The first part of the mix was the Turkish military aristocracy, who filled the top military and political offices of the kingdom. They were a small minority of power holders in a densely populated agrarian civilization, and they had no settled culture of succession to the throne, so that they were often internally divided by wars of succession. The succession was marked by an unusual frequency of violence: The turnover rate of kings was about twice that of previous Indian kings (an average reign length of about ten years, compared to more than twenty years for the earlier period) and dynasties (there were six in 320 years) were short-lived compared to those of the earlier period, many of which had continued in power for centuries. The regime depended to an unusual degree on the direct use of military force, and the liberal reward of the military elite to bind it to the sultan.

The Iranian element in the mix was crucial, because without it the rulers would have had to do what earlier Central Asian invaders of India had done—recruit Indians as their administrators and assimilate themselves to Indian culture to gain the confidence of those they ruled. As

FIGURE 15 Qutb Minar, Delhi, 12th century

it happens, the Mongol catastrophe descended on the lands of eastern Islam in the formative years for the Sultanate of Delhi, destroying the last remnants of the Abbasid caliphate and making life miserable for Iranians. A stream of Iranian émigrés flowed toward Delhi, where the sultans were famous for their wealth and generosity. Thus the Mongol threat created conditions under which the Turks had the advantage of a steady supply of Iranians literate in the Persian language who could be made into the judges, land revenue officials, bureaucrats of all kinds, scholars, teachers, poets, and artists. This is why Persian became the language of government and diplomacy, which it continued to be as late as the early nineteenth century, and many more Persian-language texts are composed in India than in Iran, with its much smaller population. The historical circumstances promoting the Iranian emigration to India shored up the Islamic character of the Turkish kingship, and gave it a Persian cast.[29]

Finally, the largest component of the mix was the Indian people themselves. Even though the Persian and Turkish element of the government held privileged positions at the top, both the army and the civil government depended on very large numbers of Indians. As to the army, whereas Turkish military power relied on Central Asian horses and horsemanship, the Indian peasantry supplied an immense body of soldiers whose services the sultans endeavored to command. The civil government, although Persian in the style of its record-keeping, inevitably depended on large numbers of scribes fluent in the native languages of India to assess and collect the land revenue that supplied the state with its vast wealth. The Sultanate required huge amounts of money to sustain the lavish gift giving that held the state together, and taxation became much more extractive. It is always difficult to be precise about taxes in ancient times, but it is significant that in the ancient period the king's share of the peasant's crop was nominally put at one sixth, whereas under the Turkish sultans it sometimes rose to as high as half.

To raise the land tax it was necessary for the tax administrators to deal with local Indian officials, and generally the Hindu rajas at the local level were left in charge of raising the revenue from their districts. Thus Hindu society and its traditional leadership continued, but the apex of the power pyramid was occupied by Turks and Iranians, especially in the Doab or the land between the Ganga and Yamuna. Outside the Doab there were Hindu rajas who continued to rule their own territories on condition of paying a tribute to Delhi. As Hinduism continued to dominate the countryside, Islam formed communities in the walled cities of North India, becoming a notably urban phenomenon. In these cities religion was under the care and guidance of the scholars of Islamic law and learning (called the *ulama*), who were notable for their orthodoxy, their concern that Islam not be contaminated by the Hinduism that surrounded them, and their full support of the kingship. Sufi organizations and craft guilds controlled city life.

These were not conditions conducive for the conversion to Islam of large numbers of Indians, and indeed even in the upper Ganga Valley from which the Delhi sultans ruled there were few rural Muslims. It is often said that the conversions that did take place were the result of direct force, and accompanied by the destruction of Hindu temples. Both did occur, but only in the path of conquest and as a kind of exemplary punishment for stubborn resistance, as Richard Eaton has shown. Once the territory had been conquered, however, the situation was quite different. The vastly outnumbered Turkish military elite could not have ruled North India had it offered continual provocation to the Indians by the regular practice of forced conversion. Not only did the sultans have no such policy, but early on they adopted the position that the Indians were dhimmis or adherents of tolerated religions, allowing them the freedom to practice their religion so long as they submitted to the rule of the sultan and paid taxes. This position became the norm for Muslim rulers in India. In general, conversion to Islam by Indians did not come from the actions of governments, which did not want to lose taxes through conversions. In the long period of Turkish and Mughal rule, mass conversions to Islam, which in an agrarian society means mass conversions of peasants, occurred not in the central territories of these rulers but rather at the edges, in the Indus Valley and in Bengal. According to Eaton, in Bengal at least, mass conversions to Islam came about with the formation of large grants of land to Muslim entrepreneurs and Sufi shrines as part of a pioneering process that spread agriculture into the forestlands, much as monastic estates in Europe spread agriculture and Christianity beyond the frontiers of settled life.[30] It was especially the devotional, mystic form of Islam called Sufism to which Indians responded, containing as it did practices of devotionalism that were similar in a general way to bhakti Hinduism, and the renunciation and mysticism of charismatic Sufi teachers had a general likeness to yoga. Many Sufis appear in Indian folklore as holy men no different than the yogis and medicants of other Indian religions.

The history of the Sultanate of Delhi can be outlined in a number of stages. The first was one of building and consolidating the kingship itself in north India, and this occupied the first hundred years. Then from about 1300 to 1350 CE the sultans extended their power to the Deccan, drawing off huge amounts of movable wealth from the kings and temples of the peninsula with which they maintained the liberality by which they held the Turkish military aristocracy and the Iranian scholarly class to them. This was certainly the high point of the Sultanate, but also the beginning of decline, for so long as sources of external wealth could meet the Sultanate's need for large amounts of money it would flourish, but when the Deccan had no more to give the Sultanate was forced to live within its means (that is, through the land tax on North Indian peasantry), and its practice of overtaxing tended to ruin agricultural productivity. The period after about 1350, therefore, was one of retrenchment and the search for a style of rule that would promote agriculture rather than damage it. Then in 1398 North India was invaded by Timur (Tamerlane, as he was called in the West), the Mongol king of Iran and Central Asia, resulting in a major catastrophe. Delhi was sacked and its artisans were carried off to build a mosque in Samarkand (modern Tashkent) for Timur. The final period of the Sultanate was a century of decline after that invasion, during which time many provincial sultanates were formed by breakaway military men, in Bengal, Kashmir, Punjab, and elsewhere, and the kingdom of Vijayanagara was formed in the South. It is in the provincial sultanates that Islam became domesticated to Indian culture, and it is in these regions that the numbers of Muslims are large today.

Vijayanagara, the capital of the empire of that name, was constructed in the dry interior of the peninsula, by a new warrior class that was created as agriculture advanced into the dry region, as Cynthia Talbot has shown. From this vantage it dominated the territories of South India through its governors. Its kings were Hindu but its structure was cosmopolitan, employing Muslim artillerymen and trading with the Portuguese for war horses, which were always in short supply in the peninsula relative to its northern neighbors. A common formula identified three major powers of the day: The sultan of Delhi was called Ashvapati, or lord of horses; the king of Orissa was called the Gajapati, or lord of elephants; and the Vijayanagara emperor was Narapati, or lord of men. This triangle of major states constituted the international order at the time, showing how the Turkish kings of Delhi had become normalized in India. Phillip Wagoner shows that the kings of Vijayanagara adopted the cap and robes of the Turkish kings as a norm of diplomatic dress.[31] In hundreds of ways, large and small, Central Asian and Perso-Islamic practices became part of the Indian scene.

Mughals

The Mughals, who dominated the history of India for the better part of two centuries and who lingered on with reduced power for another century and a half, were far more successful as a ruling family than any of the dynasties of the Delhi Sultanate, the longest-lived of which survived for only ninety years. The greater success of the Mughals was mainly due to a more cosmopolitan policy that gave a larger place in government to Indians—although noblemen and scholars from Central Asia and Iran continued to find India a land of wealth and opportunity through government service—and conciliated the interests of the Hindus to a far greater degree than the Delhi Sultanate had. Mughal emperors fulfilled their role as Indian kings by participating in Hindu ceremonies and observances such as the festival of lights (Diwali), the weighing of the ruler in gold, which was then given away in alms, ritual feeding of brahmins, "giving darshan" or showing the royal self to the public at regular intervals, and the patronage of religious scholarship and literature, including translations of the Ramayana and Mahabharata.[32]

They left an indelible imprint on India, including architectural masterpieces that still stand and continue to be admired, such as the Red Fort in Delhi and the exquisite Taj Mahal in Agra, built of white marble and set in a formal garden of the Central Asian style that the Mughals brought to India (Figure 16).

The first six Mughals, listed here, represent the period of the empire's foundation and greatness:

Babur	1526–1530
Humayun	1530–1556
Akbar	1556–1605
Jahangir	1605–1628
Shah Jahan	1628–1658
Aurangzeb	1658–1707

The name Mughal is the same as Mongol. The Mughals of India traced their descent from two famous Mongol emperors, Chingiz Khan (or Genghiz Khan), a thirteenth-century pagan Mongol, and Timur, a fourteenth-century Muslim one. Timur, who had rampaged across Iran, Central Asia, Russia, and the Middle East, also sacked Delhi in 1398 but then withdrew from India. His incursion weakened the power of the Delhi Sultanate and introduced a small population of Mongol military

FIGURE 16 Taj Mahal, Agra, 1632–1647

men into the North Indian scene. Babur, who laid the foundation of Mughal ascendancy, had an illustrious family tree but a very modest patrimony, consisting of a small territory in Ferghana in Central Asia. Circumstances and temperament made him a military adventurer, and adversity directed him toward India. What he wanted was a kingdom in Central Asia, and he failed in three attempts to capture Samarkand, the prestigious throne city of his ancestor Timur, before turning his attention to the South. What he created was a state that straddled the Hindu Kush mountains to the west of the Indus Valley, with one foot in Afghanistan and another in India, more or less like that of the Kushanas or the Hunas before him. Successive Mughal emperors lost ground in Central Asia while extending the empire more deeply into India, with the results shown in Map 7.

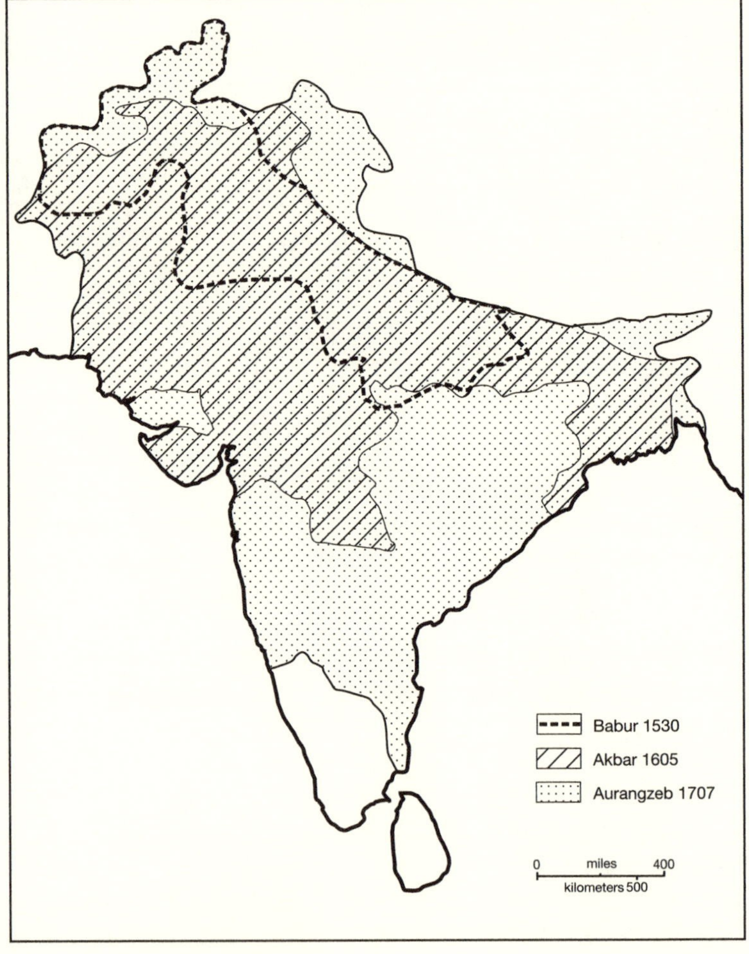

MAP 7 The Mughal empire

The era of gunpowder warfare had begun in India before Babur, but his mastery of artillery was certainly an important part of his advantage at the battle of Panipat in 1526, when he defeated the Sultan of Delhi. He also had the advantage that all Central Asian invaders of India held: an abundant supply of horses and able cavalrymen. Babur did not long outlive his victory, and although the Sultanate had been defeated, the Turkish nobility and Rajput warrior lineages were far from content to accept Mughal rule. Indeed, after Babur's death his son, Humayun, was expelled from India by Sher Shah of the Suri family, an Afghan nobleman who had briefly joined Babur's camp. He revived the power of the Sultanate for a brief, brilliant reign of only five years, before he died in an accidental explosion of gunpowder. The troubled succession to Sher Shah created an opening for Humayun, and after an exile of fifteen years, he succeeded in restoring Mughal rule of India with help from the Persian king.

Humayun's son Akbar is the greatest of the Mughal rulers (Figure 17). He was the consolidator of the empire, who secured North India and gave his empire access to the sea by conquests on the western coast, and was the architect of its cosmopolitan policy. Officers of the government, whether military or civil, held a *mansab* or rank, which bound them, in theory at least, to supply a certain number of men and horses to the military service of the state, and gave them rights to draw revenue from certain lands assigned to them (called a *jagir*) out of which this force was to be maintained by the mansab-holder or *mansabdar*. Akbar arranged these ranks in thirty-three grades, from commanders of ten to commanders of ten thousand, with the highest ranks reserved for members of the royal family. The imperial service was opened to Hindus, and Akbar made a point of including Rajput warrior lineages in his government and forming marriage alliances with them by taking Rajput wives. A single service was formed, and the emphasis was on ability, for the mansabs and the emoluments that went with them were not hereditary, and the sons of mansabdars had to prove themselves in the lower ranks. The system was meant to prevent the growth of a landed aristocracy (in which it achieved only partial success), by the rule that one could not hold a jagir in the region to which one was posted, by moving officeholders from one post to another in the course of a lifetime, and by the nonhereditary nature of the service. One effect of this policy was that Mughal officeholders, knowing they could not pass on their estates to their sons, spent their fortunes on the building

FIGURE 17 Akbar inspects the building of a palace

of elaborate and beautiful tombs, many of which survive as monuments of the exquisite architectural style of the age.

In keeping with this inclusiveness in the government apparatus, Akbar also explored the content of the many religions of his people, and of other countries as well. He was strongly attached to the Sufi, mystical form of Islam that had many broad features that resonated with

Hinduism, at least with its monistic form. He summoned to a kind of royal seminar on comparative religion scholars and teachers of Islam, Hinduism, Jainism, and Zoroastrianism, as well as Christian missionaries from the Portuguese trading station of Goa, to explain their systems and question them, and came to believe that there was something good in all of them. He retained his own ancestral Islam, and formed an imperial circle of discipleship that became known as the Din-i-Ilahi or "Divine Faith," a devotional practice made up of elements from Islam and the other religions that he had interrogated, plus ideas of sacral kingship circulating internationally. The eclectic, inclusive character of Din-i-Ilahi mirrored the ethnic cosmopolitanism of the empire. Akbar also abolished the poll tax on non-Muslims (the *jizya*), further narrowing the differences among his subjects.

The reigns of Jahangir and Shah Jahan saw the further rise of Mughal power, although Kandahar in Afghanistan was lost to the Persians in 1622, thus confining Mughal power to India. It was certainly one of the largest and wealthiest empires in the world of Islam, larger than the Persian and Ottoman Turkish empires of the time. Shah Jahan's Taj Mahal is a superb culmination of Mughal imperial architecture. With the growth of European trade, silver from the mines of the New World found its way to India, where it was turned into silver rupee coins. This was one result of the first globalization that integrated the world economy; Mughal India was part of the larger world that Islam had built by drawing disparate regions together, and of a still larger one that was coming into existence.

The declining years of Shah Jahan were troubled by a fratricidal war among his four sons, of which the principal antagonists were Dara Shukoh and Aurangzeb. These two embodied opposing tendencies of Islamic religion in Mughal India. Dara Shukoh, who was his father's choice to succeed him, had Akbar's passion for studying all the religions, and commissioned the translation into Persian of the *Atharva Veda* and some of the Upanishads, with the help of pandits. Aurangzeb, by contrast, was personally drawn to a deeply pious and austere Sunni Islam, to the point of banishing music from the court.

Aurangzeb won the contest and went on to rule for fifty-eight years. He was a very able ruler and military leader, and in a sense his reign was a huge success, for he succeeded, in a long and protracted war, in conquering the smaller states of the Deccan and bringing them under the power of the Mughals. After his death, however, Mughal power shrank drastically as his former nobility and allies waxed powerful at Mughal expense. How do we explain this decline?

Many scholars have argued that a large part of the collapse was due to Aurungzeb's personal preference for an austere form of Islam, which constituted a withdrawal from the cosmopolitan policies of his predecessors and alienated non-Muslims of all kinds. However, this explanation does not take account of the continuing presence of large numbers of Hindus in the Mughal service, including some of the leading generals, and of the continuing support by Aurungzeb of Hindu and other non-Muslim religious institutions. It is true that the Sikhs, to whom Akbar had given the plot of land where they built their Golden Temple (in Amritsar), had mixed relations with the Mughal rulers, and were turned into enemies when Aurungzeb killed the ninth guru, Teg Bahadur; his son and successor, Guru Govind, transformed the Sikhs into a formidable anti-Mughal military force. The Maratha peasantry of Maharashtra under their leader Shivaji, who had been a Mughal ally, grew to become a major continental power feeding on the declining Mughal Empire after Aurungzeb largely because Aurungzeb had missed the opportunity of keeping Shivaji on his side. In other words, missed opportunities rather than Aurangzeb's personal religious tendencies seem to have been the larger factor in the subsequent Mughal decline. Indeed, Aurangzeb had Hindu generals and continued the Mughal patronage of Hindu temples.

These disaffections in the North were taking place while Mughal power was finally successful in the Deccan, destroying the provincial sultanates of that region and placing their fragments into a Mughal *subah* (province). However, the governor Aurungzeb put in charge quickly became independent, and formed a dynastic line that ruled until the 1940s (the Nizams of Hyderabad). The fragmentation of Mughal power following the conquest of the Deccan was a replay of what had happened under the Turkish sultans. The costly and difficult conquests that successfully spread the power of the Turks and the Mughals to the greater part of India both required a concentration of resources in the Deccan, to the neglect of the economic heartland of empire in the north, the Doab and the Ganga. The successful military men and allies were enriched and empowered by the successful conquest of the Deccan to break away and make states of their own. In both cases it seems that forces leading to fragmentation were brought to a head by the very success of the conquest itself.

After the death of Aurangzeb the power of the Mughals declined and contracted to the environs of Delhi and Agra, although an aura of their imperial greatness remained through the long Mughal twilight of the eighteenth and early nineteenth centuries. As we shall see in Chapter 10, a rebellion of British-Indian soldiers in 1857–1858 swelled into a large insurgency aiming to drive the British colonial rulers into the sea. It is highly significant that the insurgents of different religions and communities rallied around the Mughal emperor in Delhi. In doing so they demonstrated vividly their belief that the Mughals were the legitimate ruling power in India and the British were not. Indians attributed to Mughal rulers eminence and authority even after the empire's effective military power had shrunk to nothing.

By its community-making power, Islam created a connection among Arab, Iranian, and Turkish people. When we ask what the relation of Islam to Indian Civilization is over the thousand years and more of their connection, the most salient feature of that history, perhaps, is the role of Iran in shaping Islamic culture.

Iran was India's cultural cousin in Vedic times, and the Iranian elite that became Muslim and gave Islamic culture its new shape in Abbasid times had been Zoroastrians, Buddhists, and Manicheans in religion, themselves having Indic features. They carried aspects of those traditions over into Islam after their conversion. We find in Iran and India Islamic equivalents of the Indic ideas of rebirth, of time cycles, and of the incarnation (avatar) of the divine in the world, such that, for example, Ismaili missionaries told their Indian converts that the fourth caliph, Ali, was the tenth avatar of Vishnu.[33]

This Iranian elite class, moreover, entertained ideas of sacred kingship embodied in the history of the pre-Islamic kings of Iran, which got blended with the tradition of the ancient prophets of the Bible in their Islamic form, ending with Muhammad. Under Islam, Iranian kingship was a second center of the sacred, parallel to the lineage of the prophets. Sacred kingship of this kind had two features that made it irreducible in a direct way to Islamic law and the religious philosophy of kingship found in the law. First, like all kings, Turkish and Mughal rulers were above the competing religions and had to arbitrate among them. There was, therefore, a continuing incentive to preserve public order and not multiply causes of civil strife and disaffection with the government. Second, the Persian conceptions of sacred kingship they brought to India were universalistic in vision and appealed to a realm of ideas that overspilled the boundaries between religions, especially ideas of astrology, millennialism, time cycles, and the interpretation of omens. Here again India and Iran were cultural cousins, Iran being a conduit of astrology and astronomy from Mesopotamia and the Hellenistic world for India, and India returning the favor at other times. Astrology in particular was a "science" that circulated freely among Muslims, Christians, and Hindus, from India to Europe.[34]

It is a mistake, therefore, to view the relation of Islam to Indian civilization through a "clash of civilizations" model, with its assumption of mutual exclusion, as if they were closed systems. On the contrary, Islam developed its distinctive Perso-Islamic culture within the penumbra of Indian Civilization, in Abbasid times. Part of the appeal of Islam to Indians was that aspects of it were already familiar, such as sacred kingship and the devotionalism and mysticism of Sufism; aspects of it, indeed, were Indian, although in a new configuration that gave prominence to the tradition of the prophets.

CHAPTER 10

Europeans

European Merchants
British Rule
India and European Civilization

India had been deeply affected by the astonishingly successful expansion of Islam and Islamic states across much of Europe and Asia from about the eighth century. This expansion had created a cosmopolitan world of trade, diplomacy, taste, and knowledge that penetrated and blended, in different ways, with Indian Civilization, drawing on it and adding to it. It was through the Islamic world that Indian ideas and inventions reached Europe in late medieval times, including what Abu Fazl called India's three contributions to the world: the game of chess; the collection of folktales and animal fables called the *Panchatantra;* and the zero, that is, the place-notation of the number system—what in English is called the Arabic numerals, although they derive, ultimately, from India.

Some eight centuries after the Asia-wide expansion of Islam had begun, from the time of Columbus, European nations began an expansion of their powers, which crossed Asia and Africa, and encompassed the New World, as well. It was a truly worldwide expansion, broader than that of Islam, but made possible by building on the accumulated geographical knowledge of the Muslim countries, and by new technologies of navigation. Indian Civilization was again profoundly affected, although by different means and in novel ways.

European Merchants

Before the worldwide expansion of European power, for medieval Christian Europe, India was the edge of the earth, a distant horizon, a strange land where things were very different. The strangeness of India for Europeans could take monstrous or pleasant forms virtually without limit, because they were unchecked by experience. It was commonly stated in medieval bestiaries or books about animals, for example, that the elephant had pillar-like legs that lacked knee joints, and had to sleep standing up, leaning against a tree, because it could not get up if it fell down. It was said that hunters would saw a tree half through in hopes that an elephant would lean against it and fall, unable to rise again.

Images of India in medieval Europe have a dream-like character, but they were not free inventions of the mind and, on the contrary, had their own history. The legacy of Greco-Roman antiquity was one great fund of such images, and from it medieval Europeans drew the most exotic pictures of India. Thus in the *Nuremberg chronicle,*[35] for example, published in 1493 at the beginning of print in the West and at the outset of the great voyages that would take European merchant venturers to India, we find pictures of fantastic races of people in India

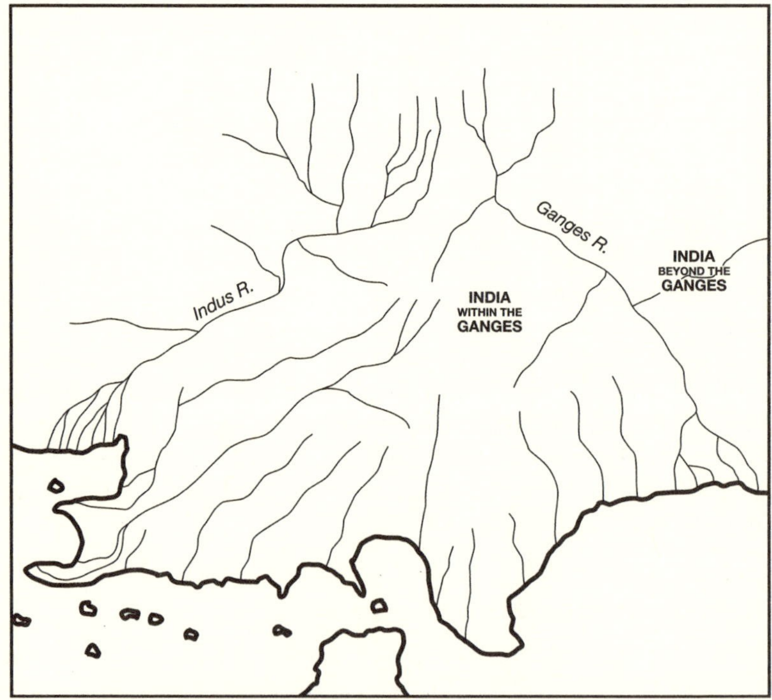

MAP 8 India in Ptolemy

such as the mouthless people who are nourished by smells and the backward-foot people, that go way back to the hearsay reports of the Greek writer Ctesias in the fifth century BCE (see Chapter 4). Besides images of repellant, freakish strangeness, Europeans also entertained pleasing images of India as a land of luxury and wealth, and the source of desirable and expensive things such as diamonds, silk, exotic animals, and spices. This reputation for wealth was certainly a function of the trade of ancient times, for, as noted earlier, only the most precious commodities could repay the very high costs of transportation over so long a distance. India had been a source of exotic and expensive items of trade since the time of Solomon in the Bible, and it was a supplier of luxuries to Rome in ancient times, such as ivory, silk, and precious stones, to a degree that caused alarm because of the drain of wealth it entailed, as we saw in Chapter 8. Indian goods again made their way to Europe as its economy recovered from the collapse of the Roman Empire and slowly began to grow in the course of the Middle Ages. Now, however, India was a part of the large Asian trading world created

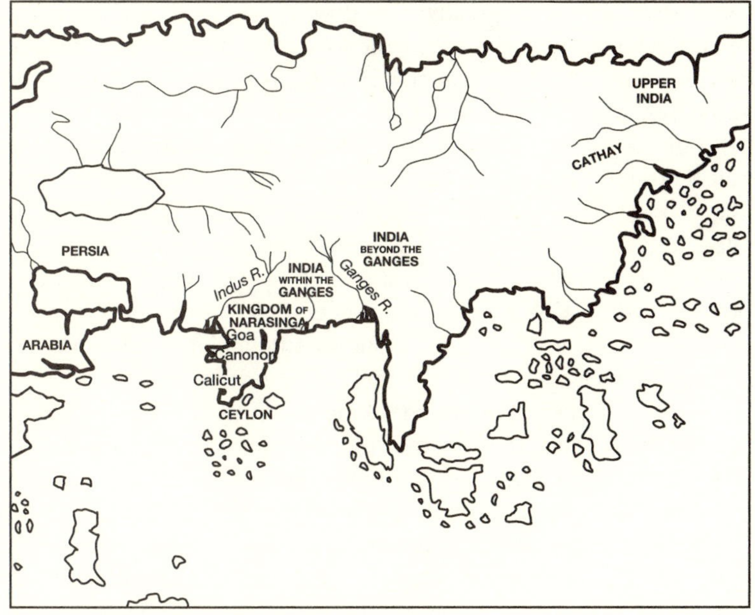

MAP 9 India as seen from Europe, 1545

with the spread of Islam, and Muslim merchants and states now intervened between Europe and India. The creation (in 1299 CE) and spread of the Ottoman Empire in Turkey, and its revival of the institution of the caliph as head of the worldwide community of Islam, further solidified Muslim centrality to the trade of Eurasia. The Islamic countries, unlike those of Europe, had direct knowledge of India and a vastly superior and more rational understanding of the geography of Eurasia developed through the trade, exploration, and conquests of Islamic forces in India and elsewhere. Europeans drew on this fund of geographical knowledge and built on it from experience as their own trade grew and expanded to India and beyond, and the real India began to come into focus.

Venice made its fortune through this trade in precious goods from the Muslim east, but other European nations and their merchants soon were searching for passages to India that would bypass the Muslims. Columbus surmised that he could reach India by sailing west around the world, and when he reached the New World he thought he was in India. This supposition was assisted by two features of early printed maps of the world, deriving from the geography of Ptolemy (c. 150 CE). On the one hand, there was no effective means of determining longitude, and world maps based on Ptolemy greatly overestimate the east–west dimension of the Eurasian landmass. By putting the coast of Asia too far east of Europe, one could infer that the distance westward from Europe to Asia, across the Atlantic Ocean, is not very great. The other feature of these maps is that countries are named but no boundaries are drawn around them, and India tends to sprawl across Asia eastward to the coast. In Ptolemy's map (Map 8) India proper is called "India within the Ganges," and something called "India beyond the Ganges" is the name for Southeast Asia (the Ganga River was thought to flow due south, separating the two Indias), and in northern China one finds "upper India"; India is practically a name for Asia as a whole. Map 9 shows a Ptolemaic map of 1545 with improved knowledge of India due to European voyages.[36]

Spain soon lay claim to the Americas and the Philippines, but Portugal made the first effective explorations in the other direction, of the southern route around Africa to the coast of India, beginning with the voyage of Vasco da Gama in 1498 (Figure 18). For about a century Portugal dominated the European trade of Asia. The Portuguese created a watery empire of trade, consisting of a few small land bases established by treaty with the local powers, reaching from Goa on the west coast of India to Macao in the south of China. Portugal enforced its domination

FIGURE 18 Vasco da Gama

of the seaborne trade through a far-flung network of armed ships that required all ships of other countries to take a *cartaz* or charter from the Portuguese and trade only with the Portuguese in certain items. In this way Portugal came to dominate the trade in spices, and much else besides. In exchange the Portuguese brought American crops to Asia that had a lasting impact: potatoes and corn (maize) that allowed farming in soils and seasons where it was otherwise difficult; new luxuries like tobacco and pineapple; and two foods so completely integrated into Indian cooking that it is hard to imagine that they are really fairly recent introductions: tomatoes and chili peppers.[37] As we saw in Chapter 9, the Portuguese played an important role in the success of the South Indian empire of Vijayanagara by supplying it with horses, which were very scarce in the south and badly needed for warfare against their northern neighbors.

The Portuguese brought Catholic Christianity with them to India, and Catholic missionaries from various countries who set about learning Indian languages and making converts, and establishing the Pope's supremacy over the ancient community of Thomas Christians in South India, who claimed to have been led to Christianity by the apostle Thomas. The missionary enterprise was pulled in different directions by contrary forces promoting assimilation with Indian culture and isolation from it. At the one extreme, the attempt of Jesuits to present Christianity in a form acceptable to Indians led to the work of the Italian Jesuit Roberto Nobili, who adopted the dress and way of life of a brahmin renouncer. This impulse was canceled by Rome, however, in the upshot of a "quarrel of the rites," in China as well as India, and the suppression of the Jesuit order by the Pope somewhat after. At the other extreme was the Inquisition instituted at Goa to enforce orthodoxy among Catholics, in response to anxiety that lingering Hindu beliefs and practices were compromising the purity of Christianity in India. During the heyday of Portuguese control of the India trade, the Portuguese language was widely used on both coasts of India as a medium of trade, and a sprinkling of Portuguese words in Indian languages, such as Hindi *almari* (Indian English *almirah*, a wardrobe or chest of drawers) and *tauliya* (towel), persist as vestiges of that period.

The ambitions of Spain and Portugal soon clashed, and their rivalry was resolved by the Pope, who drew a vertical line on the globe through South America that awarded Portugal everything eastward of Brazil and Spain everything to the west of it. Other European nations and their merchant companies began to push their way forward, however, and intra-European rivalry proved a powerful force in the expansion of European economic and political power around the world, beginning about 1600. East India companies were formed by the English, the Dutch, the Danes, the French, and some others, with monopoly rights over their nation's trade with India. The most effective of these were the Dutch and the English, and they and the Portuguese formed a three-cornered struggle for the India trade. The ultimate outcome of the struggle was that the Portuguese were confined to a few small trading stations on the Indian coast, the Dutch concentrated their power on Indonesia and the Spice Islands, and the English came to dominate the trade of India itself.

In many ways the European trade with India, leading up to colonial rule, was continuous with the old Roman trade, in the sense that India supplied Europe with rare commodities such as spices and gems, and luxurious manufactured goods, especially fabrics, in exchange for silver and gold. But while these terms of trade were in broad terms stable over a very long period, the trading methods of the period of European expansion were quite new, involving the creation of merchant companies that had monopoly powers of their country's Asian trade and arms to protect and enforce them on their rivals. These companies did not promote free and peaceful trade but instead monopolies maintained by force. They entered into political relations with Indian powers to establish and maintain small enclaves on land in which to collect tradable goods for shipment homeward, and to sell goods shipped out from Europe. East India trading companies of the different European nations had to be political actors, negotiating relations with Indian rulers, and not just commercial ventures. These circumstances led to European rule of Indian territory and people by a body of foreign merchants, something entirely novel in India's history.

British Rule

The rivalry of European nations among themselves was a driving force for the international expansion of European imperial power in the seventeenth century and after, and these rivalries were projected on the whole world. The rivalry of England and France especially had momentous consequences in the middle of the eighteenth century: the extinction of French rule in Canada by the British; the revolt of the thirteen colonies of America from British rule with French assistance; and the establishment of British territorial rule in the eastern part of India (Bengal). Conquest of Indian territories came about when armies of the British East India Company and its Indian allies fought the armies of the French East India Company and its Indian allies—the beginnings of the British Indian Empire.

In the course of the warfare in Europe and Canada of the French and English nations, the French and English East India Companies entered the fray by fighting one another in India and implicating their Indian allies in the struggle. Thus in India the rivalry between the two was not carried out by the governments of the two countries but by joint-stock corporations of merchants and the Indian princes who gave them trading privileges and leased them small patches of territory on the coast for their trading posts. These "factories," as they were called, were not places of manufacture but essentially warehousing facilities, so called because they were governed by someone called a "factor" or commercial agent of the company. Some factories were fortified and protected by Indian soldiers under European officers. These armed forces of the merchant companies now became war-making entities that drew Indian governments and their armies into the commercial and national struggle between the British and the French. The upshot of a long and complicated struggle was that the British East India Company army, under Robert Clive, defeated the Mughal governor of Bengal, Siraj ud Daula, at Plassey in 1757. Clive's victory was secured by a prior secret agreement with two of Siraj ud Daula's generals, who held back their armies, and Clive replaced Siraj ud Daula with one of them, Mir Jafar, as Bengal's governor. Within a few years the East India Company became the effective co-ruler of Bengal, and was given a charter authorizing its new powers by the Mughal emperor in Delhi. He granted it the *diwani,* or fiscal administration of the country, in concert with the existing political and military administrator. The situation was highly anomalous; a merchant company from England had become a territorial ruler in Bengal under a grant of authority from the emperor of India. In a sense the East India Company was a Mughal vassal, but that was only the legal clothing in which the military power and diplomatic maneuvering of the Company was dressed.

In later years the British liked to say that they acquired an empire in India "in a fit of absent-mindedness." The process was not so thoughtless and innocent as this phrase wants us to believe. The Company had in fact aimed at territorial dominion, following the Dutch model, in the past, although without success, and had the Dutch example before it in Ceylon (Sri Lanka), where the Dutch governed large lowland territories as the kingdom of Ceylon retreated to the mountainous interior. But the immediate cause of British rule in India was the worldwide struggle of England and France, which the English and French East India Companies joined in, the consequences of which—the diwani of Bengal—were unanticipated.

In any case the transformation of the Company was profound, from a trading company with negligible territorial holdings on the coast of India for the purposes of turning a profit, to a governing power ruling vast and increasing agrarian territory from which it had to collect taxes and over which it had to maintain law and order. It was the beginning of the period of Company rule, which lasted for about a hundred years, from 1765, when the Company acquired administrative powers in Bengal (the diwani), and ended in 1858 when, at the close of the Rebellion of 1857, the British government put an end to Company rule and imposed Crown rule, which is to say, direct rule of British India by the British government. Crown rule also lasted about a hundred years, from 1858 to independence in 1947.

An utterly new kind of empire in India was created by the British East India Company. Previous foreign rulers had come with land armies as conquering powers; this one had evolved from trading company to territorial ruler. Previous invaders came and settled in India, making it their home and the home of their descendants; the British sent out its young men, aged seventeen or eighteen, to be civil servants and military officers, but they all intended to retire to Britain at the end of their careers, and considered Britain their home—those who remained in India were mostly the rather large number of Britons who died of illness before their time and were buried there. Although ideas of colonizing India with European settlers, on the model of America, Canada, and South Africa, were floated from time to time, the East India Company strongly resisted. It wanted to avoid creating situations of conflict between a large European population with ideas of its own superiority and the much vaster population of Indians, which would unsettle British rule. For the same reason the Company assiduously prevented the admission of nonofficial Europeans, including missionaries. Indeed, the numbers of Europeans in the British Indian government were kept very small—three to five thousand in the civil service, more in the army—supervising very large numbers of Indian employees. The connectedness with the home country depended on sailing vessels of improved design and speed, but the voyage often took six months. Nevertheless the relatively faster means of communication made for an altogether new kind of empire in which small numbers of East India Company officials were born, schooled, and (if they were lucky to live long enough) buried in Britain but spent most of their adult life in India, participating in its governance or the Company's commerce, under the direction of Company headquarters, East India House, in faraway London. For all these reasons the political, institutional, and religious character of India's relation to Europe through the agency of British rule was shaped quite differently from its relation to the Islamic world. At the same time, India as a colony of the growing British empire was under very different conditions of rule than the British settler colonies of Canada, the thirteen colonies of America, Australia, New Zealand, the West Indies and, later, South Africa.

The Company's military successes in India were accomplished by large numbers of Indian soldiers under British command, and smaller numbers of British soldiers. The means of success lay not so much in military technology, which was not very different from that of the Mughals and other Indian powers, which were fully in the gunpowder era, using artillery and matchlocks or flintlocks. The European advantage lay in the rapidity and massing of firepower achieved through close formations of well-drilled men. The new organizational techniques yielded, at the beginning, outsized victories in the sense that smaller forces under British command bested much larger Indian armies. This advantage could not last forever, and indeed Indian princes very quickly learned to make use of European officers (especially those left unemployed by the defeat of Napoleon) to train their own officers and troops in the European techniques of battlefield organization. As they did so, ever-larger British and allied forces were needed to defeat their opponents in India.[38]

The other contributing factor to British military success in India was the alliances that the British made with Indian rulers against other Indian opponents. Such allies retained the rule of their own countries throughout the period of British rule, although at a price, which included leaving their foreign affairs in the hands of the British-Indian government while contributing to the maintenance of the Indian army, sometimes through ceding territories to pay their obligations. These "princely states" remained formally outside British India, and managed their own regimes of taxation and administration, and their own armed forces, but each of them had a British "resident" who kept them apprised of British policy, and often interfered with the internal governance and the succession to the kingdom. The Indian princes played a large role in the system of alliances that extended and consolidated British rule in India, but over time their political functions shrank, although the British came to regard their military forces as a valuable and inexpensive supplement to the army of British India and in the world wars. Their presence throughout the two centuries of British rule gave the political map of British India a patchwork quality, with large areas of direct British rule interrupted by the princely states, some of them large as Britain itself, some smaller than an American county (Map 10). In aggregate the princely states covered a third of the landmass of India, right up to the end of British rule.

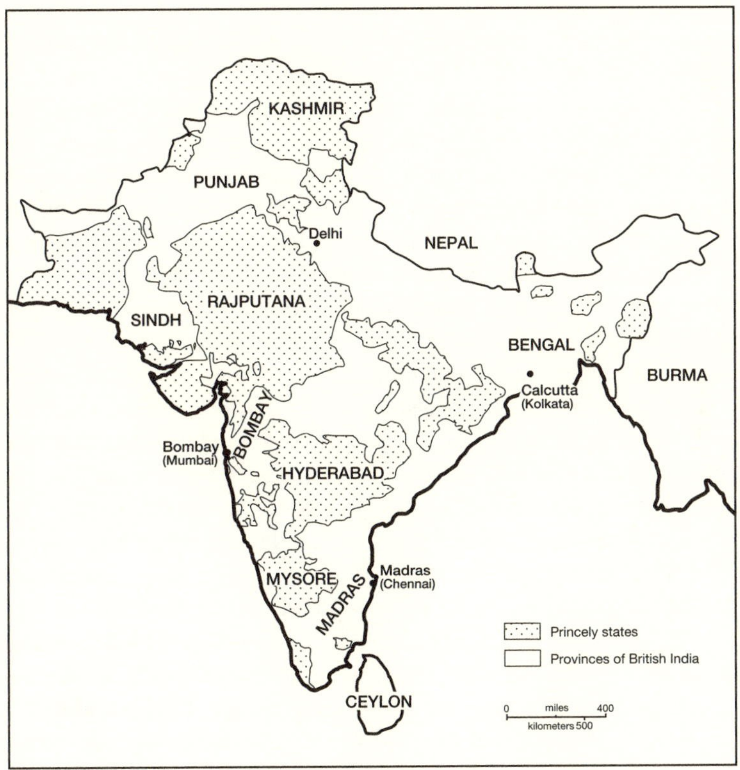

MAP 10 British India in 1939

In 1857 a mutiny of Indian *sepoys* or soldiers against their British officers in Meerut, near Delhi, spread and morphed into a broad rebellion against British rule that engulfed much of North India. Causes of discontent were many, but the immediate one was the introduction of the Enfield rifle, the cartridges of which were greased with animal fat, and the belief that they were greased with beef tallow and pig fat gave offense to Hindu and Muslim sepoys alike. Army mutinies had occurred before, and been contained, notably the Vellore mutiny of 1806 in South India. That mutiny, too, had in it an element of feeling that religion was under attack, in the form of orders imposing a new uniform code that included European hats and forbid beards, earrings, and marks of religious identity on the forehead. Whereas the mutinies at Vellore and other garrisons were quickly suppressed and did not spread, the 1857 mutiny and the resentments out of which it originated grew and fused with the bitterness that Indian princely allies felt over their treatment by the British and the continuing loss of their powers. One of the chief causes of alarm was the policy of "lapse," by which a princely state was dissolved if there was no direct heir, a policy that, in the long run, would lead to the winding up of all the princely states and their disappearance into British India. The mutiny quickly boiled into a full-scale military insurrection attempting to restore the old regime of India prior to the British, the regime of the Mughal, the ruler of the Marathas called the Peshwa, and the Indian princes, and to drive the British out of India. The insurgents took Delhi and declared the Mughal emperor Bahadur Shah II emperor of India, as indeed, he always had been in a formal sense, remembering that British India began when the Mughal emperor granted the diwani of Bengal to the Company. The Rebellion also spread to Kanpur, where it was led by Nana Sahib, discontented son of the last Peshwa, to Lucknow, and to parts of central India where the Rani (queen) of Jhansi led a heroic resistance. The mutiny spread through army garrisons in various parts of North India, but garrisons elsewhere remained loyal to the British and were used to put it down. After a year the mutiny was finally suppressed. It was a war of independence, led by the army and the elites of the old regime of the princes, but it was not unified. The Rebellion failed, and India's independence from British rule was to come nearly a century later, under the leadership of quite new elites with quite different ideas of the nation. Although the Rebellion of 1857 did not achieve India-wide extension of its power, it was India-wide in its visibility, and it served to advertise and make vivid the disaffection of many Indians from the colonial regime.

The aftermath of the failed Rebellion was a complex mixture of repression and conciliation by the British. The mutineers themselves, at least those thought to be directly involved in the killing of Britons, were harshly and publicly punished, some of them being tied to the ends of cannon and blown in half. The Mughal Empire was formally abolished, Bahadur Shah being exiled to Burma (Myanmar) to end his days there. Company rule was also brought finally to an end when, in a proclamation of November 1, 1858, Queen Victoria formally assumed the government of India, which in effect meant that India was now ruled directly by Parliament in London rather than by the Company under a charter from Parliament. The royal proclamation, in offering assurances that Indian religions would not be interfered with and that the rights and territory of the princely states would not be encroached on, identified religious alarm over British attempts to reform Indian society and the discontent of the allies as the principal causes of the insurrection, and seemed to abandon the reform program for Indian society formulated in the 1830s. The army was reorganized. In India there had always been an Indian army with British officers and Indian noncommissioned officers and sepoys, as well as a British army with British officers and troops. Now the number of British officers in the Indian army was increased, and the size of the British army was increased as well. Perhaps the most important outcome was the bitterness of feeling that divided Britons and Indians as a result of the killings of British civilians besieged by the insurrectionists and the harsh punishments that followed. Henceforth, resistance to British rule was to take new forms under new leadership, inspired by a new goal—to turn India into a nation-state like those of Europe and the Americas.

India and European Civilization

British colonial rule was the means by which India came into close contact with the civilization of Europe, and the specifics of that rule shaped the ways in which India was affected by Europe.

It was only gradually that the British developed policies that promoted the introduction of aspects of European civilization in India. The initial conditions of British rule all favored the opposite policy, namely, one of minimal of interference with the customs and traditions of the Indians. The British in India were the servants of a joint stock company that was there to make a profit for its shareholders in Britain, not to undertake costly and profitless projects for the Europeanization of Indian society. Its government was minimal, and provided little beyond a law-and-order function; it had, for example, to be forced by the British Parliament to set aside the pitifully small sum of 100,000 rupees for education and the revival of learning. It was very much a government on the cheap, and took no responsibility for the education, reform, and uplift of the people. Moreover, it was believed that British rule would not last long and its tenure could be cut short if it provoked Indian unrest by taking measures offensive to Indians. Given that foreign rule is inescapably irksome and unwelcome, the object of government was to "lessen the weight of the chain by which the natives are held in subjection," in the words of Warren Hastings, the first governor-general—to make its rule as light a burden as possible in every matter that did not touch the profit of the Company and the security of its rule. This mindset had several policy outcomes, the most telling of which concerned religion, the family, and land revenue.

Catholic missionaries, especially Jesuits, had long been resident in India and promoted the spread of Christianity, with the active assistance of the Portuguese. One of the most successful missionary ventures was the production of an abundance of Christian writings in Tamil by the Italian Jesuit Constantius Beschi, who became a virtuoso in that language. The Protestants were slower to get involved. The first were the Danes, at their trading stations in South India (Tranquebar) and Bengal (Serampore, near Calcutta). Lutheran missionaries from Halle, in Germany, were patronized by the Danish king and formed a long and continuing connection with South India.

But the East India Company prohibited missionary activity in its territories, on grounds that it would antagonize Indians, Hindu and Muslim, and so jeopardize its operations. Thus the first American missionary to sail out of New England after the War of 1812 to promote Christianity in India, Adoniram Judson, was clapped in jail when he reached Madras, and had to turn his attentions to Burma instead. The ban on missions certainly removed a potential source of dissatisfaction of Indians with British rule, but it was intensely criticized in England, so it was not maintained without cost, especially with the rising tide of evangelical religion in England in the opening years of the nineteenth century. Nevertheless the ban lasted many decades until pro-missionary opinion in England successfully pressured Parliament to end it when the East India Company's charter was renewed in 1813. By that time British

Baptist missionaries, Carey, Marshman, and Ward, had been working out of Danish Serampore (Srirampur), near Kolkata, with some success, long before the Church of England had missions in the field. Although the numbers of conversions were tiny in relation to the whole population of India, the missions had a number of significant effects, most notably through their schools, but also through their critiques of Hinduism, as we shall see.

Although the Company's policy of keeping missionaries out had at last to give way, its noninterference stance toward the family had consequences that last to this day. In England, matters of family law were adjudicated in ecclesiastical courts of the Church of England, and in India the colonial government, with the English pattern in mind, undertook at an early stage to recognize in India a distinct Hindu law and Mohammedan or Muslim law governing matters of marriage and inheritance in its courts, whereas criminal and contract law were made uniform for all Indians. Thus in family matters the colonial regime perpetuated the authority of the ancient Sanskrit law books (Dharmashastra) for Hindus and the Sharia law of the Islamic jurists for Muslims, and if anything the authority of these ancient texts became greater, insofar as it tended to replace local customary practices. The British government was wary about interfering with these bodies of law, and legislated on family matters in only a very limited way. One of the consequences was that at a time when the possibility of civil marriage (i.e., marriage outside of religion) was being invented in Europe, there was and remains limited scope for civil marriage in India and most marriages are performed by religious authorities. Although Parliament in independent India has taken charge of creating new laws for marriage and inheritance for Hindus and others, Muslim law in India remains a separate domain, essentially unchanged from the Anglo-Mohammedan law (as it was called) of the colonial period. The Indian Parliament, with its Hindu majority, undertook to set aside the authority of the Dharmashastra and legislate on family matters for Hindus, but it has felt it too politically sensitive to interfere with the existing religiously based law for Muslims because of their being in the minority, with the result that there is no uniform law of marriage and inheritance for all Indians. (By contrast, the parliaments of Pakistan and Bangladesh, where Muslims are the majority, have not hesitated to legislate concerning marriage.) This impasse has been a source of continuing friction between Hindus and Muslims in the Republic of India, as the law for

Hindus has been reformed to bring it in line with current sentiment, but the law for Muslims remains in the hands of religious authorities and is deemed unchangeable by Parliament.

Finally, in the matter of land revenue the early tendency of the Company was also in the direction of minimal interference, and it decided on a policy of permanently settling the revenue obligation of large landlords, called *zamindars,* holding hundreds of villages. The idea behind the Permanent Settlement, as it was called, was that the zamindars, having a fixed, unchanging amount of revenue to be paid every year, would be induced to increase the output of agriculture by investing in improvements, because every additional increment of production by the peasantry would yield the zamindar a pure profit that he would not have to share with the government. The Permanent Settlement was also convenient to the British rulers in that it put the burden of collecting revenue from the cultivators on the shoulders of the zamindar, and relieved the government of the obligation to maintain large numbers of petty officials for this purpose.

In various ways the policy stance of minimal interference and no reform came under increasing pressure in the opening decades of the nineteenth century, when various independent forces converged to create an overwhelming British interest in reform of India along European lines. The change began with the land revenue. Because the overwhelming majority of Indians were farmers it was the main form of government income. The way in which agricultural production was taxed had large consequences both for the rulers and the ruled. When territories of the interior of South India fell to the British in 1792, Thomas Munro was one of the army officers involved in surveying the newly acquired tracts and settling the revenue from them. He settled it, not on large landholders or zamindars, but on individual cultivators or *ryots* (Hindi *raiyat*). Through Munro's advocacy the *Ryotwari* system became the standard for future revenue settlements in South India and the region of Mumbai, rather than the *Zamindari* system. It sought to give the cultivator a strong property right in his land and so make the land-owning peasant, not some rich zamindar, into an agent for the improvement of agriculture. This entailed a revolution in government. To hold the individual cultivator responsible to pay the land tax, the government needed an army of petty revenue officers to measure each individual field to assess and collect the taxes, under a British collector appointed in each district of every province. Because these revenue officers had low pay and abundant opportunities for peculation and extortion, the collector was given virtually unlimited powers to investigate and dismiss members of his staff. In addition, whereas the executive powers of collectors were originally separated from the judicial powers of the courts set up by the East India Company, collectors now were given extensive judicial powers as well, which was a substantial departure from British governmental principles of separation of powers between the executive, legislative, and judicial functions. This, then, was the pattern of rural government from then on: a highly paid British collector with great executive and judicial power fielding a lowly paid and numerous army of Indian revenue officials. In this way government reached every cultivator directly and not through the intermediacy of a large land owner.

Besides the reform of land revenue, with its liberal ideology of promoting improvement through private property rights and the incentive of personal gain (under the oversight of a distinctly nonliberal collector), the turn to reform was also promoted by the convergence of two distinct strands of liberal reform coming out of England: Utilitarianism that sought government reform and the evangelical movement that sought social reform. These forces as they concerned India were represented by James Mill, leader of the Utilitarians, and Thomas Babington Macaulay and Charles Trevelyan, who had evangelical connections. They were not natural allies, and in fact Macaulay had published a devastating attack on Mill's famous essay on government. Circumstances brought them together, however, especially in India. Mill greatly favored the Munro system of revenue; Macaulay and Mill promoted education of Indians in English rather than the classical languages of Indian law, Sanskrit, Persian, and Arabic. Both sides promoted a policy stance of changing India for their perception of India's good by the massive introduction of European ideas. The decade of the 1830s was a period of massive reform in England as well, with the broadening of voting rights and the reform of parliamentary government to make it more representative and responsible to the voters. It is a paradox that the great era of liberal reform in England promoted in India the idea of liberalism directed from above by a government that was not responsible to the people it ruled, but rather to the Parliament in faraway Britain, a kind of liberal despotism. This new policy stance was justified by a new theory of government in India. Whereas earlier British rulers in India were under no illusions that they were there for the good of anyone but the stockholders of their company, the new reform-minded rulers persuaded themselves and others that they were there for the good of the Indians, to prepare them for self-rule in some distant future, through a policy of gradual social and political reform toward a European model of civilization.

Over the course of British rule the tide of reform and Europeanization ebbed and flowed. For example, after the Rebellion of 1857 the British concluded that Indian resistance to British rule had been provoked by too much Europeanizing reform and that a more conservative policy was needed to calm Indian fears about their religion and way of life being eroded by government policy. Thus matters of religion and social custom, especially family law, were to be closed off from reform along European lines. Despite this policy, European power and the circulation in India of ideas from Europe created revolutionary effects on Indians. Let us draw up a list of these, which were not always clear-cut and often were contradictory.

As to family and kinship, the impulse to maintain ancient laws of marriage and inheritance perpetuated the existence of separate legal spheres for Hindus and Muslims and, if anything, extended the scope of the Sanskrit shastras and the Muslim Sharia law in Indian society. Thus in the main family and kinship matters remained firmly under religious authority, upheld by government law courts, and were little touched by reform through the making of new law, except through the decisions of judges in lawsuits. In this respect the effect of British rule was deeply conservative. On the other hand, the critique of Hinduism and Islam by Christian missionaries had a strong focus on the family and on the place of women, fastening on such issues as child marriage and the seclusion of women. This missionary critique of Hindu social practices did not create large numbers of conversions to Christianity, but it did provoke a movement among Indians for the reform of family law that issued eventually in important changes, such as a raising of the age of marriage and the equal inheritance of sons and daughters.

It was in the political realm that the effects of European civilization were most deeply felt, because the British, without wishing to, brought before Indians the idea of popular sovereignty as a model of government. The government of India was under the sovereignty of the people of Britain, not of India, and in that sense we could say that with respect to India the government was a despotism, the opposite of the popular sovereignty ideal. Increasingly exposed to European practices and ideas in the newly created colonial institutions of higher education through the English language, Indians could not help learning that popular sovereignty as an ideal was sweeping Europe and the Americas, creating what has since become the international norm for government. Indians had known republican forms of government (*sangha*) in the ancient past, but kingship (*rajya*) had long since won out as the normative form, so that by the time of colonial rule the idea of popular sovereignty was both very old and indeed largely forgotten, and at the same time very new in India. In a sense popular sovereignty was at the heart of the liberal ideology of empire, as Indian self-governance was the endpoint of the idea of British tutelage. However, the idea that the people are the only legitimate source of government authority was certainly in contradiction to the colonial relation, and it soon inspired a movement for national self-government, the first stirrings of which were seen by the middle of the nineteenth century. This led to the nationalist struggle against British rule and, ultimately, independence.

The third main head of the effects of European civilization on India concerns higher learning, science especially, and technology. Here the timing of empire had significant consequences, because just after Britain acquired territorial rule in India it underwent the Industrial Revolution, making it the first industrial country in the world. The effects of the Industrial Revolution profoundly reshaped Britain, and they changed Britain's economic relations with India just as profoundly. Up to about 1800 Europe had paid dearly for luxury goods from India, especially fine textiles of all kinds, and a great many words for textiles came into English from that trade, such as *calico, muslin, chintz,* and *bandana.* The English were great traders of woolen cloth in Europe, but could not sell it in India, and had to acquire New World silver in the Amsterdam markets to trade for Indian textiles. These terms of trade were largely unchanged from the times of the Roman trade with India, in which again India supplied manufactured goods in exchange for coined money. After 1800 the terms of the India trade began to change, and change drastically, as English industrialists in Manchester developed a machine-based textile industry for the manufacture of cotton cloth. This new industry made cotton cloth so cheap that it undercut handloom-made cotton cloth in India, even with the transportation costs of shipping American or Mediterranean cotton to Manchester, and Manchester cloth to India added on. Moreover, British rule ensured that cotton cloth from Manchester met no tariff barriers in India, as it would have if Indians had been ruling their own country. To be sure, the effects of industrialization were also socially disruptive in Britain, whose handloom industry was also destroyed, and whose self-employed weavers lost their livelihood and were forced to become industrial factory workers at a wage. These effects have spread worldwide and could not be stopped, although they could have been slowed and made less harsh in their social effects in India if it had had national self-government. The overall result was that India became a supplier of raw materials and an importer of (now machine-made) manufactured goods, a complete reversal of the former terms of trade. The destruction of the handicraft industry of cloth production was not, however, the end of the story. Over the long run, Indian entrepreneurs, importing English machinery at first, created a machine-based textile industry in India that has since undercut the textile industry of England. Thus the long-term effect has been a spread of the new technology that, under conditions of free trade, favored India's entrepreneurial know-how and its low industrial wages.

The story of textiles is one of the major ways in which new technologies from Europe were dramatically changing India; the introduction of railways was another, which has since become completely domesticated to the Indian scene, and indispensable to the daily life of people everywhere. Indians quickly took to engineering and science and made them their own. India's former advancement in mathematics and astronomy had made a contribution to the scientific eminence that Europe achieved in the Renaissance and provided a fund of knowledge on which Indians could draw in coming to terms with the new science and technology emanating from Europe. India's ancient engagement with science had left an imprint on the Indianate world it created in Central, East, and Southeast Asia, and its engagement with phonology and grammar now shaped Europe through the European study of Sanskrit and the discovery of Indo-European. The exchange of ideas was not an equal one, but it was not all one-sided, either.

In the end, perhaps the profoundest effects of European learning on India lie in the idea of history. European scholarly study of ancient India completely revolutionized the understanding of India's deep past, from its representation in the Mahabharata, the Ramayana and the Puranas, and connected it with the history of the other countries and civilizations of Eurasia. The new history, and the new political ideal of the nation-state, could be combined to create a new idea of India and of its trajectory toward the future, toward independence.

CHAPTER 11

The Nation-State

The Emergence of Indian Nationalism
Gandhi and Jinnah
Partition and Independence

The nation-state is a political idea that has become the international norm in the last few centuries. What do we mean by the nation-state? "Nation" is a word that has been used for a very long time, long before it came to be believed that every nation should have a state of its own. Thus British rulers at the outset thought of the Indians as composing a nation, without believing that nationhood somehow gave Indians a moral claim to be free from foreign rule. However, beginning with the American Revolution in 1776, and then the French Revolution in 1789, the ideal of popular sovereignty was propagated among European peoples; that is, the idea that the will of the people, and not the will of a king, is the proper basis for government and the only legitimate source of law, enacted by representatives of the people in a parliament. Popular sovereignty is the glue that holds together the two pieces that make up the nation-state: If the people are the source of sovereignty, every people or nation should have a state of its own. The ballot box is the means of divining the popular will through election of representatives. This idea ripened and spread during the nineteenth century, and in the twentieth century it became dominant. Thus at the end of World War I, the idea of self-determination, enunciated by Woodrow Wilson at the peace talks, expressed this ideal and served to institutionalize it. The League of Nations and the United Nations are the institutions that, in the twentieth century, enshrined the idea that the normal political units are self-governing nations.

The gradual growth of the nation-state idea affected India profoundly, and stimulated Indian resistance to British rule. The way was prepared by various forms of religious reactions to British rule and European civilization, reactions that took the form of absorbing some of the new political ideas coming out of Europe and the Americas.

The Emergence of Indian Nationalism

Rammohan Roy

Raja Rammohan Roy (1774–1833) is one of the most interesting products of his historical moment, the twilight of the Mughal Empire and the early years of British India (Figure 19). He was a Bengali brahmin whose paternal ancestors had for several generations taken up service to the state under Muslim rulers, not as priests or religious teachers (as were the ancestors on his mother's side) but in a secular capacity. Hence he was educated in Persian and Arabic as preparation for this government service, and in Sanskrit as well. This formation, and his travels through India beyond British rule, made him a scholar and enlightened Indian gentleman of late Mughal type, with a cosmopolitan outlook, holding a strong interest both in the affairs of the world and in the reform of Hinduism. The impulse toward the reform of Hinduism came first, he tells us, through his exposure to Islam and its opposition to the worship of images. He came to advocate against the worship of images in Hinduism in a text he composed at the age of sixteen.

Rammohan Roy at first felt, as he tells us in a brief autobiographical piece, a great aversion to British rule, but he eventually came to believe that, although it was the rule of a foreign power, it "would lead more speedily and surely to the amelioration of the native inhabitants," and took up service to the East India Company.[39] He mastered English and became a forceful and eloquent writer and speaker in a number of causes of social and political reform. The interest he took in Islam then extended to Christianity. He studied the Bible in Hebrew and Greek and wrote a work called "The precepts of Jesus, the guide to peace and happiness" in English, with translations into Bengali and Sanskrit, in which the words of Jesus were presented directly, without historical and miraculous context, as a rational, ethical system—similar to a work Thomas Jefferson wrote at about the same time in faraway America.

Rammohan's conception of the amelioration of the Indians was both political and religious in nature, and his actions, accordingly, involved him in lobbying the government on various issues of political reform, on the one hand, and creating a reformed Hindu religious movement,

FIGURE 19 Rammohan Roy

the Brahma Sabha, on the other. On the political front, for example, his petition against the Jury Act of 1827 eloquently stated the bitter complaint of Indians against a law that introduced religious considerations and European privilege into the English tradition of trial by jury. "Any natives, either Hindu or Muhammadan," he said, "are rendered by this Bill subject to judicial trial by Christians either European or native, while Christians, including native converts, are exempted from the degradation of being tried either by a Hindu or Mussulman juror, however high he may stand in the estimation of society."[40] Toward the end of his life he undertook a voyage to England to communicate his views on the better government of India to Parliament, which was holding hearings on the renewal of the charter of the East India Company. He died in England.

Rammohan Roy promoted social reform in several arenas into which the British government of India, with its noninterventionist philosophy, was reluctant to enter. Most of these had to do with the legal disadvantages suffered by low castes and women in Hindu society. For example, he advocated for the inheritance of family property by women and the remarriage of widows, and against polygamy. Most notably, he was a major voice in the abolition of the practice of *sati* (or *suttee*, as it is often spelled). This practice, by no means common but certainly spectacular, by which a Hindu widow burned herself to death on the funeral pyre of her deceased husband, was an extreme expression of the ideal of eternal fidelity of a woman to her husband. It provoked strong pressure from Christian sentiment in England to abolish sati by act of government, and this act committed the East India Company government of India to an intervention into Hindu custom that it was most reluctant to undertake. Rammohan's advocacy for the abolition of sati took the form of an inquiry into the question of whether it was required by Hindu law, specifically whether it was an injunction of the Veda, and he marshaled Sanskrit texts and Mimamsa principles of interpretation (Chapter 7) to argue that it was not.

This stance on the question of sati was consistent with his idea of the reform of the Hindu religion, and he formulated an interpretation of the history of Hinduism and of India that supported the reform agenda. Rammohan Roy believed that many of the social and religious practices he opposed were corruptions that were not found in the Veda but had crept into Hinduism bit by bit in later periods; and his idea of reform, therefore, was to return to a purified, Vedic or Vedantic form of

Hinduism, reformed of its social abuses and with a minimum of ritual. Thus the critique of Hinduism that he met in Islam and in Christianity became stimuli not for conversion from Hinduism but to the reform of Hinduism, from resources within itself. The form this took was the Brahma Sabha in which recitation of the Veda was the central activity, as distinct from the acts of worship before images in a Hindu temple. More important than the Brahma Sabha itself was the reform idea and the historical conception of Hinduism that it advanced.

Religious Reform

The Brahma Sabha was a small, elite affair confined to Calcutta, and it languished after the death of its founder. But Devendranath Tagore was inspired to develop it into a missionary movement, with the somewhat similar name of the *Brahma Samaj*, with initiation, paid preachers, and a printed journal, the *Tattvabodhini patrika*, to propagate its message. Through these means it quickly spread, opening branches in various parts of Bengal. It never became a mass movement but certainly was a highly visible example and proponent of Hindu reform, dedicated to the idea of a unitary God to be worshipped without images, and to the reform of Hindu social laws and customs. By 1865 the movement had split into two camps, the more extreme of which, under the leadership of Keshab Chandra Sen, took on a more devotionalist, less Sanskritic and brahminical cast and became an effective proponent on the national stage for social reform. It played a large role in the passing of legislation abolishing child marriage and polygamy, and in giving legal sanction to the remarriage of widows and creating a window for civil marriage, albeit a tiny one, for those who did not belong to any organized religion.

The Brahma Samaj had some India-wide visibility and even opened branches in Madras, Bombay, and the Punjab. Although it remained largely a Bengali movement, its influence spread beyond Bengal, especially in the large cities of British India and among the classes of professional people most exposed to the new European ideas. In Bombay a somewhat similar movement was formed, the Prarthana Samaj, with the support of Keshab Chandra Sen, as a reform movement solidly within Hinduism and devoted to the Hindu saints of medieval Maharashtra, but dedicated to practical works for social reform. Justice Mahadev Govinda Ranade became a lifelong advocate for the programs of the movement, and became one of the founders of the Indian National

Congress, illustrating the way in which religious and social reform evolved into nationalist politics.

In the Punjab, the religious reform movement took a very different form, under the inspiration of Dayananda Saraswati (1824–1883), who founded the *Arya Samaj*. Dayananda did not come from the English-educated urban elite exposed to European learning; he was a *sannyasi* (ascetic), knowing no English but well-versed in Sanskrit, and his movement spread widely in the Punjab and the Ganga Valley. His idea of reform was, in a word, "back to the Veda," and he had a conception of the Veda and Vedic society that was free of caste, image worship, multiple divinities, temples, and elaborate rituals, and was based instead on simple acts of worship centering on the sacred fire. He was opposed to the vast literature of the Puranas that had built up after the Vedic period, and viewed them as corruptions. He spread his movement through publications, vigorous preaching, and a movement of active conversion of Indians of other religions to Hinduism.

In the meantime, a quite different movement opened up in Calcutta, an order of monks called the *Ramakrishna Mission*, taking its name from that of a religious mystic and priest of the Kalighat Temple. Ramakrishna Paramahamsa (1836–1886) found that he could reach God through the practice of other religious paths, within Hinduism and also those of Islam and Christianity. He was a teacher of little education but great charisma and natural gifts, and he attracted to himself the university-educated Bengali youths who became the founders of the movement that bears his name, especially Narendranath Datta, who took the religious name of Swami Vivekananda (1863–1902). Vivekananda became a figure of international renown when he attended, in 1893, a convocation of religious leaders from many countries, called the Parliament of Religions, held in Chicago. His saffron robe and turban made a striking image for Americans, and his speeches were followed back home in India, where he returned in triumph as a national and indeed international figure. Vivekananda came to resolve the two sides of his formation, university education and the teaching of his guru Ramakrishna, in the belief that the West was superior in material matters, meaning especially science and technology, but that the East, and especially India, was superior in spiritual matters; both were needed. This formulation proved immensely effective among Indians, and among the Westerners who became followers. The Ramakrishna Mission soon opened branches all over India, and it was the pioneer in spreading yoga and reformed Hinduism in the United States and Europe.

The responses to new conditions emanating from Europe were various. The constraints of colonial rule under which this coming to terms with European models took place were such that direct expression of political views was limited by the state, and the state largely took a hands-off attitude toward religion. Religion, therefore, was a sphere of relatively free speech so long as it did not directly confront the foreign rulers of India, and this circumstance made religion an increasingly important sphere of public debate and action. The reformist movements just described were visible and influential but by no means mass movements. They had a very notable role in the shaping of a national consciousness, but in some ways various movements for the revival of traditional ways of religion, which were developing at the same time, had a larger reach and deeper consequence. Thus among Hindus movements promoting cow protection, which had an anti-Muslim effect, and the revival of devotionalism, which directly rejected the European influence while making use of the new means of communication, were very popular.

On the part of Indian Muslims, responses to European ideas were also various. One important monument of the time was the Muhammedan Anglo-Oriental College founded at Aligarh by Sayyid Ahmad Khan (1817–1898). The Muslim elite, having for long been part of the ruling power and large land owners, did not take to the new university education as quickly as did Hindus, and fell behind in mastery of the new knowledge coming out of Europe. Aligarh College was meant to rectify that relative backwardness of Muslims, giving them a college of their own at which they could receive an Islamic education, but also instruction in English and modern science. A quite different response to Western ideas and the forces of modernism was the formation of the Deoband school of traditional Islamic learning, one that accepted British rule so long as it upheld Anglo-Muhammadan family law, and was exclusively dedicated to the promotion of Islamic learning. Deoband created a formal organization that printed religious works in Urdu rather than Arabic and encouraged religious discourse in Urdu, thus broadening its social base and widening access to its version of traditionalist Islam. Deobandi schools (madrasas) are numerous in India and Pakistan.

The Indian National Congress

The Rebellion of 1857 had quickly developed into a war to restore the old regime of the Mughals and the Hindu princes. It had been quelled at great cost and with a brutal repression of the insurgents, as well as the formal demolition of the last vestige of the Mughal Empire and the exiling of the last Mughal ruler. Although the Company had ruled India under a grant of authority from the Mughals, more or less extracted by force, that fiction was gradually replaced by another: that the Mughal emperor was a pensioner of the British, which reversed the relation. This playing with symbols was now at an end, and so was Company rule. The government of India came under the British Crown, which is to say, the British Parliament, and, by a different kind of symbolic performance: Queen Victoria, a constitutional monarch of no real power, became Empress of India and her face appeared on the rupee coin.

In the aftermath of the Rebellion a new kind of political activity was being taken up by a new kind of political actor. These new politicians were not, for the most part, drawn from the elites of the old regime, the Mughal nobility and the large landlords (zamindars) centered on Delhi and the inland cities. They came instead from a new leadership, educated in the new universities of the new coastal cities that had grown large as centers of colonial government, namely, the three "presidency" cities of Calcutta, Madras, and Bombay (now Kolkata, Chennai, and Mumbai). Thus they were more fluent in European ideas. Indeed, a great many of them were lawyers, and their legal expertise gave them the technical knowledge of the colonial government that was needed for effective political action. They became the self-conscious leaders of a new conception of India, of what India could be in the modern age, so powerfully shaped by British imperialism and European civilization.

Although the British rulers of India punished advocacy of the overthrow of the government, it had always followed the practice of the Mughals and the old Hindu kingdoms in receiving petitions from its subjects, and the petitioning of government had, therefore, always been an accepted avenue for the expression of demands for government action or reform. The new Indian elites at the presidency cities were adept at using this means of political action, from the time of Rammohan Roy, as we have already seen. Single-issue advocacy of this kind gradually increased its resonance and developed a wider, in some cases an India-wide, audience, taking advantage of newspapers and other improved means for the magnification of communication. The thickening and deepening of a movement articulating a new sense of India under modern conditions eventually issued in the formation of the Indian National Congress in 1885. This group was originally a talking club of the new leadership, dispersed in the three presidency cities and many lesser ones, but now, for the first time, it gathered each year to formulate positions to present to government as the unitary voice of the Indian people. It was the first institutional form of the idea of an Indian nation in the new political sense.

There are several things to notice about this formation. In the first place it was not a mass movement, and only became so in the twentieth century, at the instigation of Mahatma Gandhi. Nor was it representative in any real sense. Its claim to represent the Indian people was scarcely democratic, but based rather on the idea that the elite had the right to lead. As the head governs the body, so the new leadership saw itself as the head of the Indian nation, speaking for the vast body of its people, by virtue of its advanced education and knowledge. In the second place, it was politically moderate and pursued its ends entirely through constitutional means. Like Rammohan Roy, it acted on a belief that the British government of India was, or could be, the best instrument for the amelioration of the lot of the Indian people, at least for the time being. It was, therefore, loyal to the government; but it increasingly sought an India that had self-rule, while remaining within the British Empire. In the third place, it conceived of the Indian people as one nation, in spite of differences of religion, and especially sought to include Muslims as well as Hindus in its movement. These were the features of Indian nationalism as it took shape in the last quarter of the nineteenth century.

Gandhi and Jinnah

It is worth reiterating that British India was a very large country with many different political and religious movements. The push for self-rule was a complex process with no single overall leadership or direction, and we cannot truly understand it by treating it as if it were the result of one or two leading personalities. At the same time, understanding Gandhi and Jinnah, the two most prominent leaders, and the parties they were connected with, the Indian National Congress and the Muslim League, is an essential first step in understanding the complexities of the independence struggle.

Gandhi

The political action of the Indian National Congress was profoundly reshaped by Mohandas K. Gandhi (1869–1948), the Mahatma (Great

Soul) as he came to be called, who was the dominating figure in twentieth-century Indian nationalism. Gandhi turned an elitist talking shop, the Indian National Congress, into an activist mass movement, the political actions of which were based on the ancient principle of nonviolence (*ahimsa*).

Like many in the political leadership of the nationalist movement, Gandhi was trained as a lawyer. His father was the prime minister (*diwan*) of Porbunder, a small princely state in western India, and Gandhi himself went to England to study law. Thereafter he spent many years in South Africa, first going there as a lawyer to a wealthy Indian Muslim client, the owner of a large grocery business. Gandhi was a profoundly religious person, but by no means traditional, and he was highly original in devising new means of nonviolent political action. In South Africa he led several nonviolent mass actions on behalf of the Indian community there to secure their equal treatment and oppose discriminatory laws. Gandhi became the undoubted moral leader of the Indians in South Africa, and his ability to mobilize them for nonviolent action that defied laws they deemed unjust, and their willingness to fill the jails to bursting under the glare of international publicity, which established the justice of the cause in the eyes of the world, was a brilliant new way of bringing ahimsa into the modern world. He called such actions *satyagraha* ("truth force" or "truth power"). Although Gandhi never held political office, by the end of his stay in South Africa he was negotiating with the prime minister the settlement of Indian grievances through changes in the laws. These actions received extensive press coverage both in India and worldwide, and Gandhi, like Vivekananda before him, became famous in India long before his return. When he arrived he was treated as a national hero. The year was 1915. He was middle aged when he returned to India and began his momentous work there.

By this time many forces had come together to draw the nationalist movement into more activist directions, and away from the loyalist and reformist politics of petition that had been the style of the Congress at the start. Government partition of Bengal into smaller provinces in 1906 had been deeply unpopular and mobilized great opposition. The *swadeshi* movement promoted a boycott of imported goods, and a repudiation of the terms of trade that British rule had imposed, in favor of Indian-made products. The outbreak of World War I created resentment when the British government of India drew India and the Indian Army into a war without Indians having any voice in the decision, a war in which Indians had no stake. In the 1919 Jallianwala Bagh massacre in the Punjab, when public gatherings were prohibited in Amritsar during a period of great unrest, General Dyer ordered his military force to fire on an unarmed crowd of Indians, killing more than three hundred and wounding more than a thousand, the soldiers firing until they ran out of ammunition. This action raised a storm of protest and generated growing Indian antagonism toward British rule, made sharper when British citizens indicated their support for General Dyer after he was relieved of his command by raising a purse of £30,000 for him and calling him the savior of the Punjab.

In the swirl of these events, Indians engaged in many different kinds of action against the regime, and Gandhi was by no means the master of events. He was certainly the most visible symbol of the nationalist movement, however, and the one who engaged the Indian people in their masses to the task of securing a better future for the country, so we need to understand his ideas and methods. It was at this historic moment that Indians seized the initiative and put the British in a position of reacting to events.

In the first place there was the matter of Gandhi's personal style. He did not present himself as an Indian gentleman, as he had years before on his arrival in South Africa, when he wore a three-piece English suit with watch chain and turban. He now adopted the dress of the ordinary peasant of Gujarat: half-*dhoti* of homespun cloth, bare chest or at most a shawl for an upper garment, shaved head with tuft, sandals, and long staff for a walking stick (Figure 20). Second, and feeding off the wide appeal of the movement in favor of native Indian (*swadeshi* or "own-country") goods and the boycott of foreign imports, he promoted the spinning of cotton thread and the weaving of homespun (*khadi*) cloth. As we have seen, cheap, machine-made cotton cloth from England had served to destroy India's homespun cloth industry, causing a great loss of jobs and a deindustrialization of the country, so that the boycott of foreign-made cloth was an apt symbol of taking back control over the national economy. Third, Gandhi formed an ashram for himself and his closest followers, a utopian community serving as a model for the nation and a political center; it was far from the highly Westernized cities, deep in the countryside, and yet connected to the country as a whole through the issuing of a magazine, *Young India*. Fourth, he held daily public prayer meetings that drew massive attendance wherever he traveled. Finally, Gandhi devised highly visible satyagrahas that galvanized the country and put the British government of India on the defensive.

FIGURE 20 M. K. Gandhi

The overall tendency of Gandhi's methods was an opening up of the Congress Party, turning it into a mass movement that drew in people of all classes, and not just the English-speaking elites. Women took active roles in the nationalist movement and found prominence in it.

This mass participation fed three major events, one in each decade, in which Gandhi was the leading force: the *Noncooperation* movement of 1920–1922, the *Salt March* of 1930, and the *Quit India* movement of 1942.

The Noncooperation movement was adopted by Congress in 1920, calling on Indians everywhere to withdraw from engagement with colonial government and its institutions. It asked government officeholders to leave office, university students to withdraw, consumers to boycott foreign goods, and so forth. This concept of a massive disengagement and refusal to cooperate with government also involved the defiance of law by peaceful means, and the courting of arrests on a large scale.

The Salt March was the most inventive of Gandhi's satyagrahas. Salt from underground deposits and salt making from seawater were considered the monopoly of government from ancient times. The British government of India vigorously upheld the monopoly and insisted on licensing and taxing the taking or making of salt. In the nineteenth century, for example, the government went to great trouble to create a thick hedge around the borders of British India in an attempt, largely futile, to control the widespread smuggling of salt that such a tax provokes. Because salt is a necessity of life for poor and rich alike, and because everyone consumes about the same amount of salt, a salt tax is highly regressive because it falls most heavily on the poor, being a higher proportion of their income. Gandhi's Salt March was devised to deliberately and with maximum publicity make sea salt in defiance of the government monopoly, and so force the government to imprison him and his following. Gandhi and his followers began, on foot, from his ashram in Central India, and ended on the seashore at Dandi in Gujarat, about 400 kilometers (240 miles) away. Each day's march concluded with a public prayer meeting drawing crowds of local people and coverage by the Indian and international press. As he marched, Gandhi drew an ever-larger following, and at the end of the march some 80,000 marchers were jailed by the British. Although the law-breaking involved was trivial—making seawater into a bit of salt—the public nature of the march virtually forced the government to crack down on such blatant defiance of its laws, and in doing so it further discredited itself in the eyes of Indians and the world.

The Quit India movement of 1942 was Gandhi's response to the outbreak of World War II, during which, as at the outset of World War I, the colonial rulers again committed India to a war without consultation with or consent of the Indian people. "Quit India" was a slogan expressing a demand that the British quit India at once, in the midst of war, and leave India to its own devices before the advancing forces of Japan. Under wartime conditions the government felt it could not but jail participants, beginning with Gandhi himself, and including nearly all of the Congress leadership. The larger context of this movement is that, in the 1930s, the British had moved in the direction of greater power-sharing with Indians, and during the period from 1937 to 1939 Congress members had taken offices in provincial governments, with powers over most matters other than security and defense. With the advent of World War II members of Congress resigned in protest, but in doing so they left government positions open to other parties, including the Muslim League. Through the Quit India movement Congress removed itself further from political action, and deepened the growing rift between itself and the Muslim League, a rift that would soon result in the Partition.

Jinnah

Muhammad Ali Jinnah (1876–1948) was, like Gandhi, a lawyer; but there the similarity ends. He had an outstanding legal mind that gave him a highly successful practice in Bombay, where his legal skills attracted the wealthiest clients. He brought to political life a mastery of the art of negotiation, at which he was virtually unbeatable. He was urbane and stylish, dressed elegantly in Western clothes, with refined tastes, decidedly liberal and secular in his leanings (Figure 21), and there was an artistic side of his sensibility—he had wanted to be a Shakespearean actor in his early days. In these matters he was virtually the opposite of Gandhi, and although they worked together from time to time, no bond of sympathy developed between them, even during the periods in which they were on the same side. When they were not on the same side he was a formidable adversary, with a brilliance that made for great success even when he was holding a weaker hand.

Events conspired to make Gandhi and Jinnah the leaders of opposing visions for India's future. From the start (and, indeed, to this day) the Indian National Congress conceived itself to be a big-tent party representing Indians of all religions. It took up a "one-nation" view of Indian history, according to which the Indian nation is an amalgam of peoples who have come together in the course of history. That was not the only view, however. V. D. Savarkar (1883–1966), from the Hindu side, took the view that true Indians were those for whom India was not only the land of their ancestors (*pitr-bhumi*), but also the land of their religion (*punya-bhumi*), which meant that Muslims, Christians, and others, even

FIGURE 21 Jawaharlal Nehru and Muhammad Ali Jinnah

though they might have been Indian by birth and ancestry, were not fully Indian by virtue of following religions with places of origin that lay outside India. This position can be called Hindu nationalist. On the Muslim side, a different version of the two-nation theory held that Muslims made up a separate nation that needed a separate nation-state.

Although Hindus formed the large majority of Indians, the Congress did not consider itself a Hindu party and wished to hold all Indian communities together in its ideal for India. The thorniest issue for the nationalist movement was the position of the Muslim minority in India's future. Undivided British India had a huge Muslim population of nearly a hundred million, the largest Muslim population within a single political entity at the time, constituting 25 percent of the whole population. What made the issue thorny was the new ideal of popular sovereignty and its "one man, one vote" logic of ballot-box democracy. This logic would make Muslims a permanent minority, subject to Hindu majorities in the legislatures of an independent India. It was the British-Indian version of the perennial problem of representative democracies, namely, how to secure the needs of minorities against oppression by the democratically elected majority. Of the myriad details that made the relations between the Congress and the Muslim League difficult and delicate, this structural fact was the most fundamental source of friction. Moreover, as we have seen, Indian Muslims largely consisted of a small, wealthy landed elite deriving from Mughal times and a large, poor class of artisans and landless laborers, with little by way of a middle class having a university education; there were few modernizing professionals like Jinnah. These conditions gave reason to consider a future governed by an Indian nation-state as problematic for Muslims.

Relations between Congress and the Muslim League varied over time. The high point of their cooperation was the period of World War I, when Britain, and perforce India, was at war with the Ottoman Empire of Turkey by virtue of Turkey's alliance with Germany. The Khilafat movement in India supported the Ottoman ruler, who was considered to be the *khalifa* or caliph for the entire Muslim world, and this was an anti-British issue around which both the Congress and the Muslim League could unite. But when, after the war, Turkish secular nationalists overthrew the Ottoman Empire and brought the caliphate to an end, the Khilafat movement died, too.

Cooperation between the two parties ceased and their different conceptions of the Indian nation were an increasing source of conflict.

Beginning in the first decade of the twentieth century, the British, increasingly pressed by nationalist action, sought to find formulae that all parties could agree to for sharing power with elected Indian officials. These included the idea of reserving a certain proportion of seats for minority groups such as Muslims who might be underrepresented by winner-take-all elections. During the period of shared rule from 1937 to 1939, called *Dyarchy*, elections were held so that Indian governments could be formed that shared power with the British, and these resulted in an overwhelming Congress victory and the formation of Congress governments in many provinces. This outcome tended to reinforce the doubts of the Muslim League about their prospects of getting sufficient powers and adequate protection of Muslim interests under a democratic future. The idea of Pakistan was floated as an alternative future, under the idea that Muslims and Hindus formed two nations and that Indian Muslims needed their own nation-state. When World War II broke out and the Congress governments resigned to protest India being drawn into it without the people's consent, Jinnah and the Muslim League declared a day of national rejoicing for a miraculous deliverance from Congress rule.

In Britain's postwar national elections, Churchill's Conservatives were swept out of power by the Labour Party under Clement Attlee. Churchill was dead set against India's independence, whereas Attlee and the Labour Party favored it, and sought to push it through quickly. There were several reasons for urgency. Attlee's government considered that it had to be done before the next national elections, which might bring Churchill back into power, which gave at most five years in which to come to a settlement for India's future. Moreover, England was economically drained by the war and could not afford an India that was also a drain on its resources. Finally, the state of unrest in India was such that it was on the verge of civil war. The last of the many proposals for a constitution for a independent and unified India, the last formula to keep the Congress and the Muslim League together within an undivided India, was the called the Cabinet Mission Plan. It proposed a federal plan, consisting of a central government with only the most basic powers over national defense and foreign affairs, and provinces with very large powers of self-government, subject only to these limited powers of the center. The special feature of this plan was that provinces could choose to combine, forming intermediate blocs of provinces with governments and powers of their own. This would allow Muslim majority provinces to band together to form superprovinces under the rule of Muslims, and Hindu majority provinces might do likewise. (This is similar to recent proposals for the government of Iraq, devised to hold Sunnis, Shias, and Kurds together under a federation.) When this proposal failed to get the agreement of the parties, partition was the only remaining option.

Partition and Independence

Lord Louis Mountbatten was sent out to be British India's last viceroy and to preside over the partition and transfer of power, a transfer that came on August 14 and 15, 1947, for Pakistan and India, respectively. The partition itself was a curious affair. A judge was sent from Britain to draw the line of partition on the map, his qualification for this delicate job being that he had never been to India and had no connection whatsoever to it, so that he could be presumed impartial. The line defining the boundaries of the independent republics of India and of Pakistan was prepared in secret over several months and then announced all at once, by radio. At the same time, preparations were made to divide up the assets of the British-Indian government in amounts mirroring the proportions that the new governments would represent. Thus 17.5 percent of army uniforms, railroad engines and wagons, bank deposits, and pencils went to Pakistan, 82.5 percent to India. A vast movement of peoples took place, with Hindus and Sikhs in Pakistan trying to get to India and Muslims in India trying to get to Pakistan. In the process millions left their homes behind forever, and hundreds of thousands were killed in conditions of interreligious hatred and lawlessness fomented by the partition. Not long after, in 1948, both Gandhi and Jinnah were dead, Gandhi by an assassin's bullet, Jinnah by cancer. Gandhi, who had tried valiantly to hold all communities together, above all Muslims and Hindus, had failed to do so; and the secular Jinnah became the leader of a religiously based state.

Under conditions of mass violence and dislocation, two new nation-states came into the world. It was a momentous occasion for South Asia and for the world. The formation of India and Pakistan opened the path to independence for other colonies of Europe. In the next two decades or so, the colonies of the European empires became independent nation-states, creating the international order in which we now live.

CHAPTER 12

New Nations

The Republic of India
Pakistan and Bangladesh
Nepal, Sri Lanka, Bhutan, and the Maldives
Indian Civilization and the Future

The independence of India and Pakistan led the way toward the dismantling of the British, French, Dutch, and Portuguese empires. The era of *decolonization* in the 1950s and 1960s redrew the map of the world along the lines of the nation-state model, which had became normative and remains so to this day. The newly created United Nations was admitting dozens of new nation-states as members, and the appearance of their flags in front of the UN building and their representatives in UN deliberations made visible this new reality of the postwar world.

In South Asia the Republic of India is very much the largest of the nation-states that emerged at the Partition and after, namely, India, Pakistan, Bangladesh, Nepal, Sri Lanka, Bhutan, and the Maldives. The new international order within South Asia was strongly shaped by the Partition of British India into India and Pakistan, and the uneasy relations between them. The Partition was a solution to a difficult and volatile situation approaching civil war, but it did not prevent violence. A vast exchange of populations that immediately followed, affecting some fifteen million people mostly in Punjab and Bengal, was accompanied by lawlessness, violence, and bloodshed on a huge scale along the new international borders, and created massive refugee populations living under conditions of desperate poverty in each country, whose resettlement took decades to accomplish. The two countries went to war almost immediately over Kashmir, a Muslim-majority region ruled over by a Hindu king, which both countries claimed, and which remains disputed territory, with parts of it dominated by each country. India and Pakistan have gone to war three times, in 1948, 1965, and 1971, and engaged in a miniwar over the border territory of Kargil in 1999. Thus the differences that separated independent India and Pakistan have not ended, but on the contrary have continued, and been internationalized, so to say. Each side now has a nation-state and an army; and each has in more recent times created a capacity to make and deploy an atomic bomb. In this way the Partition has not solved the problem it addressed, but if anything exacerbated it by giving each side the

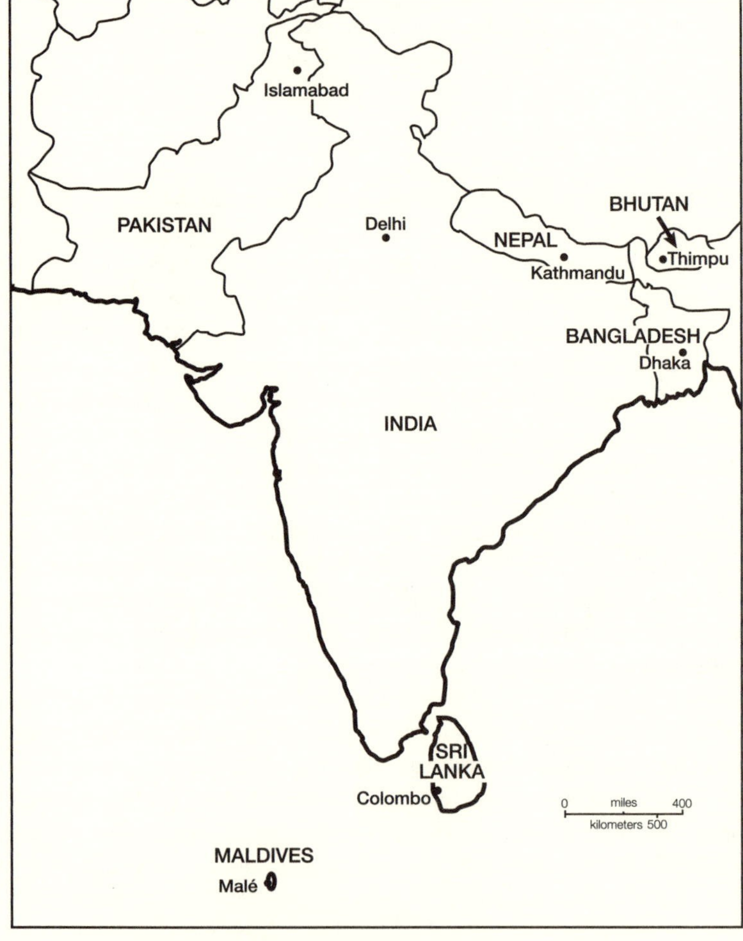

MAP 11 The nation-states of South Asia

means of making war. The evident evils of war have been a restraining factor for both countries for most of the time, and there have been long periods of uneasy truce and small-scale border conflict. The tension between India and Pakistan is a large structural condition of South Asian life today, but only one. To get a deeper picture we need to examine the region's new nations one by one (Map 11), starting with India.

The Republic of India

The Republic of India (Map 12) has changed a great deal over the six decades of its existence. Although we cannot do justice to all the complexities of these changes in this brief account, we identify the most important of them under three headings: the nation-state, economy, and society.

As to the state, the most salient fact is that the Republic of India has been from the outset, and remains, a representative democracy with effective and credible elections. This is a considerable achievement for a number of reasons. First, it is the largest country, by far, with a working democracy—so large that balloting for national elections is spread over several weeks. Whereas Europe is divided up into much smaller nation-states of less than one hundred million people, and the United States has just over three hundred million inhabitants, India has a population of more than one billion. Modern representative democracy has evolved in Europe and America under a regime of small, competing nations, whereas India, even after partition, is large enough to be many separate nation-states. Many states of the less developed world have had periods of military rule or one-party rule under which competing parties have been suppressed, a pattern from which India is the great exception. India's military has remained firmly subordinate to its civilian government. Although there was a period of two years under Prime Minister Indira Gandhi, called the Emergency (1975–1977) during which civil liberties were suspended and the executive ruled effectively without Parliament, the military did not take control and the country successfully returned to elections and parliamentary rule. As to one-party rule, it is true that the Congress Party dominated national elections for decades, and the family of its first prime minister, Jawaharlal Nehru, became a kind of political dynasty that even today is still a factor within it, but other parties were not suppressed and have played an important part in national life. The country has made a peaceful, ballot-box transition to non-Congress governments and back at the national level

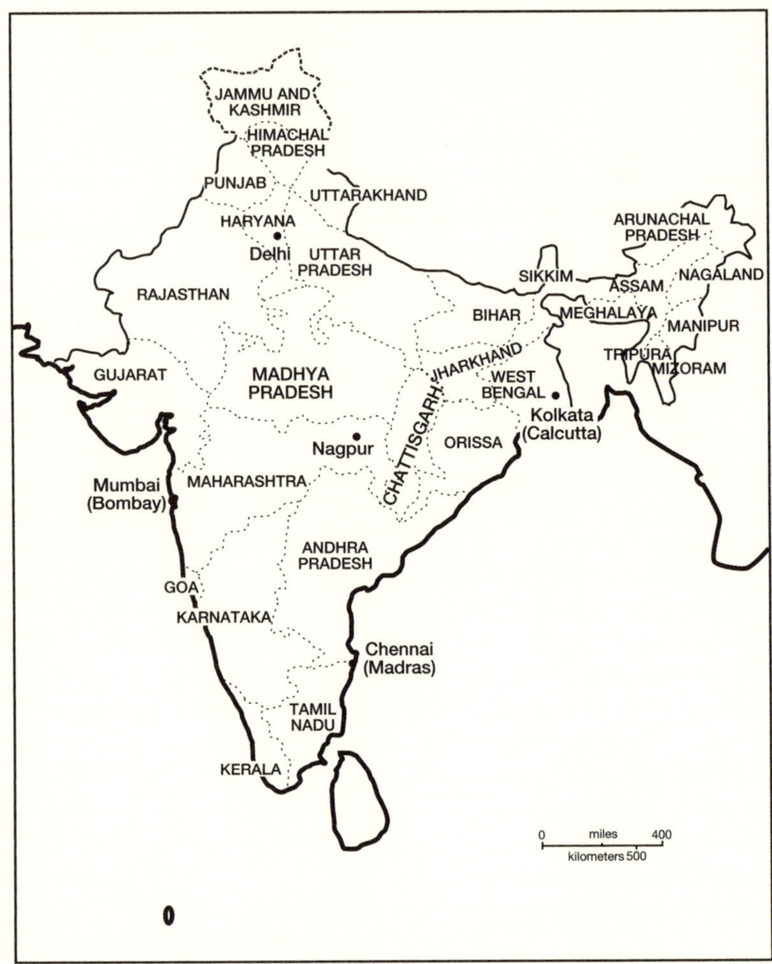

MAP 12 The Republic of India

more than once, and there have been many state governments ruled by parties other than Congress. Much as we might like to think that representative democracy is the normal and desirable form of government in this age, the truth is that in many superlarge countries and less developed countries, as well as oil-rich countries, representative democracy has been absent or unstable. India is the great exception. Part of the reason might be the exposure to British parliamentary practices and ideals, but some former British colonies have not had the same result. Part might be due to the fact that, in a sense, Indian society, divided up into many languages and castes, has no ready-made majority, so that all politics in India is inevitably a politics of coalition making, to which representative democracy is well-suited.

Jawaharlal Nehru (1889–1964), the first prime minister, was a young leader of the Congress during the nationalist struggle for independence (Figure 21). He was a great favorite of Gandhi, but led the country in very non-Gandhian directions. Like many of the first generation of the leaders of newly independent states that came out of the unwinding of the British Empire, he was educated in England, and he was the scion of a well-to-do family long involved in nationalist politics. Nehru wanted an India with a strong military and a strong industrial base, quite different from the utopian alternative to prevailing Western models for which Gandhi stood. His exposure to British socialist politics gave him a different model for an alternative to the West. Politically the Nehru model took the form of nonalignment; economically it took the form of state-led economic development featuring nationalization of basic industry and regulation of the rest.

The *Non-Aligned Movement* (NAM) was created in 1955 by Nehru, Tito, and Nasser, the leaders of India, Yugoslavia, and Egypt. It was a creature of the Cold War period, that is, of the prolonged rivalry of the United States and the Soviet Union that tended to divide the world into two camps. Nonalignment was to be a third way, one that refused to take sides in the Cold War and promoted alternatives. Although it had some effect in the world, the nonalignment idea was not a strong enough force to hold the movement together, and indeed some of the leading members of the movement—China, Cuba, and Yugoslavia are examples—were not everywhere recognized to be truly nonaligned. India's border war with China in 1962 drove a wedge between NAM's two largest members, and although it still exists, the end of the Cold War has deprived it of its logic.

Of far greater consequence was the quasi-socialist form that Nehru gave to the problem of industrializing India. As we have seen, India had been made a colony of Britain at the very time that Britain was undergoing the Industrial Revolution. The fact that the ruler of India was the first industrial nation in the world led, as we have seen, to a deindustrialization of India, under which the pre-machine-age industries of India, especially weaving, were destroyed and India was turned into a supplier of raw materials to British industry, which in turn sold its industrial products to India. An independent India had to do everything it could to change that pattern by promoting the industrialization of India, or perhaps we should say (as its earlier industry had been destroyed) its reindustrialization on modern lines.

Nehru opted for a regime in which state-run industries were largely responsible for the more basic products, such as electricity, coal, and steel, and many consumer durables; other consumer goods were left to private industry under heavy government regulation. The development of the economy was to be directed by government through economic planning, adopting the five-year plan model of the Soviet Union. The aim was to protect infant industries from foreign competition by strongly limiting foreign access to Indian markets (the reverse of the colonial terms of trade), and to develop Indian industries along the lines of *import substitution;* that is, creating Indian industries to replace imported foreign goods, in such consumer durables as automobiles. In this industry the Indian government allowed a private firm, Hindustan Motors (created by the Birla family) to acquire foreign technology by agreement with the British company Morris for the manufacture of the Ambassador car, and the German company Mercedes-Benz, through a similar arrangement, supplied technology for the manufacture of trucks. During the Nehru era one model of automobile and truck were found throughout the country, vehicles that did not change much over time, with simple engineering making for easy reparability and a ready supply of spare parts from older vehicles.

The logic of this quasi-socialism was that, in a country that was poor but large, and that had only small amounts of private capital for starting new industries, the government was the only source for the formation of large pools of capital (through taxation) that the industrialization of the country required. (The great exception was the Tata company, a private firm that had led the way in modernized steel production during the colonial period.) This logic seemed compelling in the early years, but as time went on Indian state-run industries became notorious for inefficiency, underproduction, and technological stagnation. Indian consumers had to wait for years to buy a car or motor scooter, and the technology of these products was more and more outdated. Indian industrial self-development did not look good in the light of East Asian industrial tigers. Finally, the fall of the Berlin Wall in 1989, and of the Soviet Union in 1992, accompanied by a foreign exchange crisis in India, led the then Congress government of India to abandon the Nehru model and liberalize the economy. India opened its markets to foreign companies by ending tariff barriers, divested government ownership of some industries, cut back the government regulation of private industries, and ended the attempt to direct economic growth through government planning of the economy. This movement toward a laissez-faire model led to a great influx of foreign capital and a massive die-off of those Indian brands with technological backwardness that could not survive the new competition, and the survival of others that proved up to the mark. India is now deeply into the new era of market liberalization and globalization, and enjoys a high rate of economic growth and the rapid creation of firms and jobs.

We turn now to the social changes of independent India. The colonial rulers, wishing not to interfere in the Indian family, left matters of marriage and inheritance to what it understood to be existing religious law, much as in England these subjects were under the jurisdiction of religious courts of the Church of England. Thus while the British rulers of India felt themselves free to frame criminal laws and laws of contracts that were secular and the same for everyone, family matters were under so-called personal law that was specific to each religious community. So Hindu law based on Sanskrit dharmashastra texts and Muslim law based on the Sharia law of Islam were codified in British India and cases in each were adjudicated by British-Indian courts. The regime of personal law presumed that everyone belonged to one religious community or another, and that one married within that community; civil marriage had very little place, and existed, in effect, only for those who married outside their religion or renounced religion altogether. Although the colonial rulers felt themselves competent to codify and adjudicate personal laws for the different religious communities, they were very reluctant to legislate new law for people of religions that were not their own, and so very little reform of family law occurred during the colonial period. During the freedom struggle, leaders of the nationalist movement also felt it was necessary to postpone the divisive business of social reform until after independence was achieved.

Thus at independence there was a pent-up demand for reform that had been held in abeyance, even while missionaries were pointedly criticizing aspects of Indian family life such as child marriage and family law in Europe was rapidly being secularized and modernized. The new

Indian government, therefore, had social reform high on its agenda. After contentious hearings on the reform of Hindu law, it passed a set of acts on family law of which the principle ones were the Hindu Marriage Act (1955) and the Hindu Succession Act (1956). This finally put an end to the authority of the Sanskrit dharmashastra texts in Indian courts. Hindu family law was from now on to be made by Parliament, acting as representatives of the Indian people, and Parliament could revise it at any time; it was no longer based on the eternal dharma. Moreover, for purposes of the law "Hindu" was specified to include all Indians but those who were Muslim or Christian; that is, for legal purposes Jains, Buddhists, and Sikhs were put in the same category as Hindus, a legacy of colonial practice. Among the most important changes in the law was that rights of inheritance of landed property were conferred on daughters, strongly departing from the ages-old pattern of the patrilineal joint family.

We see in these laws a strong push away from the colonial pattern of personal law and toward a uniform family law for India. However, with respect to Muslim law especially, the Parliament, being Hindu in the majority, is unwilling to legislate for Muslims in these intimate matters, and among Muslim scholars there is strong pressure to retain the status quo and perpetuate the Muslim law of the colonial period. The result is a stalemate, and the ideal of a uniform code for family law can go no further for the time being. This has been a matter of much public debate and political division between the Congress, which has tended to uphold the status quo out of deference to the wishes of the Muslim leadership, and the Bharatiya Janata Party (BJP, or "Indian peoples' party," Hindu nationalist in character) and its allies, who have been vocal in their wish for uniformity in family law.

Pakistan and Bangladesh

The partition line that divided British India into two nation-states divided the large Muslim population of South Asia into three parts. In Hindu-majority areas Muslims became a large minority of the new India, and Muslim-majority areas in the Indus Valley and in Bengal became Pakistan. Thus at its birth Pakistan was an anomalous country with two large wings, West Pakistan in the Indus region and East Pakistan in Bengal, separated by several hundred miles of India, held together by air flights over foreign territory. This was somewhat like the relation of Alaska and the lower forty-eight states of the United States, except that the two parts of Pakistan were of more or less equal size in population. At its outset Pakistan had to deal, like India, with problems of poverty and underdevelopment, resettlement of refugees created by partition, and the warfare over Kashmir that broke out almost immediately between the two countries. It also had the added problem of holding the two distant wings of the country together.

The peculiar geographical configuration of Pakistan reflected the striking fact that Islam struck its deepest roots not in the Gangetic region of Delhi and Agra, which were the capitals of the Turkish and Mughal rulers, and where Islam was largely an urban phenomenon, but rather in the two regions at considerable distance from those centers, where Islam was adopted by the masses of society in the countryside as well as the city. This historical distribution, when subjected to the process of trying to form two nation-states out of British India along religious lines, created this unusual outcome. Apart from religion, the two wings of Pakistan were very different, especially in language. East Pakistan began to accumulate grievances. The central government was located in West Pakistan, at Islamabad. The army was dominated by the West, especially the Punjabis of West Pakistan. Government expenditure favored the West over the East. Finally, in 1971 these grievances erupted into civil unrest that was put down by the army, but it boiled up into a civil war in which India intervened with its army on the side of the East Pakistanis. The outcome was the creation of an independent country of Bangladesh, and as a result Pakistan was reduced by half and confined to the Indus Valley.

The independence of Bangladesh from Pakistan had several effects. It created two countries that were more geographically coherent than before. In strategic terms it altered the balance of power in South Asia, in that Pakistan was now very much smaller in relation to India, and India now had a greater dominance within its region. And it created a new refugee population: Urdu-speaking emigrants or Muhajirs from the valley of the Ganga in emerging Bangladesh, as non-Bengalis, were identified by Bengalis with the hated army and central government of Pakistan. They were now made refugees a second time and fled to Pakistan. The Bangladesh War of 1971 was a tremendous blow to Pakistan and heightened India's military dominance in the region. Pakistan's push to develop an atomic bomb, demonstrating technological and scientific capabilities of a high order, was successfully achieved soon after India had done so; it was an attempt to restore a balance of force between the two countries that Pakistan could not achieve through numbers of soldiers.

Pakistan has an array of political parties of which the largest are the Muslim League and the Pakistan Peoples Party, and its parties participate vigorously in electoral contests. Partly because of its military rivalry with a much larger India, the military in Pakistan looms proportionally larger in public life than it does in India, and the United States aided it as a military ally in the Cold War against the Soviet Union. The military owns a great deal of investments, real estate, and industries, giving it a good deal of financial autonomy. Civilian governments have had to defer to the military; the military has often stepped in to maintain order, and periods of civil rule have alternated with periods of military rule under leading generals, in 1958 (Ayub Khan), 1977 (Zia-ul-Haq), and 1999 (Pervez Musharraf), not to speak of a number of attempted coups that failed. In addition to the large role of the military in Pakistan's political life, religion has also loomed large in politics. At the outset Pakistan had the form of a liberal state, although one in which Islam had a central role, but its guarantee of religious freedom was not backed by state action and the flight of Hindus and Sikhs to India immediately after partition left Pakistan (then West Pakistan) nearly wholly Muslim. Religion offers a common ground to unite the country, and political figures both civilian and military have often appealed to religion for political purposes. The shortage of state-supported schools and the mushroom growth of religious schools offering free education to poor youths, aided by large donations from Saudi Arabia, has further enlarged the power of religion in public life and politics and has contributed to the formation of political parties along religious lines. Finally, in recent times the Supreme Court has emerged as a fourth center of political power that has proven difficult for either civil government or the military to control. In sum, Pakistan has a vigorous political life in which the views and interests of different sectors get expressed but governments are pulled in different ways by the partially autonomous centers of political power.

Finally one must mention the relation of Pakistan to Afghanistan, which has had an even rockier history and was the site of large international interventions by the Soviet Union and by the United States and its allies. Afghanistan, with a population of about thirty million people, is much smaller than Pakistan, with about 170 million, and so Pakistan plays a large role in Afghan affairs. Yet much of the Pakistan–Afghanistan border runs through tribal regions that are not directly controlled by either the Pakistani or Afghan governments. The Afghan insurgency against Soviet-aided rule of a Marxist Afghan government (1979–1989) created a large Afghan refugee population in Pakistan. The religious schools of Pakistan that educated the refugee children were an important source of the Taliban movement that forced the Russians out and created a religious government in Afghanistan; the Taliban government of Afghanistan that followed Soviet withdrawal was allied with the Arab fighters in the anti-Soviet insurgency who formed the al-Qaeda movement. After al-Qaeda's September 11, 2001 attacks in the United States, America made war on the Taliban government and destroyed it, sending al-Qaeda fighters across the border into Pakistan for refuge, especially into the regions more inaccessible to the control of the Pakistan government. The war against the Taliban brought about a further involvement of the United States with the Pakistani government, still in progress at this writing.

What the future holds for Pakistan we cannot tell, but it should be said that, despite the many problems the country faces, it has many strengths as well, including the rich wheat-growing agricultural lands of the Indus Valley, a rapidly growing economy and a well-educated elite; in short, it has many assets making for a rising level of prosperity. What is evident is that the military and religion will continue to play large roles in government, although we cannot predict what exactly the roles will be.

In Bangladesh, too, religion and the military have played large roles. Like the Indus Valley, Bengal is a rich agricultural region, made the richer by the alluvial deposits of the Ganga and the Brahmaputra rivers. Over the centuries it became a densely populated region based on wet-rice agriculture; the success of its agriculture has made it one of the world's most populous and poorest countries. Much of Bangladesh lies only a few meters above sea level, and is subject to devastating floods from cyclones over the Bay of Bengal and its funnel shape, the narrow end of which is aimed at the Bengal coast, which serves to intensify flooding when major storms hit. Moreover, global warming threatens to raise the sea level, making this effect still worse. Bangladesh has the problem of a large, mostly rural and agricultural population constantly pressing outward to occupy new coastal lands of rich topsoil deposited by the rivers, ever more vulnerable to devastating floods, and all the other ills that beset a poor country with a large population.

Nevertheless, and in spite of intervals of military rule, Bangladesh has succeeded in instituting a parliamentary government that has changed hands between the two main parties, the Awami League and the Bangladesh Nationalist Party (BNP), several times in recent decades. Moreover, Bangladesh has been achieving sustained economic growth thanks to export earnings from its growing garment industry, which employs large numbers of women, and remittances from its expatriate workforce, which is largely male. There is, as a result, a noticeable increase of the middle class. Bangladesh has also made progress in slowing the rate of population growth, which acts to consolidate these economic gains. Finally, it has devised an original and effective form of microcredit to finance small-scale entrepreneurship by women, through what is called the Grameen Bank, for which its inventor, Muhammad Yunus, was awarded the Nobel Prize.

Nepal, Sri Lanka, Bhutan, and the Maldives

The remaining states of South Asia, in order of population size, are Nepal, Sri Lanka, Bhutan, and the Maldives.

As recently as 2008 Nepal went through a tremendous change, from a kingdom to the *Federal Democratic Republic of Nepal*, making it, for a time, the newest republic in the world. Nepal had been under monarchy for centuries, and in recent times, until the forced abdication of the king, called itself the last Hindu kingdom, taking the ancient Sanskrit word for kingdom (*rajya*, or rather an extended form of the word, *adhirajya*) in its official self-designation. Now it takes one of the Sanskrit words for the ancient tribal republics (*gana*) in the form *ganatantra*.

Nepal was an independent state throughout the period of British rule of India, but the British did have for much of that period a British resident in Nepal who represented British interests and exerted British influence on the government. Since the end of the colonial period India had taken up that role in Nepali affairs. One example of this continuity is that the British-Indian government had come to recruit Gurkha soldiers from among the Tibeto-Burman-speaking soldier-peasants of Nepal, and both the British and the Indian armies continue to have Gurkha units, by agreement with the Nepal government. That Nepal shares long borders with both India and China has made it a strategic region for India ever since the late 1950s, when the relations between India and China deteriorated and turned to armed conflict.

Nepal is the country of the tallest mountains of the world, the Himalayas (Sanskrit for "abode of snow"), a mountainous country with highly varied geographical regions and climates sustaining a population of about thirty million, most of them farmers. Although it was until recently a Hindu kingdom with a national language (Nepali) of the Indo-European language family, it has large populations speaking languages of the Tibeto-Burman language family and large numbers of Buddhists and other, localized religions. Over the last several decades political parties inspired by the nation-state ideal struggled to impose constitutional limits on the monarchy, a process that was thwarted by the large number and disunity of different political parties and various forms of resistance on the part of the monarchy. Most recently Maoist fighters mounted an increasingly effective insurgency, and the increasingly autocratic actions of the king (Gyanendra) provoked a large popular uprising in the capital, Kathmandu. This led to the formation of a constituent assembly that mandated the abdication of the king. The nation-state, therefore, is very much a work in progress in Nepal, and what form it will take is uncertain.

The *Democratic Socialist Republic of Sri Lanka* formerly called Ceylon or Sinhaladvipa, the island of the Sinhala people, was a crown colony of Britain beginning in 1802, and became independent soon after the independence of India and Pakistan, in 1948. Its last kingdom, that of the central highland region, Kandy, was extinguished by the British in 1815 and the government took the form of a republic upon independence. It is a large island, just north of the equator and only 30 kilometers (20 miles) from the southern tip of India, with a population of about twenty million.

Sri Lanka has a single dominant community, the speakers of Sinhala, which is an Indo-European language (related to those of North India), who are Theravada Buddhists and whose co-religionists are found in Thailand and Burma. But like India and Nepal, it has a large minority, in this case the speakers of Tamil, who are Hindu, and who make up about 18 percent of the population. The smaller communities are the Moors (Muslims), Burghers (Eurasian Christians), and Veddas (indigenous peoples). The Tamils are of two groups: those whose forbears have resided in Sri Lanka for hundreds or even over a thousand years, who are found throughout the island but constitute a majority in the northern region of Jaffna, and the tea-estate workers of the highlands, who came from India as labor migrants during British rule, many of them settled there for several generations. After independence the grievances of Tamils against the government of the ruling majority were provoked by a number of measures, including a Sinhala language policy for government and universities, which put barriers in the way of the well-educated Tamils, and denial of citizenship to many of the tea-estate Tamils. A virulent insurgency ensued, spearheaded by the LTTE or Liberation Tigers of Tamil Eelam (a Tamil name for Sri Lanka) which sought an independent Tamil state. The government of India was drawn into the conflict in a number of ways, aiding Sri Lanka with a military force for a while, and drawing the enmity of the LTTE. The latter has been implicated in the 1991 murder of the Indian prime minister, Rajiv Gandhi (grandson of Nehru), by a suicide bomber, whose act was emulated by suicide bombers in Israel, Iraq, Afghanistan, England, the United States, and elsewhere. After a long insurgency the LTTE was defeated by the Sri Lankan armed forces in 2009, and its leadership was killed in the fighting. Time will tell whether the minority and the majority populations of Sri Lanka can find ways of promoting the common good together and healing the bitterness that the violence has left.

The *Kingdom of Bhutan* is a country of perhaps seven hundred thousand in the eastern Himalayas between India and China, and close to Nepal and Bangladesh. Its small population consists almost entirely of speakers of the Tibeto-Burman language Dzongkha who are followers of a form of Tibetan Buddhism. Like Nepal it was never under British rule, but it has had treaty relations with Britain and a substantial British interest in its affairs. Because of its relative isolation in a mountainous region far from the sea, it has a degree of cultural uniformity that is remarkable in this age of international migration, and its rulership has created representative institutions, so that it seems well on its way toward the ideals of the nation-state form. We could call it a constitutional monarchy, and it had its first elections for Parliament in 2008. However, Nepali labor migrants into Bhutan have created a significant minority of linguistically and culturally different people with grievances against the majority, who were forcibly deported to Nepal and put into refugee camps. So, in spite of its isolation and relative homogeneity, Bhutan has not escaped the quandaries of the nation-state form. Bhutan is famous for its policy of preferring to maximize the gross national happiness rather than the gross national product.

The *Republic of Maldives* is the smallest of the self-governing countries making up South Asia, with a population of about three hundred fifty thousand. Its territory, straddling the equator in the Indian Ocean west of Sri Lanka, consists of coral atolls making up some one thousand islands, of which only about two hundred are inhabited. Its language, Dhivehi, is Indo-European but with a considerable Dravidian (Tamil) substratum. Its people were Buddhist in the remote past, but became Muslim in the twelfth century when a sultanate was created there. European powers—Portugal, the Netherlands, and Britain—ruled it successively as a colony, but it became independent in 1965 and three years later the sultanate was wound up in favor of a republic. The Maldives are a tourist destination for Indians and Europeans, with beaches and tropical sunlight that are much liked by fashion photographers and music video makers. The main anxiety of its people has to do with the fact that their land is so close to sea level, and that the sea level is rising with global warming.

Indian Civilization and the Future

The nation-state is quite new in history, the first having been created by the American (1776) and French (1789) revolutions. In South Asia it began with partition and independence in 1947. The independence of India and Pakistan inaugurated the era of decolonization, which emptied out the European empires and cast the colonies into the mold of the nation-state. Thus the nation-state form became virtually universal after the partition of British India, and has been in place as a worldwide political norm for little more than the last six decades. During this period empires and monarchies have lost their legitimacy as political forms and kingship has largely died out, except as window dressing for the nation-state, as in Britain.

It is apparent that the nation-state has become normative in South Asia and has strongly shaped political forces within the region, but we have seen that each of the new states has its own difficulties achieving or maintaining the nation-state ideal. It is unclear how we should interpret these problems, but some possibilities can be suggested. We need to remember how very difficult it has been for the older nation-states to maintain the ideal. America went through a long civil war that threatened to split it in two, and France has had interludes of dictatorship and monarchy, and is in its fifth republican constitution. This history reminds us that there is no magic in the nation-state form and its democratic methods to achieve consensus. Indeed, it is not consensus but majority rule that the nation-state achieves, and minorities must give way to the will of the majority. When minorities feel their core interests are endangered they might turn to strong means of pursuing them, or to pressure the majority to make concessions. Much as we might believe in the nation-state and popular sovereignty as the desirable form of political life in the current age, we need to recognize that the problem of the minority is a structural weakness of the form. It is not that other political forms have ready-made ways of speaking to the needs of minorities, but the election process seems to intensify the minority problem. This effect will be minimized or magnified by the particulars of the situation, of which the major ones in South Asia are caste and religion.

The effect of the nation-state on caste has been to dissolve the caste *system* and to turn castes into so many independent interest groups. That is because popular sovereignty requires equality before the law for citizens, so that the hierarchy that orders the castes into a system of cases is intolerable for a nation-state. Discrimination in the public sphere on the basis of caste is no longer supported by the state, and, to the contrary, is made illegal. Nevertheless the castes remain, no longer the elements of a state-supported system as in the ancient kingdoms but as individual entities, and take political action to pursue their interests through the ballot box. In the early days of India's independence the experts regularly predicted that caste would undermine democracy, but the opposite has been the case. Because of the multiplicity of castes, majorities have to be formed out of coalitions of people of different castes, and this has tended to ensure that majorities and minorities are always changing in their internal composition, so that there is no permanent established majority. Although castes have found a viable place in democratic politics, however, forms of social and economic inequality and discrimination remain severe problems that will not disappear in the foreseeable future.

Although ballot-box politics has proven compatible with castes, it has tended to promote religious identity as a means of forming national legislative majorities in South Asia. Although the nation-state has reduced the influence of caste, it has solidified and magnified the importance of religion, and this effect has acted to intensify the disaffection of minorities. Most of the nation-states of South Asia show this effect.

We return, in conclusion, to the concept with which we began, that of Indian Civilization, and ask what its future might be, in the face of the nation-state form, and the heightened salience of religion.

The universalization of the nation-state concept has created multiple nation-states in South Asia, and each has its own version, or competing versions, of the past. Bronislaw Malinowski, an anthropologist, has said that myth is *social charter*, meaning that myths justify and sanctify the way society is organized and bounded. In an age of nation-states, history tends to be pressed into the role that myth served in the past, and functions as the charter of the nation. Thus the nation-state strongly shapes the view (or views) of the past. In South Asia the idea of Indian Civilization tends to be viewed quite differently by the different nations. In the Republic of India there is a deep and general sense of the ownership of the whole of Indian Civilization and its history. It is widely agreed that Indian Civilization begins in the Indus Valley, with the Indus Civilization, even though the bulk of it lies outside of India, in Pakistan. On the other hand, there is a sharp difference in the majority community of Indians over whether the rule of the Turkish sultans and Mughal padshahs represents the domestication and Indianization of Islam or incursion of a foreign civilization. These two interpretations are highly politicized, being attached to competing political parties, Congress and the BJP.

In Pakistan, on the other hand, the sense of the past is quite different. Pakistan occupies the greater part of the territory of the Indus Civilization of old and the Vedic Civilization in its earliest phase. Through the work of the Archaeological Survey of Pakistan and such directors-general as Ahmad Hasan Dani and Rafique Mughal, archaeological work on the Indus Civilization of the first scientific importance has been carried out. Shortly after independence the British archaeologist Mortimer Wheeler (the last director-general of the Archaeological Survey of India under the British) wrote a book with the paradoxical title, *Five thousand years of Pakistan*, that projects the name of the new nation-state on the ancient past.[41] But in spite of these developments, on the whole the national sense of history in Pakistan is not strongly engaged with that ancient past, and the religious logic of the boundaries of Pakistan has tended to link the nation-state with the coming of Islam to South Asia, and to render the more remote past as a kind of prehistory. Each other nation of South Asia likewise has its own stake in and its own "take" on the history of Indian Civilization, so that the unity of that history is subjected to differing national pulls and pushes. The need of nation-states for history guarantees that the history of Indian Civilization will remain a matter of great political importance and continuing debate among the nations of South Asia.

The numerous conflicting views of the past of Indian civilization are, at the same time, conflicting visions for its future. It is characteristic of older forms of history that they included prophecies, the history not only of the past, but the history of the future as well. But history has advanced by abandoning claims to foretell the future and sticking to the close examination of evidence from the past. That is not, however, the end of the story, for although we cannot foretell the future, we cannot act in the world without an idea of a desirable future toward which we direct our actions; and it is in relation to imagined futures that we investigate the past. All our history-making serves the purpose of finding out where we are now and helping us face the future. With respect to Indian Civilization, history tells us that the nation-state form, appealing as it is, has problems as well, problems specific to it, leading to conflict, problems that need to be recognized and that need to be mitigated.

We cannot say what will be the future of the world's civilizations, formed in a very different past, in the world of today, an age of incessant movement and intermixtures of populations. Substantial populations of South Asia have formed a diaspora beyond the homeland, unevenly distributed around the world (Map 13). The pattern of migration in modern times has largely been to the colonies of the British Empire (on the map: Jamaica and Trinidad, Guyana, Canada, Britain, Kenya, South Africa, Singapore, Malaysia, Australia, and Fiji), labor countries of the Persian Gulf, and the United States. However, it is important not to think of civilizations as sharply bounded objects with a fixed nature; they are *processes* that overlap and draw into themselves lots of ideas and things

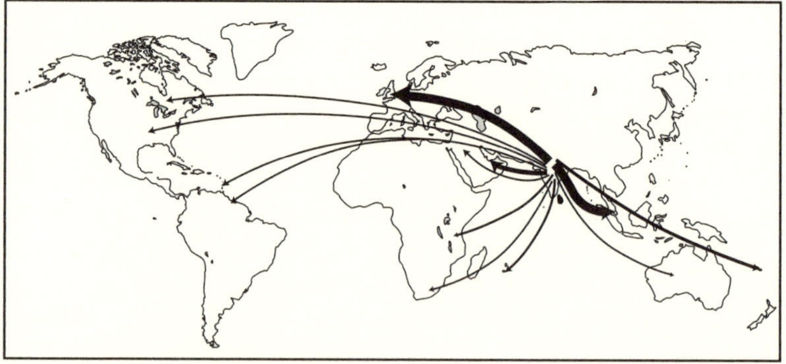

MAP 13 The South Asian diaspora

coming from elsewhere. In other words, the cultural mixtures of today are new only in their scope and intensity. Mixture has been going on ever since civilizations began, and has been part of the civilizational process from the start. It is by no means clear that what we think of as the newness of the age we live in will put an end to such civilizational processes, and in many ways it has given them new direction and scope. Little as we can see into the future, it seems likely that the history of Indian Civilization will continue for some time to come to serve as an object of historical investigation and political debate.

FURTHER READING

This is not intended as a systematic bibliography of the field, but a few suggestions of books newcomers to the history of Indian Civilization might find useful after reading this book, or to read along with it.

For ancient India, A. L. Basham (1954), *The wonder that was India,* is an invaluable guide, still very sound even though it was first published more than fifty years ago. See especially its long chapter on religion, and its appendixes on the sciences. For classical India, Turks, and Mughals, Asher and Talbot (2006), *India before Europe,* is an excellent new synthesis. For modern India, Metcalf and Metcalf (2006) is first rate, as is Bose and Jalal (1998), and there are a number of others as well. On aspects of the Indian population, Sumit Guha's *Health and population in South Asia* (2001) is a magnificent survey of the entire period, and *Environment and ethnicity in India* (1999) examines human ecology from 1200 to the present. Essays of the economist Amartya Sen (2005) have the quality of addressing present and future problems within a long view that uses the ancient past as a resource.

On the beginnings of European scholarship on India, see Thomas R. Trautmann (1997), *Aryans and British India.* On the study of religions, see the title essay of Lorenzen (2006). On matters of language, Deshpande (1993) is essential.

There are many good books on the Indus Civilization, notably that of Gregory Possehl (2002).

For Indo-European, two books are essential: Mallory (1989) gives a fine synthesis of historical linguistics and Renfrew (1987) gives a controversial archaeology-based view that associates the spread of Indo-European languages with the spread of agriculture. A recent book by David Anthony (2008) is a magnificent treatment of the archaeology of the Indo-European-speaking peoples, following the domestication of horses and the spread of the chariot. Trautmann, ed. (2005), *The Aryan debate*, gives sources on both sides of the question about the relation of the Indus Civilization and the Vedic Aryans. Fustel de Coulanges's (1864/1980; many editions of the English translation are available) *The ancient city*, is a classic work on the Greek and Roman city, the opening chapters of which are a comparative study of Greek, Roman, and Vedic Indian family structure and ancestor worship. Stephanie Jamison, in *Sacrificed wife/sacrificer's wife: Women, ritual and hospitality in ancient India* (1996), offers new methods for getting at gender relations in the Vedic tradition.

On the Mauryas, Romila Thapar's (1961) *Asoka and the decline of the Mauryas* is indispensable, and includes translations of Asoka's edicts. Megasthenes' book on India has been translated by McCrindle (e.g., 1961). *The Indo-Greeks* by A. K. Narain (1962) is a classic on the topic. Courtly love poetry of the ancient period (Sanskrit, Prakrit, Tamil) is translated and analyzed in the anthology of Martha Selby (2002), and we have excellent translations of the Tamil courtly poetry by A. K. Ramanujan in *The interior landscape* (1967) and George Hart and Hank Heifetz in *The four hundred songs of war and wisdom* (1999). Daud Ali's *Courtly culture and political life in early medieval India* (2004) is excellent on the connection of kingship and ideas of refinement. P. V. Pillai's (1977) comparison of kinship in ancient India and China, *Perspectives on power: India and China*, has many useful insights. Translations of the Chinese Buddhist travelers to India, Faxian (1956) and Xuanzang (1969), give eyewitness accounts of India in the times of the Guptas and of Harsha. Gupta inscriptions can be found in Fleet (1981), and coins are described in the catalog of the British Library collection by Allan (1967).

On family structure, marriage, and inheritance, see Trautmann (1981), *Dravidian kinship*, especially Chapter 4. On gender, Susie Tharu and K. Lalita, *Women writing in India, 600 B.C. to the present: Vol. 1* (1991), is an important contribution and an interesting anthology. Indrani Chatterjee, ed. (2004), *Unfamiliar relations: Family and history in South Asia*, is a highly useful collection of articles. For the modern period, Mrinalini Sinha's (2006) *Specters of Mother India: The global restructuring of an empire* is a superb analysis of the relation of gender, imperialism, and nationalism.

On Dharmashastra, the best single book is that of Robert Lingat (1973), *The classical law of India,* and the monumental work of P. V. Kane (1968), *History of Dharmasastra,* in many volumes, is comprehensive. David Pingree's many works on Indian astronomy, astrology, and mathematics (for example, 1963, 1974) are the most authoritative, although unrelentingly technical. There is an overview of Indian analysis of language in Trautmann (2006), *Languages and nations,* Chapter 2.

Amartya Sen's (2005) chapter on India and China in *The argumentative Indian* is very good; Georges Coedès's (1968) *The Indianized states of Southeast Asia* is a classic, although data-heavy and somewhat dated. *The Periplus of the Erythraean Sea* is a Greek sea-captain's manual of the ancient trade (translation, 1980). S. D. Goitein (1973) gives translations of letters of Jewish merchant families trading between Egypt and India in late classical times.

On Turks, we have a number of good studies lately, in addition to Asher and Talbot (mentioned earlier): Sunil Kumar (2007), Gilmartin and Lawrence, eds. (2008), *Beyond Turk and Hindu* (a collection of articles), Phillip Wagoner (1996) on Islamicate dress and titles, and Richard Eaton (2000) on temple destruction. There are many good books on the Mughals—too many to list—but Irfan Habib's (1999) magnificent study of the agrarian system is fundamental, Jos Gommans (2002) on Mughal warfare is especially good on environmental effects, and Eaton (1993) is the leading study of conversion.

Good histories of modern India are even more numerous. We can only mention a small handful. On intellectual exchanges with Europe, Wilhelm Halbfass (1988) is especially good. Rommohan Roy's writings (1995) are available in recent editions. Uday Singh Mehta (1999) on the liberal theory of empire in British India is essential. Gandhi's autobiography (1983; many editions), called *The story of my experiments with truth,* is very accessible. For Jinnah there are biographies by Wolpert (1984) and Jalal (1985). Nehru's *Discovery of India* (2004; many editions) is very readable and interesting for the first Indian prime minister's conception of Indian Civilization. On princely states, Barbara Ramusack's (2004) *The Indian princes and their states* is the classic study, and Nicholas Dirks' (1993), *The hollow crown: Ethnohistory of an Indian kingdom* is a classic study of a single princely state. The fundamental work on Deoband is Barbara Metcalf's (2005) *Islamic revival in British*

India: Deoband, 1860–1900. More advanced (and demanding) reading on the modern period would begin with the scholars of the Subaltern Studies school, above all Ranajit Guha.

On the Republic of India there is now a full-length history by Ramachandra Guha (2007). Diane Mines and Sarah Lamb, eds. (2002), give numerous anthropological microstudies of everyday life in contemporary South Asia.

NOTES

Chapter 1

1. The classic work of Elias (1994) views civilization as a process—"the civilizing process" spreading from a trendsetting center rather than a staircase of stages.
2. Huntington (1996) argues that following the end of the Cold War, during which the world order had been structured by the rivalry of the United States and the Soviet Union, the international sphere has been shaped by a "clash of civilizations."
3. The map is after Gommans (2002), who analyzes the effects of the arid and wet zones on Indian history in the Mughal period.

Chapter 2

4. Fairservice (1975).
5. Marshall (1973).
6. Possehl (2002).
7. Raikes (1964) and Dales (1965).
8. Wheeler (1960).
9. Bryson and Baerreis (1967) and Bryson and Murray (1977). On the ITD, Das (1968) and Bryson and Murray (1967, Chapter 7).
10. Divyabhanusinh (2008).
11. Lal (1997) and Gupta (1996).

Chapter 3

12. Wasson (1968) on the fly agaricus mushroom; Falk (1989) on ephedra.
13. After Piggott (1950).
14. Dumézil (1952).
15. Anthony (2008).

Chapter 4

16. Basham (1954).

Chapter 5

17. As Lattimore (1988) says, speaking of how nomadism forbids accumulation of property, "The pure nomad is a poor nomad."
18. This is the formulation of P. V. Pillai (1977).
19. This interpretation is that of Richard D. Saran (c. 1969, unpublished).

Chapter 6

20. On women in Vedic religion, see Jamison (1966).
21. On the Nayar, see chapters by Gough in Schneider and Gough (1961).

Chapter 7

22. Tharu and Lalita (1991).
23. Pingree (1963, 1974).
24. The Brahmi chart was made by Anshuman Pandey.

Chapter 8

25. Trautmann (2006).
26. Sen (2005, Chapter 8, "China and India").
27. Coedès (1968).
28. Barnes (1993).

Chapter 9

29. I owe this interpretation to the late Allen Luther (personal communication).
30. Temple destruction: Eaton (2000); conversion: Eaton (1993).
31. Wagoner (1996).

32. Azfar Moin (personal communication).
33. Asani (2003).
34. On Muslim kinship in relation to Hellenistic and Christian polities, see Al-Azmeh (1997); on Mughals and Iran, see Azfar Moin (2010 and personal communication).

Chapter 10

35. Schedel (1493/1966).
36. Ptolemaeus (1545) is an early printed atlas based on the geography of Ptolemy, and is the basis for Maps 8 and 9. In Map 9, Ptolemy's geography has been modified by the addition of new information acquired by the voyages of discovery.
37. My thanks to Sumit Guha for this point.
38. Ness and Stahl (1977).

Chapter 11

39. Rammohan Roy (1995).
40. Rammohan Roy (1995).

Chapter 12

41. Wheeler (1992).

BIBLIOGRAPHY

Ali, Daud (2004). *Courtly culture and political life in early medieval India.* Cambridge, UK: Cambridge University Press.

Allan, John (1967). *Catalogue of the coins of the Gupta dynasties.* London: British Museum.

Anthony, David W. (2008). *The horse, the wheel, and language: How Bronze-age riders from the Eurasian steppes shaped the modern world.* Princeton, NJ: Princeton University Press.

Asani, A. (2003). Creation tradition through devotional songs and communal script: the Khojah Isma'ilis of South Asia. In *India's Islamic Traditions, 711–1750*, ed.R. M. Eaton, pp. 285–310. New Delhi, Oxford University Press.

Asher, Catherine B., and Cynthia Talbot (2006). *India before Europe.* Cambridge, UK: Cambridge University Press.

Barnes, Ruth (1993). *Indian block-printed cotton fragments in the Kelsey Museum, the University of Michigan.* Ann Arbor: University of Michigan Press.

Basham, A. L. (1954). *The wonder that was India: a survey of the culture of the Indian sub-continent before the coming of the Muslims.* London: Sidgwick & Jackson.

Bose, Sugata, and Ayesha Jalal, eds. (1998). *Modern South Asia: history, culture, political economy.* New York: Routledge.

Bryson, Reid, and David A. Baerreis (1967). Possibilities of major climatic modification and their implications: Northwest India, a case for study. *Bulletin of the American Meterological Society* 48(3): 136–42.

Bryson, R. A., and T. J. Murray (1977). *Climates of hunger: mankind and the world's changing weather*. Madison: The University of Wisconsin Press.

Chatterjee, Indrani., ed. (2004). *Unfamiliar relations: family and history in South Asia.* New Brunswick, NJ: Rutgers University Press.

Coedès, Georges (1968). *The Indianized states of Southeast Asia.* Honolulu, HI: East-West Center Press.

Dales, G. F. (1965). Civilization and floods in the Indus Valley. *Expedition* 7(2): 10–19.

Das, P. K. (1968). *The monsoons.* New Delhi, India: National Book Trust.

Deshpande, Madhav M. (1993). *Sanskrit and Prakrit: sociolinguistic issues.* Delhi, India: Motilal Banarsidass.

Dirks, Nicholas B. (1993). *The hollow crown: Ethnohistory of an Indian kingdom.* 2nd ed. Ann Arbor: University of Michigan Press.

Divyabhanusinh (2008). *The story of Asia's lions.* 2nd ed. Mumbai, India: Marg.

Dumézil, Georges (1952). *Les dieux des Indo-Européens.* Paris: Presses Universitaires de France.

Eaton, Richard M. (2000). Temple desecration in Indo-Muslim states. *Journal of Islamic Studies* 11(3): 283–319.

———. (1993). *Rise of Islam and the Bengal frontier, 1204–1760.* Berkeley: University of California Press.

Elias, Norbert (1994). *The civilizing process.* Oxford, UK: Blackwell.

Fairservice, Walter A. (1975). *The roots of ancient India: the archaeology of early Indian civilization.* Chicago: University of Chicago Press.

Falk, Harry (1989). Soma I and II. *Bulletin of the School of Oriental and African Studies* 52(1): 77–90.

Faxian (1956). *The travels of Fa-hsien (399–414 A.D.).* Trans. H. A. Giles. London: Routledge and Kegan Paul.

Fleet, John Faithful (1981). *Inscriptions of the early Gupta kings.* New Delhi, India: Archaeological Survey of India.

Fustel de Coulanges, N. D. (1864/1980). *The ancient city: a study on the religion, laws and institutions of ancient Greece and Rome.* Baltimore: Johns Hopkins University Press.

Gandhi, Mohandas K. (1983). *Autobiography: The story of my experiments with truth.* New York: Dover.

Gilmartin, David, and B. B. Lawrence, eds. (2008). *Beyond Turk and Hindu.* Gainesville: University Press of Florida.

Goitein, S. D. (1973). *Letters of medieval Jewish traders.* Princeton, NJ: Princeton University Press.

Gommans, Jos. L. (2002). *Mughal warfare: Indian frontiers and highroads to empire, 1500–1700.* London: Routledge.

Guha, Ramachandra (2007). *India after Gandhi: the history of the world's largest democracy.* New York: HarperCollins.

Guha, Sumit (1999). *Environment and ethnicity in India, 1200–1991.* Cambridge, UK: Cambridge University Press.

———. (2001). *Health and population in South Asia, from earliest times to the present.* New Delhi, India: Permanent Black.

Gupta, S. P. (1996). *The Indus Saraswati civilization.* Delhi, India: Pratibha Prakashan.

Habib, Irfan (1999). *The agrarian system of Mughal India, 1556–1707.* New Delhi, India: Oxford University Press.

Halbfass, Wilhelm (1988). *India and Europe: An essay in understanding.* Albany: SUNY Press.

Huntington, Samuel P. (1996). *The clash of civilizations and the remaking of world order.* New York: Simon & Schuster.

Jalal, Ayesha (1985). *The sole spokesman: Jinnah, the Muslim League, and the demand for Pakistan.* Cambridge: Cambridge University Press.

Jamison, Stephanie W. (1996). *Sacrificed wife/sacrificer's wife: women, ritual, and hospitality in ancient India.* New York: Oxford University Press.

Kane, P. V. (1968) *History of dharmasastra.* 2nd ed. Pune, India: Bhandarkar Oriental Research Institute.

Kumar, Sunil (2007). *The emergence of the Delhi Sultanate, 1192–1286.* New Delhi, India: Permanent Black.

Lal, B. B. (1997). *The earliest civilization of South Asia: Rise, maturity and decline.* New Delhi, India: Aryan Books International.

Lattimore, Owen (1988). *Inner Asian frontiers of China.* Hong Kong: Oxford University Press.

Lingat, Robert (1973). *The classical law of India.* Berkeley: University of California Press.

Lorenzen, David N. (2006). *Who invented Hinduism? Essays on religion in history.* New Delhi, India: Yoda Press.

Mallory, J. P. (1989). *In search of the Indo-Europeans: Language, archaeology and myth.* London: Thames and Hudson.

Marshall, John Hubert (1973). *Mohenjo-daro and the Indus civilization.* Delhi, India: Indological Book House.

Megasthenes (1961). Ancient India as described by Megasthenes and Arrian. Trans. J. W. McCrindle. Calcutta, India: Chuckervertty, Chatterjee.

Mehta, Uday Singh (1999). *Liberalism and empire: A study in nineteenth-century British liberal thought.* Chicago: University of Chicago Press.

Metcalf, Barbara D. (2005). *Islamic revival in British India: Deoband, 1860–1900.* New Delhi, India: Oxford University Press.

Metcalf, Barbara D., and Thomas R. Metcalf. (2006). *A concise history of modern India.* Cambridge, UK: Cambridge University Press.

Mines, Diane P., and Sarah Lamb, eds. (2002). *Everyday life in South Asia.* Bloomington: Indiana University Press.

Moin, A. Azfar (2010). Islam and the millennium: sacred kingship and popular imagination in early modern India and Iran. Ph.D. dissertation, University of Michigan.

Narain, A. K. (1962). *The Indo-Greeks.* Oxford, UK: Clarendon.

Nehru, Jawaharlal (2004). *The discovery of India.* New Delhi, India: Penguin Books.

Ness, Gayle. D., and William Stahl (1977). Western imperialist armies in Asia. *Comparative studies in society and history* 19(1): 2–29.

Periplus Maris Erythraei (1980). *The periplus of the Erythraean Sea.* London: Hakluyt Society.

Piggott, Stuart (1950). *Prehistoric India to 1000 B.C.* Harmondsworth, UK: Penguin.

Pillai, P. V. (1977). *Perspectives on power: India and China.* New Delhi, India: Manohar.

Pingree, David (1963). Astronomy and astrology in India and Iran. *Isis* 54:229–46.

———. (1974). History of mathematical astronomy in India. In *Dictionary of scientific biography*, vol. 15, ed. Charles Coulston Gillispie, 533–633. New York: Scribner.

Possehl, Gregory L. (2002). *The Indus civilization: a contemporary perspective.* London: Altamira Press.

Ptolemaeus, C. (1545). *Geographia universalis, vetvs et nova complectens Claudii Ptolemaei Alexandrini ennarationis libros viii.* Basel, Switzerland: H. Petrvm.

Raikes, R. L. (1964). The end of the ancient cities of the Indus. *American Anthropologist* 66(2): 284–99.

Ramanujan, A. K. (1967). *The interior landscape: Love poems from a classical Tamil anthology.* Bloomington: Indiana University Press.

Rammohan Roy, Raja (1995). *The essential writings of Raja Rammohan Ray.* Delhi, India: Oxford University Press.

Ramusack, Barbara N. (2004). *The Indian princes and their states.* Cambridge, UK: Cambridge University Press.

Renfrew, Colin (1987). *Archaeology and language: The puzzle of Indo-European origins.* London: Penguin Books.

Saran, Richard D. (c.1969). Rajput state formation. Unpublished manuscript.

Schedel, Hartmann (1493/1966). *The Nuremberg chronicle.* New York: Brussel and Brussel.

Schneider, David M., and Kathleen Gough, eds. (1961). *Matrilineal kinship.* Berkeley: University of California Press.

Selby, Martha (2002). *Grow long blessed night: love poems from classical India.* Oxford, UK: Oxford University Press.

Sen, Amartya (2005). *The argumentative Indian: writings on Indian history, culture and identity.* New York: Farrar, Straus and Giroux.

Sinha, Mrinalini (2006). *Specters of Mother India: the global restructuring of an empire.* Durham, NC: Duke University Press.

Thapar, Romila (1961). *Asoka and the decline of the Mauryas.* Oxford, UK: Oxford University Press.

Tharu, Susie, and K. Lalita, eds. (1991). *Women writing in India: 600 B.C. to the present.* 2 vols. New York: Feminist Press at the City University of New York.

Trautmann, Thomas R. (1981). *Dravidian kinship.* Cambridge, UK: Cambridge University Press.

———. (1997). *Aryans and British India.* Berkeley: University of California Press.

———, ed. (2005). *The Aryan debate.* New Delhi, India: Oxford University Press.

———. (2006). *Languages and nations: The Dravidian proof in colonial Madras.* Berkeley: California University Press.

Wagoner, Philip B. (1996). "Sultan among Hindu kings": dress, titles, and the Islamicization of Hindu culture at Vijayanagara. *Journal of Asian studies* 55(4): 851–80.

Wasson, R. Gordon (1968). *Soma: divine mushroom of immortality.* New York: Harcourt Brace Jovanovich.

Wheeler, R. E. M. (1960). *The Indus civilization.* Cambridge, UK: Cambridge University Press.

———. (1992). *Five thousand years of Pakistan: an archaeological outline.* Karachi, Pakistan: Royal Book.

Wolpert, Stanley A. (1984). *Jinnah of Pakistan.* New York: Oxford University Press.

Xuanzang (1969). *Si-yu-ki: Buddhist records of the western world.* Trans. S. Beal. Delhi, India: Oriental Books Reprint Corp.

INDEX